The Unacceptable

Also by John Potts

AFTER THE EVENT: New Perspectives on Art History (*co-edited with Charles Merewether*)

A HISTORY OF CHARISMA

CULTURE AND TECHNOLOGY (*with Andrew Murphie*)

RADIO IN AUSTRALIA

TECHNOLOGIES OF MAGIC (*co-edited with Edward Scheer*)

Also by John Scannell

JAMES BROWN

The Unacceptable

Edited by

John Potts
Professor, Macquarie University, Australia

and

John Scannell
Macquarie University, Australia

palgrave
macmillan

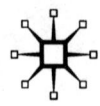

Introduction, selection and editorial matter © John Potts and
John Scannell 2012, 2014
Individual chapters © Contributors 2012, 2014

All rights reserved. No reproduction, copy or transmission of this
publication may be made without written permission.

No portion of this publication may be reproduced, copied or transmitted
save with written permission or in accordance with the provisions of the
Copyright, Designs and Patents Act 1988, or under the terms of any licence
permitting limited copying issued by the Copyright Licensing Agency,
Saffron House, 6–10 Kirby Street, London EC1N 8TS.

Any person who does any unauthorized act in relation to this publication
may be liable to criminal prosecution and civil claims for damages.

The authors have asserted their rights to be identified as the authors of this
work in accordance with the Copyright, Designs and Patents Act 1988.

First published in hardback 2012
First published in paperback 2014 by
PALGRAVE MACMILLAN

Palgrave Macmillan in the UK is an imprint of Macmillan Publishers Limited,
registered in England, company number 785998, of Houndmills, Basingstoke,
Hampshire RG21 6XS.

Palgrave Macmillan in the US is a division of St Martin's Press LLC,
175 Fifth Avenue, New York, NY 10010.

Palgrave Macmillan is the global academic imprint of the above companies
and has companies and representatives throughout the world.

Palgrave® and Macmillan® are registered trademarks in the United States,
the United Kingdom, Europe and other countries.

ISBN 978–1–137–01456–6 hardback
ISBN 978–1–137–44019–8 paperback

This book is printed on paper suitable for recycling and made from fully
managed and sustained forest sources. Logging, pulping and manufacturing
processes are expected to conform to the environmental regulations of the
country of origin.

A catalogue record for this book is available from the British Library.

A catalog record for this book is available from the Library of Congress.

Transferred to Digital Printing in 2014

Contents

Acknowledgements vii

Notes on Contributors viii

Introduction: What Is the Unacceptable? 1
John Potts and John Scannell

Part I The Socially Unacceptable

1 Power and the Unacceptable 23
   Mitchell Dean

2 'Schooling Scandals!': Exploring the Necessity of Cultural Disgust 45
   Chris Haywood

3 Presumed Innocent: Picturing Childhood 68
   Catharine Lumby

4 The Sombrero Comes Out of the Closet: Gay Marriage in Mexico City and a Nation's Struggle for Identity 80
   Santiago Ballina

5 The Drug Cultures in France and the Netherlands (1960s–1980s): Banning or Regulating the 'Unacceptable' 103
   Alexandre Marchant

6 'When the Smoke Clears': Confronting Smoking Policy 119
   John Scannell

Part II Representing the Unacceptable

7 The Monstrous-Familial: Representations of the Unacceptable Family 137
   John Potts

8 Unacceptability and Prosaic Life in *Breaking Bad* 156
   Elliott Logan

9	Sade's Constrained Libertinage: The Problem of Disgust *Naomi Stekelenburg*	168
10	Freedom of Expression has Limitations: Censorship of Performance in the USA *Timothy R. Wilson*	187
11	Why Saying 'No' to Life Is Unacceptable *Claire Colebrook*	203

Index   223

Acknowledgements

The editors wish to thank the authors who have contributed stimulating essays to this book. Many of the chapters were developed from papers initially given at The Unacceptable conference held at Macquarie University, Australia in 2011. We acknowledge the input of Nick Mansfield, Sabine Krajewski, Sarah Keith and Becky Shepherd in the formulation and organisation of this conference, as well as the financial support of the Department of Media, Music, Communication and Cultural Studies. For the development of this book, we are indebted to Felicity Plester at Palgrave Macmillan, whose encouragement and guidance helped to translate this research into publication.

Contributors

Santiago Ballina has served as an independent translator, political affairs adviser for diplomatic representatives, and Deputy Consul at the Consulate of Mexico in Yuma. He is currently a freelance writer, with a deep interest in cultural and socio-economic affairs from an international and comparative perspective.

Claire Colebrook is Edwin Erle Sparks Professor of English at Penn State University, USA. She has published books and articles on contemporary European philosophy, feminist theory, literary theory and poetry. Her most recent book is *William Blake and Digital Aesthetics*.

Mitchell Dean, author of *Governmentality: Power and Rule in Modern Society*, is Professor of Public Governance in the Department of Management, Politics and Philosophy at Copenhagen Business School. His previous books include *The Constitution of Poverty: Toward a Genealogy of Liberal Governance*; *Critical and Effective Histories: Foucault's Methods and Historical Sociology*; and *Governing Societies: Political Perspectives on Domestic and International Rule*. He is currently working on a book on substantive approaches to power.

Chris Haywood is Senior Lecturer in the Department of Education at the University of Newcastle, UK. He has published widely in the areas of sexuality, gender and age relations, with a particular focus on the cultural analysis of schooling and education. His latest book (with Mairtin MacanGhaill) is *Masculinity and Education: Social and Cultural Transformations*.

Elliott Logan researches television and film aesthetics and criticism in the School of English, Media Studies, and Art History at the University of Queensland. He is the author of 'Flashforwards in *Breaking Bad*: Openness, Closure, and Possibility' in the forthcoming *Global Television: Aesthetics and Style*, co-edited by Jason Jacobs and Steven Peacock.

Catharine Lumby is Professor in the Department of Media, Music, Communication and Cultural Studies at Macquarie University. She is the author of seven books. She has a broad research background with degrees in Fine Arts, Law and Media Studies. Her current project is a literary biography of the Australian author Frank Moorhouse.

Alexandre Marchant is Lecturer at the University Paris Ouest – Nanterre La Défense. He is researching social, cultural and political aspects of the 'drug epidemic' problem, on the basis of public archives.

John Potts is Professor in Media at Macquarie University, Australia. He is the author of *A History of Charisma*, *Radio in Australia*, and *Culture and Technology* (with Andrew Murphie). He has published widely on media, digital technology, art history and intellectual history. He is a founding editor of *Scan Online Journal of Media Arts Culture*.

John Scannell is Lecturer in the Department of Media, Music, Communications and Cultural Studies at Macquarie University, Australia. He has published articles on popular music, new media, contemporary philosophy and cultural studies and has integrated these research interests into his recent interdisciplinary book on the musical icon James Brown.

Naomi Stekelenburg has worked as a research psychologist at the Mental Health Research Institute and St Vincents Hospital in Melbourne, and now integrates her love of literature and science through her research on disgust, evolution and transgressive fiction.

Timothy R. Wilson is Professor of Theatre in the Department of Dance and Theatre at the University of North Texas. His work as a choreographer, performer and director has involved commissioned creations of original contemporary works for stage as well as site-specific environmental performances.

Introduction: What Is the Unacceptable?

John Potts and John Scannell

This book probes the issue of the unacceptable as a social and cultural category.

The unacceptable is explored in fields including censorship, pornography, free speech and hate speech, moral panics, drug culture, religious cults, fears surrounding paedophilia and the family, same-sex marriage, childhood sexuality, power, smoking and the representation of criminal or transgressive behaviour. The essays in this volume reveal the ways in which the category of the unacceptable reflects the sexual, racial and political fault-lines of a society.

To consider how images, texts, behaviours and practices might be judged 'unacceptable' is key to understanding how culture, communication and creativity fit into society. This issue of what is fit to present has always haunted culture, especially in relation to social institutions: the proscription of heresy, the erasure of bodies (due to gender, race, age), the silencing of sexualities, the purging of languages, the classification of desires as pathologies. Mainstream society constructs a set of values, supported by law, expressing its idea of acceptable behaviour. The unacceptable is that which transgresses this moral code, that which needs to be criticised, censored or suppressed in civil discourse.

As the essays collected in this book demonstrate, the unacceptable varies widely across cultures. Case studies from the UK, the USA, Australia, Europe and South America provide distinctive perspectives on the theme of what is deemed socially acceptable. The dividing-line between the acceptable and the unacceptable also shifts over time within a specific culture; the contributors to this book are attentive to the cultural dynamic in which the notion of the unacceptable is contested.

Designating the unacceptable proves a difficult challenge, as it is fundamentally an impediment to the productive difference of life. To pose the question of unacceptability is to propose limits upon the visible and the sayable. Of course, many would argue that it is important to intervene in human activity, and that to limit acceptability is the function of a civil society. To suggest that 'anything goes' in a society is to contravene its most vital mode of constitution, the stability of law. The unacceptable, then, may be regarded as the necessary limit of social production. It is the point where bodies, images and practices are deemed to be without merit or value and thus extricated from the realm of the social. It is at this limit of acceptability that this book has its place; it seeks to comprehend, and perhaps intervene, in some such divisive contemporary issues.

In the following discussions of the unacceptable, we attempt to evaluate and rationalise points of intervention, terminations, matters of law, reactionary forces. Central to our concerns is the pursuit of the unacceptable. Does it remain with us? Is the outlawed simply an object of voyeurism? What does the unacceptable reflect of a society that has exercised censorship or repression?

Out of these discussions, we can begin to question the function of the unacceptable. At what point is regulation necessary? When does reaction simply exist for its own sake? Who has the capacity to designate that which is unacceptable, and, moreover, do we have the chance to overturn it? How can we tell the difference between productive social policy and fashion, fad or fable? What role has censorship played in the definition and proscription of unacceptable behaviour?

Censoring the unacceptable

The word 'censor' derives from Ancient Rome: the first censors were appointed in 443 BC. The initial task of the two censors was to conduct a census of Roman citizens, but their powers extended to a general level, where they 'exercised a supervision of the morals of the community'.[1] The censors were authorised to assess the conduct of citizens, placing a mark of censure against any man whose behaviour – public or private – they considered 'reprehensible'.[2] The Roman censors exerted significant authority and influence: they could punish unacceptable conduct by removing the offending individual from his tribe, the social division to which all Romans belonged.

When Christianity was accepted as the official religion of the Roman Empire in AD 380, the Christian church became the guardian of moral values in the West. Bishops assumed great authority, recognised by the state as leaders with a civil status similar to that of magistrate. After the fall of Rome, the church maintained its role as the source of moral authority in European societies. Church leaders defined the code of social behaviour expected of good Christians; the church was also energetic in proscribing the unacceptable. In its early centuries, the church devoted much of this energy to repressing interpretations of Christianity which it deemed theologically unacceptable. The orthodox theological position was established in part through the expulsion of alternative viewpoints, which were outlawed as heresies. The violent suppression of the heretical Catharist sect in France in the twelfth century was only one instance of the continuing persecution of unorthodox views. The notorious Inquisition, founded in the thirteenth century, was a religious court authorised to use torture and death in the punishment of heretics. The Inquisition's repressive programme also included censorship: an Index of proscribed books – texts condemned as heretical – was compiled in 1557, was continuously updated, and remained in effect until 1966.

In the development of the modern state, many of the functions of censorship and regulation were assumed by state authorities. Another significant process in the defining of the unacceptable was the rise of the middle class as the dominant class within newly urbanised, industrialised societies. The ascendancy of bourgeois values in the wake of the Industrial Revolution was first evident in Great Britain in the early nineteenth century, when the middle class 'started to develop a strong sense of identity and of self-worth and virtue'.[3] As Roger Osborne has remarked, middle-class values were defined by Protestant ideals of 'self-help and public virtue'.[4] Thrift, hard work and moral decency were highly valued in public and private behaviour. This newly hegemonic social class was critical of both the aristocracy, which it deemed 'corrupt and lazy', and the working class, which it considered 'ignorant, lazy and morally lax'.[5]

Much of the drive to social 'improvement' in the Victorian era was driven by the bourgeois class, which throughout the nineteenth century gained representation in parliament, government bureaucracies, local councils and – most importantly – the press. As the self-appointed custodian of national virtue, the middle class regarded as its public duty the correcting of the behaviour of the lower classes. Temperance movements were launched in a bid to rectify moral failures within the working class. Rules were created for sport and leisure activities such as boxing and the football codes, previously considered unruly. Social services bureaucracies were empowered to intervene in families suspected of failing to raise children in an acceptable manner. Middle-class values became mainstream social values in the Victorian period – and this legacy remains in contemporary Western societies. Decency, the value of hard work, the importance of respectable public behaviour, the sanctity of the nuclear family, the need to protect children: these principles are at the core of mainstream society's idea of acceptable behaviour. The unacceptable is that which transgresses these moral values, generating censure or suppression in response.

Across the contemporary world, the definition and regulation of the unacceptable varies enormously. In a theocratic state such as Iran, the function of proscribing and policing unacceptable behaviour rests with religious authorities; the dividing-line between acceptable and unacceptable social behaviour or cultural production is determined according to the interpretation of religious texts and values. In a secular communist state such as China, the right to define and punish unacceptable behaviour or publication is reserved by the governing Communist Party, which actively censors publications – including the internet – and subjects dissidents to detention and punishment. In the liberal-democratic nations, freedom of speech and freedom of the press are prized values – yet these freedoms have never been absolute. There are definite limits, legislated and policed by the state, to freedom of expression. Racial vilification, for example, is forbidden by law in many countries, as is incitement to violent behaviour. The civil rights and feminist movements of the 1960s and 1970s achieved hard-won victories against discrimination on the grounds of gender and race; these victories are reflected in anti-discrimination legislation, setting legal boundaries around unacceptable civil behaviour.

Yet the role of the state in censoring unacceptable behaviour through 'hate speech' laws has been questioned by civil libertarians. Julian Assange, whose WikiLeaks has earned the enmity of the US government and corporate power, nevertheless prefers the protection of free speech guaranteed by the First Amendment in the USA to the 'acceptable' censorship model favoured in the UK and Commonwealth nations such as Australia and Canada. For Assange and human rights lawyer Jennifer Robinson, the Commonwealth nations' laws support a form of censorship justified 'by the perceived need to protect historically persecuted minorities and maintain racial harmony'.[6] Yet from the civil libertarian perspective, any form of censorship, no matter how well intended, remains a constraint of freedom of expression. Democracy is healthiest, according to Assange, where free speech is least impeded, and where the state's intervention into unacceptable speech and behaviour is minimal.

The function of censorship and classification of published materials in liberal democracies is exercised by state authorities – although religious pressure groups continue to exert significant influence. This was nowhere better demonstrated than in the adoption of self-regulating censorship by the Hollywood film industry in the early 1930s, a response to intense pressure from the 'League of Decency' and other religious groups concerned at the licentious and violent content of US films. The Hays Production Code, installed by Hollywood to assuage the concerns of moral crusaders, limited the ways that crime and sexual relations could be portrayed, creating – in the words of film historian David Robinson – 'standards for screen morals which condemned American films to a kindergarten scope of discussion for the next 40 years'.[7]

Censorship of books, films and other works in Western societies remained a contentious issue throughout the twentieth century. Major works of literature, including *Ulysses*, *Lady Chatterley's Lover* and *Howl*, were the subject of high-profile prosecutions on the grounds of obscenity. A turning point came in the 1960s and 1970s, when classification and censorship of films, literature and other media forms – including pornography – entered a permissive phase in many Western nations. This liberalisation of standards concerning what was acceptable to publish was the subject of a backlash in the 1980s in the USA, the UK, Australia and other nations, when moral crusaders aligned with feminist advocates to campaign against pornographic content. The grounds for objection to pornography were divergent – Christian decency and protecting family values on the one hand, opposition to the objectification and degradation of women on the other – yet both groups of advocates were vocal in defining the unacceptable in media representations.

In the early twenty-first century, the representation of children has become a flashpoint for concerns about childhood and sexuality, as several contributors to this volume examine in their chapters. Paedophilia is at the centre of a volatile moral panic, ready to erupt whenever it is feared that children have been sexualised in works of art, film or television, advertising or fashion. The representation of children runs across one of the fault-lines of contemporary Western societies, where consumerism, the cult of youth, permissiveness and marketing to the young oppose the need to protect children, the demand to preserve moral decency and the call to regulate media industries to prevent the sexualised depiction of the young. The tussle between conflicting social imperatives reflected in this opposition is also the struggle over the definition of acceptable and unacceptable representations of children.

There are other contentious issues straddling other fault-lines in contemporary Western societies, in which legislation and policing by the state are hotly debated. One of these fault-lines is found in the clash between mainstream social values and the alternative values of an immigrant culture. In 2010, the French senate passed legislation banning veils covering the face, a ban forbidding the wearing in public of the niqab and burqa worn by some Muslim women. This law, which came into effect in 2011, introduced fines for women wearing such veils in public (as well as fining men who forced women to wear full face veils). Another punishment for those individuals transgressing this law is compulsory lessons in French citizenship. The French state, resolute in its secular identity and the separation between religion and the state, has decreed that this Islamic practice is unacceptable within its borders. Opposition to the law insists on the primacy of religious freedom and civil rights, arguing that the state has imposed its authority on individuals, and on a religious minority, in an unacceptable manner.

Another fiercely debated issue concerns same-sex marriage. In 2011, New York became the seventh and largest state in the USA to legalise same-sex marriage, sparking celebrations from gay rights activists – and lamentations from religious and conservative groups. The right for same-sex couples to wed is a contemporary battle-ground for advocates of equal rights for gay, bisexual and transgender individuals. Pitted against such groups are conservatives who consider marriage an exclusively heterosexual rite, and religious organisations claiming moral authority over the institution of marriage. The Catholic Archbishop of New York, for example, condemned the 2011 legislation as 'immoral' and an 'ominous threat'.[8] This attitude is the continuation of a centuries-long prejudice against homosexuality supported by religious leaders.

Discrimination against sexual minorities received a public counter-force only in 1970, with the inaugural Gay Pride Marches in the USA following the Stonewall Riot in New York the previous year. Activist groups for gay, lesbian and transgender rights succeeded in overturning much of the discrimination and persecution embedded in social institutions and policies, yet same-sex marriage has remained a stumbling-block. In the USA, 29 states have constitutional bans on same-sex marriage, while another 12 have laws banning it. State referendums outlawing same-sex marriage have never been defeated. Yet the balance of power on this issue appears to be shifting in the wake of the New York legislation. *The New York Times* reported that a 2011 Gallup Poll found that 53 per cent of Americans believed that the law should recognise same-sex unions.[9] This was the first Gallup poll to show a majority in favour of legalising same-sex marriage. The majority of states in the USA have decreed by law that same-sex marriage is unacceptable; but this state of affairs, like many others before it, may well be in the process of undergoing change.

Theorising the unacceptable

As the preceding examples have demonstrated, the socially unacceptable is often a fiercely contested category, subject to conflicting pressures and change over time. Any attempt to theorise the unacceptable must therefore take into account the manifold social forces contributing to the establishment and transformation of cultural values. The various contributors to this volume all subscribe to a critical perspective on cultural studies, in which culture is conceived as 'dynamic and multiple', as characterised by Murphie and Potts in their study of culture and technology. According to this critical perspective, culture is dynamic because 'ideas and values change, often quite quickly, over time'.[10] As a result of activism, lobbying, media strategies and other mechanisms, 'older attitudes to culture may be superseded', leading to new definitions of what is acceptable and unacceptable. Culture is multiple because 'it contains the activities of different classes, of different races, of different age groups'.[11] Culture is riven by oppositions and contradictions, manifest in government policies, alternative political viewpoints, religious teaching, and the spectrum of attitudes found in the media and on the internet. The values of mainstream culture are defined in part by political means, including legislation; this political expression of cultural values is, as we have seen, subject to pressures from oppositional groupings, often resulting in legislative change. These processes, in which the dividing-line between acceptable and unacceptable is continually re-assessed, are part of a larger cultural dynamic.

The various chapters in this book approach the unacceptable in a range of ways. There are a number of theoretical frameworks on which to draw in analysing the unacceptable; one of the more pertinent points of connection is the psychoanalytical theory deriving from Freud. The key idea in Freud's formulation of the psyche was that of repression, which bears directly on the social definition of unacceptable behaviour. According to the Freudian model, the primary drives, largely sexual or aggressive and seeking only self-satisfaction, enter into conflict with the 'reality principle', the socialising force that adapts the subject to the social order. Freud's analysis of the unconscious, through the interpretation of dreams and the process of analysis, revealed the unconscious as an unruly, illogical site for the primary processes that are repressed from expression in conscious behaviour. The unacceptable, in the Freudian conception, is that which is censored from the secondary processes of thought, the domain of civilised behaviour and the rules of society.

Freud expanded on this theory first in studies of 'the psychopathology of everyday life', then in a generalised extension to the operation of civilisation. In *Civilization and its Discontents*, published in 1930, Freud proposed an 'irremediable antagonism between the demands of instinct and the restrictions of civilization'.[12] In this largely pessimistic account of civilisation, Freud's focus was on 'the discrepancies between people's thoughts and their actions, and to the diversity of their wishful impulses'.[13] Freud regarded civilisation as a system of 'achievements' and 'regulations' which serves two main purposes: 'to protect men against nature and to adjust their mutual relations'.[14] For Freud, the 'adjustments' of civilisation were doomed to produce multiple discontents because civilisation is built on the restraining of human desires. This process includes the repression of drives which, if carried out uncensored, would result in socially unacceptable behaviour.

All human societies enact regulation and social control: Freud noted that the 'taboo-observances' of tribal societies 'were the first "right" or "law"'.[15] The incest taboo was for Freud 'perhaps the most drastic mutilation which man's erotic life has in all time experienced'.[16] Other 'taboos, laws and customs' impose 'further restrictions' in setting the rules of acceptable behaviour within the social formation.[17] Freud observed that the Western civilisation of his time imposed a set of limitations on sexual enjoyment; this meant that 'sexuality as a source of pleasure in its own right' was not acceptable, and sexual activity was restricted to heterosexual monogamous relationships sanctioned by marriage.[18] The 'frustrations of sexual life' were the source, for Freud, of neurotic behaviour, but he argued that civilisation 'demands other sacrifices besides that of sexual satisfaction'.[19] These include the curbing of instinctually aggressive behaviour, which constitutes 'the greatest impediment to civilization'.[20] The mechanisms of guilt and conscience, as well as the state's social authority, were for Freud the means of restricting unacceptably aggressive or selfish behaviour. Civilisation will continue to generate its 'discontents' because it is fundamentally based on repression, and 'when an instinctual trend undergoes repression, its libidinal elements are turned into symptoms, and its aggressive components into a sense of guilt'.[21] The best Freud could hope for was that this libidinal struggle might be better accommodated in future civilisations, 'however much that civilization may oppress the life of the individual to-day'.[22]

The Freudian model of psychology, readily applicable to the social order and civilisation itself, exerted significant influence across a range of intellectual and cultural activity in the twentieth century, even though Freud's influence on the field of psychology itself declined appreciably in the second half of that century. The proponents of a more permissive society in the 1960s argued along Freudian lines when they asserted that repressive censorship and restrictions on sexual expression had created an unhealthy society. The opposing approach, advocating increased restrictions, had failed spectacularly earlier in the twentieth century, most notably during the Prohibition of alcohol in the USA in the 1920s. Prohibition was the answer to problems too difficult to address, to questions left unanswered and put aside; it increased the 'oppression' of the individual lamented by Freud. The social lesson learned from this attempt to ban the unacceptable was that extreme prohibition is ill-conceived and destructive, that banning activities does not make them disappear, but simply pushes them farther underground. Freud's concept of 'reaction formation' – the reactionary defensiveness borne of the fear of one's own desires – has also been critically applied to those conservative advocates crusading against the unacceptability of others. The unacceptable is often attached to myth and misrepresentation, the pretext of moral panics and hysteria, the culprit accused in lieu of more deep-seated and elusive social problems.

Of the many refinements and adjustments of Freudian theory, the most influential in cultural studies and critical theory has been the fusion of Freudian psychoanalysis and structuralist linguistics achieved by Jacques Lacan. By emphasising the field of language – most famously in his dictum 'the unconscious is structured like a language' – Lacan shifted the Freudian scenario into what he called the Symbolic order, in which the Name of the Father represents the Law inscribing the subject within a social and symbolic system. Lacan conceived desire as being driven by lack, often as the desire of the other, as the subject is 'split' and alienated within the Symbolic order. The Lacanian model would hold that prohibition – to use our earlier example – created desire in attempting to repress it; the regulation produces the transgression. The unacceptable is thus a product of law rather than nature. Lacan's development of Freud has in turn been applied in the field of cultural theory, most notably in the work of Slavoj Zizek and Julia Kristeva. Zizek's deployment of Lacan within a Marxist social critique has yielded a range of insights and analyses, including a focus on the 'violence' enacted on subjects – even within liberal democracies – through the imposition of prohibitions and the social order.[23]

Kristeva's theory of the 'abject' has been highly influential in a number of disciplines, and relates directly to the idea of the unacceptable. Kristeva defines the abject as that which is excluded from subject and object: the abject is 'radically excluded and draws me toward the place where meaning collapses'.[24] Food loathing is identified as an archaic form of abjection, along with disgust for filth, waste, excrement, corpses, the unclean and the improper. The significance of the abject for Kristeva is that it disturbs 'identity, system, order'[25]: the corpse is death infecting life, and premeditated crime displays the fragility of law. The abject is 'the in-between, the ambiguous', and exercises a paradoxical fascination in that it both repels and attracts. Prohibition and law open up the 'perverse interspace' of abjection,[26] which exercises a seductive appeal even though it is categorised as socially unacceptable. Kristeva proposes that the historic role of religion – to purify the abject – has been assumed by art in the modern secular era; her theory of the abject has been applied in literary and film theory to analyse the representation of the abject – the horrific, the unacceptable – in contemporary cultural works.

Another productive theoretical approach has been developed within the field of critical theory, beginning with the work of the Frankfurt School in the early 1930s. The research of Max Horkheimer, Theodor Adorno and other theorists applied a Marxist critique to the mass culture of contemporary capitalism, drawing at times on psychoanalysis in a synthesis of Freud and Marx. Herbert Marcuse's radical interpretation of Freud in works such as *Eros and Civilisation* (1955) and *One-Dimensional Man* (1964) redefined the Freudian conflict within civilisation to a struggle between an oppressive technological-economic apparatus, driven by rationalisation, and latent human desires. These works provided a theoretical grounding for the sexual politics and activism of the 1960s; Marcuse also offered, with his concept of 'repressive tolerance', an analysis of the way that the cultural upheaval of the 1960s was negotiated by the established social order. Marcuse argued that liberal claims for tolerance of dissenting or permissive behaviour were invalidated by the 'invalidation of the democratic process itself', due to the 'concentration of economic and political power and the integration of opposites in a society which uses technology as an instrument of domination'.[27] Tolerance of dissent or of unacceptable public behaviour was for Marcuse ultimately repressive because it is 'deceptive and promotes co-ordination' rather than the radical overturning of the social system: 'tolerance itself serves to contain such change rather than to promote it.'[28]

The critical thought of Michel Foucault, focusing on the intersection of power, knowledge and social behaviour, has been extremely influential in a wide range of disciplines. From his earliest works such as *Madness and Civilisation*, Foucault analysed the formation of knowledge and accepted codes of behaviour from the perspective of that which was marginalised or excluded: forms of mental illness, forms of sexuality, expressions or activities either 'disciplined or punished' by the workings of power/knowledge. Foucault's historical investigations, and his reflections on the present, were concerned with how the acceptable has come to be defined in modern societies, as he remarked: 'the target of analysis wasn't "institutions", "theories" or "ideology", but *practices* – with the aim of grasping the conditions which makes these acceptable at a given moment.'[29] Foucault described his critical method as analysis of the 'regime of practices', practices being understood 'as places where what is said and what is done, rules imposed and reasons given, the planned and the taken for granted meet and interconnect'.[30]

One of the consequences of this form of inquiry is the opening up of opportunities for resistance or refusal within practices such as psychiatry or the prison system. The intolerable activities of everyday life were of significant interest for Foucault, whose study of some of the more insidious but seemingly acceptable institutional mechanisms were the focus of his own concept of unacceptability. The philosopher Gilles Deleuze said that for Foucault 'thinking was an experiment, but it was also a vision, a grasping of something intolerable'.[31] Referring to the intolerability of the prison system as revealed by Foucault's analyses, Deleuze stated that 'it was not a question of being unjust. Something was intolerable precisely because no one saw it, because it was imperceptible (even though everybody knew about it)'.[32]

The critical analysis of the workings of power has been continued in the writing of Giorgio Agamben, who in a series of works beginning with *Homo Sacer* (1998), has focused on the operations of 'sovereign power'. Agamben's notion of 'bare life', a concept he discovered in classical Greek thought, relates to the limits of the acceptable in contemporary societies. Agamben points to those 'states of exception' in the form of the camp – refugee detention centres, camps for 'unlawful enemy combatants' – where appalling conditions, amounting to nothing more than 'bare life', are tolerated. In these officially sanctioned spaces, the unacceptable, in the form of human misery, is rendered acceptable as a 'state of exception'.[33]

Perhaps what is most unacceptable about everyday life is that which is not even recognised as such. The unacceptable includes the unacceptability of poverty, homelessness and starvation, which permeates our daily lives, yet is so neatly folded into our social order that it barely warrants recognition. At what point do we begin to see the intolerable activities that are simply an inherent part of the everyday?

Deleuze discussed the notion of 'the intolerable' in his work, which, he argued, might in some cases reflect the truly catastrophic, but may also just as readily refer to the banality of the everyday: 'The intolerable is no longer a serious injustice, but the permanent state of a daily banality. Man is not himself a world other than the one in which he experiences the intolerable and feels himself trapped.'[34] Perhaps it is in such daily banality, the banality which is intolerable because it does nothing about those most intolerable aspects of our lives, that the concept most properly resides. Being trapped in the common sense of the world has always been a concern for Deleuze, and is central to a philosophy that attempts to rethink a politics devoid of orthodoxy and dogma, which, as the catalysts of stasis and banality, are anathema to him. Both alone and in conjunction with Felix Guattari, Deleuze considered what it might take to break free of these 'intolerable' forces of a life otherwise imposed upon by the 'common sense' of thought.

In *What is Philosophy?* Deleuze and Guattari proposed that art plays a crucial role in breaking free of the intolerability of life, and it is the intolerable which motivates artistic change and response. An intolerable situation can shock thought into irrational connection, however traumatic this might be, because emerging from such an affective event can set in motion the body's rebirth as well. Thrown into this 'chaosmos' the body must emerge 'somehow', and it is this process itself that forces one into new methods of responding to the world. There are many instances of the world of art and culture in the discussions contained in this book. Many of them provoke a sense of deliberate chaos and a shock to thought, which is not always met with the same spirit in which it is intended. They constitute an affront to dogma, and it is dogma that destroys creative thought. In this regard, representation of the unacceptable is seen to challenge the limits and constraints of the acceptable.

The structure of this book

The Unacceptable is divided into two sections. Chapters in the first section, 'The Socially Unacceptable', explore the limits of the permissible in social formations, with reference to issues of censorship, regulation, media, power and policing. The second section, 'Representing the Unacceptable', examines the ways in which taboo subjects and behaviour deemed unacceptable have been represented in literature, art, film, television and other media forms.

The first chapter in Part 1 is 'Power and the Unacceptable', in which Mitchell Dean asks whether political power has entered into the domain of the unacceptable. Dean begins with a consideration of the controversy surrounding film director Lars von Trier's 'Nazi' comments at the Cannes film festival in 2011, and the praise for Marc Jacobs' 'Night Porter' Louis Vuitton Fall/Winter 2011 show in Paris. He then inquires about the conditions of acceptability and unacceptability of power in forms of speech and visual culture, and returns to questions of fascist desire and the pleasure of forms of power and domination raised first in the 1970s by theorists such as Deleuze and Guattari. This chapter contrasts the juridical-theological logic of law, ban and transgression with the visual-aesthetic one of economies of power, pleasure and desire. Due to legal proscription, it has become harder to address publicly the investments and attractions of 'extreme' politics, from fascism to terrorism, while, paradoxically, such politics underlies the production of taboos that can be openly played with, exploited and turned into profit.

In the next chapter, ' "Schooling Scandals!": Exploring the Necessity of Cultural Disgust', Chris Haywood explores cultural representations of the unacceptable that circulate through media reports of schooling and sexuality. Researchers have argued that media reports on sexuality and schooling are primarily concerned with the control and regulation of sexuality divisions. This chapter seeks to build upon this work by suggesting that such media reports are intricately connected to the fragmentation of a cultural imaginary that is constituted by idealised teacher/pupil and adult/child boundaries. However, media scandals do not simply threaten the imaginary and reinforce the acceptable; they also create a cultural disgust that is abhorrent, unacceptable, exciting and necessary. To explore this further, Haywood draws upon UK news reporting of school sex scandals from the last 25 years and focuses on representations of sexually 'voracious teachers', 'precocious pupils' and 'predatory paedophiles'. The analysis of these representations helps us to understand how the shock and horror of media accounts is not simply about the closure or the repression of the unacceptable, but rather the mobilisation of abject and subjunctive sexual subjectivities. The chapter concludes by suggesting that representations of sexual unacceptability in schools impel and contribute to narratives of future social and economic prosperity.

In 'Presumed Innocent: Picturing Childhood', Catharine Lumby considers the images of children that have become the site of increasing public concern, debate and regulation over the past decade. From fears that children are being sexualised in advertising, to the public outcry in Australia about artist Bill Henson's photographs of naked young people, we are living in a time of heightened anxiety about how children are represented and who has the right to represent them. This chapter explores the extent to which discourses of protection mask discourses of control and what the consequences are for our understanding of children and young people's social and political rights. The chapter examines recent research into children's use of emerging online, social and mobile media technologies.

In 'The Sombrero Comes Out of the Closet: Gay Marriage in Mexico City and a Nation's Struggle for Identity', Santiago Ballina examines the issue of same-sex marriage in the context of Mexico. In 2010, in a swift move that caught by surprise both supporters and foes, the Local Assembly of Mexico City legalised gay marriage, making it the first city in Latin America to allow civil weddings between same-sex partners. The assembly went one step further, including adoption rights in the law that was finally approved.

In a country where the share of Catholic population is well above 80 per cent and deeply bound by traditional values, the issue, not surprisingly, became the centre of a heated debate. This chapter addresses the controversy aroused by the approval of gay marriage in Mexico City, with a particular focus on the arguments put forward by its opponents, who either overtly or subtly portrayed this type of union as a hazard to the social fabric of traditional Mexican society and values, and hence, as unacceptable. The case of Mexico is unique insofar as it reflects the broader context of a nation struggling to reshape its own modern identity. Caught between a predominantly conservative and Catholic Latin America and a neighbouring, flamboyant – and frequently intimidating – North America, fault-lines are not infrequent among Mexican society. The debate about same-sex marriage is the latest expression of a national quest for identity.

Alexandre Marchant explores the issue of drug use in 'The Drug Cultures in France and the Netherlands (1960s–1980s): Banning or Regulating the "Unacceptable"'. At the turning point of the 1960s–1970s, Western societies were confronted with a sudden upsurge of youth drug consumption. Drug scenes, the first cultural happenings (beatnik *provos* in Amsterdam, 'underground' in Paris) including the sight of young junkies in the streets, appeared in every Western city. In reaction, drug abuse was termed an 'epidemic' by the media, designated a 'social plague' by politicians and conceptualised by intellectuals as a threat to civilisation. The new drug subcultures, making wandering and drug-taking a lifestyle, were a true negation of what had become the modern Western world. Based on French and Dutch public archives, this chapter aims to question the cultural logics which make a practice and a subculture unacceptable. In France, in an atmosphere of moral panic, public authorities set up a prohibitionist logic in 1970. In contrast, Dutch authorities, more receptive to counter-cultural claims and young protestations, established a model of toleration of soft drugs and harm reduction policies in 1976, finally adopting a model of 'repressive tolerance', accepting certain deviant behaviours for a better overall social control. The comparison highlights a common opposition of Christian and conformist societies to drug underworlds which denied, by their simple existence, the traditional symbolic order.

The final chapter in the 'Socially Unacceptable' section concerns the issue of smoking. In ' "When the Smoke Clears": Confronting Smoking Policy', John Scannell draws on the philosophy of Gilles Deleuze, a well-known victim of smoking. Scannell does not try to defend the practice, but instead uses the recent trend of enforced smoking bans in public spaces to ruminate upon the 'encounter' that ensues. As such, this chapter seeks to dissect the point of intervention between smoker and assailant, a complex assemblage of multiple worlds thrown together by chance, and necessarily guaranteed by law. As ongoing smoking bans impel further collisions between habit and policing, such unmitigated encounters have driven the more indignant of the nicotine-addicted to widely reported incidents of 'smoke rage'-related physical violence. Yet the biggest victim of all in this power struggle over public space is community itself, with law enforcement taking precedence over camaraderie, and where the punitive work of an increasingly litigious society is freely undertaken by private volunteers. With the growth of open-air smoking bans, and a commensurate growth in the individual policing that necessarily ensues, it is argued that the detrimental social side effects of such overzealous prohibition has reached its limit of effectiveness in the community at large.

The first chapter in 'Part Two: Representing the Unacceptable', concerns representation of the family. In 'The Monstrous-Familial: Representations of the Unacceptable Family', John Potts takes a historical perspective on the changing structure and status of the family, culminating with the normative status attributed to the nuclear family in Western societies since the mid-twentieth century. This chapter focuses on representations in film and television of the nuclear family's other, which has often been depicted as monstrous – that is, both repulsive and fascinating. Variations of this monstrosity include the extended family, portrayed as constricting and violent (*The Godfather*), the polygamous family, patriarchal and illegal (*Big Love*) and the rural/cannibalistic family depicted in numerous horror films since the 1970s. Each of these family types is represented as unacceptable, to varying degrees, yet each generates a strong fascination for audiences. Potts considers why depictions of alternatives to the conventional nuclear family have exerted such appeal.

Elliott Logan's chapter, 'Unacceptability and Prosaic Life in *Breaking Bad*', examines the handling of boundaries between acceptability and unacceptability in the television series *Breaking Bad*, a hybrid modulation of gangster, Western and domestic melodrama. Identifying the operation of acceptability and unacceptability as thematic oppositions in Hollywood gangster and Western melodrama, Logan shows how *Breaking Bad* unsettles their opposition. Contemporising and resituating these genres to the prosaic sociality of the bourgeois modern world, *Breaking Bad* stages its conflict between the socially acceptable and unacceptable in modulations of self-performance. Logan suggests that in this programme a conflict rages beneath veneers of acceptability, as heroic desires struggle with the prosaic demands of the modern self.

Naomi Stekelenburg turns attention to fiction in 'Sade's Constrained Libertinage: The Problem of Disgust'. Transgressive fiction is a genre that is thought to flaunt its capacity to challenge societal conceptualisations of acceptability. Works by transgressive authors such as the Marquis de Sade and Georges Bataille frequently represent the 'unacceptable' via the overt portrayal of the products of the body, bodily states (such as filth and death) and ways of bodily functioning that place it under threat of contamination. In this sense, they create an aesthetic of disgust that has, to some extent, prevented their participation in mainstream literary society. Stekelenburg draws on an understanding of the emotion of disgust from an evolutionary psychology perspective, suggesting that works by Sade present a quite conventional view of human nature; that the portrayal of corporeality is, paradoxically, a distraction from and a conduit for his contribution to the conversation regarding morality. It is suggested by evolutionary scholars that disgust originated as a response to protect humans from pathogens and disease, and from this particularly corporeal and material focus, it was co-opted into the more abstract purpose of protecting the soul from moral contamination. Reading transgressive fiction in the light of this nexus provides insights into how authors manipulate the connection between corporeal aspects of disgust and the associations they have with notions of moral purity and cleanliness, in order to evoke a commentary on sexual and moral 'acceptability'.

Stekelenburg investigates how the libertine fiction of Sade negotiates the fraught textual space of libertinage, where images of excessive corporeality constantly threaten to undermine the central didactic aim of enlisting new libertines. Her analysis eschews focus on Sade's capacity to shock and repulse, as this has been explored sufficiently by past scholarship. Instead, by using a perspective informed by evolutionary psychology, the textual strategies that Sade uses to attenuate the negative affect and effects elicited by explicit representation of the 'unacceptable' are illuminated.

Timothy R. Wilson addresses the issue of censorship in his chapter, 'Censorship in Performance in America: Freedom of Expression Has Limitations'. Wilson argues that although freedom of speech is a basic tenet of US foundation and philosophy, contemporary artists in performance, theatre, film and television are consistently faced with issues of censorship. Government grant agencies may refuse funding based on 'the decency clause'. Concerns that an artist's individual expression may violate 'common standards of decency', a vague and openly prejudicial concept, may and does prevent full enjoyment of freedom of speech – not only for the artist, but also for the potential audience. One contemporary example considered in this chapter is the case of the 'NEA 4', four individual artists who took their cases of implied censorship by a government agency to the United States Supreme Court. Wilson also discusses the American Film Rating System, which appears much more concerned with sexuality, nudity and language rather than with the effect of violence. The sense of arbitrarily assuming what may/may not offend the American viewer becomes even more difficult to understand in television. The practice of concealing body parts with black bars or fuzzy ovals confounds the contemporary audience and distracts from the artistic intent. In further 'protection' of our sensibilities, television censors will simply 'bleep out' what is considered an expletive in contemporary language. The language is a vital part of the contemporary writer's intent, but various networks will choose to edit someone else's work. On the other hand, as Wilson points out, it appears to be acceptable for the American viewer to experience violence and brutality. This chapter is a timely reminder of the power of censorship in defining what is unacceptable in contemporary society.

The concluding chapter in this book confronts the ultimate issue related to the unacceptable: life itself. In 'Why Saying "No" to Life is Unacceptable', Claire Colebrook focuses on the limits to questions of life and death. In 2008, *The Day the Earth Stood Still* featured a dead-pan alien (played appropriately by Keanu Reeves) who informed humanity that its violence and destructive modes of consumption no longer entitled it to life on earth. A common motif in science fiction narratives of alien invasion, the judgment of humanity as life-denying and life-unworthy is neither refuted nor answered, but simply set aside as the plot hurtles toward redemption. By contrast, only a few years later, in series three of the TV programme *True Blood*, the villainous anti-hero Russell Eddington asserts that a vile, destructive, violent and planet-destroying humanity must give way to another more worthy species. How has the common figure of the self-evident value of human life as life itself given way to an increasing sense of species guilt and preliminary mourning? Why, just as humanity begins to have some sense of its end, are policies of survival, adaptation, mitigation and climate change accompanied by a wide sense and figuration of the unacceptable nature of human life? Colebrook explores the limits of acceptability in her meditation on the permissible – and unacceptable – questions posed of humanity and life itself.

Notes

1. John Roberts (ed) *The Oxford Dictionary of the Classical World*, p. 139.
2. Ibid., p. 30.
3. Roger Osborne, *Civilisation: A New History of the Western World*, p. 352.
4. Ibid.
5. Ibid.
6. Julian Assange and Jennifer Robinson, 'Play Ball, not Bolt, in Free Speech Debate', p. 15.
7. David Robinson, *The History of World Cinema*, p. 105.
8. Michael Barbaro, 'Start Spreading the News: New York Legalises Gay Marriage', p. 11.
9. *New York Times*, 'New York Decision Sparks Hope for Gay Marriage Movement', p. 10.
10. Andrew Murphie and John Potts, *Culture and Technology*, p. 7.
11. Ibid., p. 8.
12. Albert Dickson, 'Editor's Introduction' to *Civilization and its Discontents*, p. 246.
13. Sigmund Freud, *Civilization, Society and Religion*, p. 251.

14. Ibid., p. 278.
15. Ibid., p. 290.
16. Ibid., p. 293.
17. Ibid., p. 293.
18. Ibid., p. 294.
19. Ibid., p. 298.
20. Ibid., p. 313.
21. Ibid., p. 332.
22. Ibid., p. 335.
23. Slavoj Zizek, *Violence: Big Ideas/Small Books*.
24. Julia Kristeva, *Powers of Horror: An Essay on Abjection*, p. 2.
25. Ibid., p. 4.
26. Ibid., p. 16.
27. Herbert Marcuse, 'Repressive Tolerance', p. 310.
28. Ibid., p. 324.
29. Michel Foucault, 'Questions of Method', p. 225.
30. Ibid.
31. Gilles Deleuze, 'The Intellectual and Politics: Foucault and the Prison', p. 20.
32. Ibid.
33. Giorgio Agamben, *Homo Sacer: Sovereign Power and Bare Life*.
34. Gilles Deleuze, *Cinema 2: The Time Image*, pp. 169–170.

References

Agamben, Giorgio, *Homo Sacer: Sovereign Power and Bare Life*, tr. Daniel Heller-Roazen, Stanford, CA: Stanford University Press, 1998.

Assange, Julian and Robinson, Jennifer, 'Play Ball, not Bolt, in Free Speech Debate', *Sydney Morning Herald*, 28 October 2011, p. 15.

Barbaro, Michael, 'Start Spreading the News: New York Legalises Gay Marriage', *The New York Times*, reprinted in *The Sydney Morning Herald*, 27 June 2011, p. 11.

Deleuze, Gilles, 'The Intellectual and Politics: Foucault and the Prison' (interview by Paul Rabinow and Keith Gandal) in *History of the Present*, 2 Spring 1986.

Deleuze, Gilles, *Cinema 2: The Time Image*, tr. Hugh Tomlinson and Tobert Galeta, Minneapolis, MN: University of Minnesota Press, 1989.

Deleuze, Gilles and Guattari, Félix, *What Is Philosophy?* tr. Hugh Tomlinson and Graham Burchell, New York: Columbia University Press, 1994.

Dickson, Albert, 'Editor's Introduction' to *Civilization and Its Discontents*, in *Civilization, Society and Religion* (Pelican Freud Library Volume 12), New York: Penguin, 1985, pp. 245–249.

Foucault, Michel, 'Questions of Method', in James D. Faubion (ed) *Essential Works of Foucault, 1954–1984 Volume 3*, tr. Robert Hurley et al., New York: New York Press, 2000, pp. 223–238.

Freud, Sigmund, *Civilization, Society and Religion* (Pelican Freud Library Volume 12), New York: Penguin, 1985.

Kristeva, Julia, *Powers of Horror: An Essay on Abjection*, tr. Leon S. Roudiez, New York: Columbia University Press, 1982.

Lacan, Jacques, *Ecrits*, New York: W. W. Norton, 1977 [1966].

Marcuse, Herbert, 'Repressive Tolerance', in Paul Connerton (ed) *Critical Sociology: Selected Readings*, New York: Penguin, 1978, pp. 301–329.

Murphie, Andrew and Potts, John, *Culture and Technology*, Basingstoke: Palgrave Macmillan, 2003.

New York Times, 'New York Decision Sparks Hope for Gay Marriage Movement', reprinted in *The Sydney Morning Herald*, 28 June 2011, p. 10.

Osborne, Roger, *Civilisation: A New History of the Western World*, London: Jonathan Cape, 2006.

Roberts, John (ed) *The Oxford Dictionary of the Classical World*, Oxford: Oxford University Press, 2005.

Robinson, David, *The History of World Cinema*, New York: Stein and Day, 1981.

Zizek, Slavoj, *Violence: Big Ideas/Small Books*, New York: Picador, 2008.

Part I
The Socially Unacceptable

1
Power and the Unacceptable

Mitchell Dean

The unacceptable is a grey zone. We are used to identifying the unacceptable with what is proscribed, forbidden, censored and banned. Yet this implies a juridical model of power as command and repression and a 'police' complex to secure and enforce the ban. What is unacceptable often finds itself under the ban, such as a film rejected by a censorship board. On many occasions, however, the unacceptable falls short of what essentially is a juridical-theological model.

Often, the utterance 'this is unacceptable', is a performative one that may belie the incapacity of the actor making the statement to issue and secure a prohibition. It enacts a condition of censure, of disapproval and perhaps annoyance. An example would be when a politician says, 'Unemployed people have no right to reject available jobs'. It also performs, more or less successfully, the authority of the speaker to decide on questions of acceptability. Of course, the same politician in government might seek to compel the unemployed person to accept a menial or low-paid job by removing their right to benefits if they decline it. However, in a condition of wage-labour, which formally depends on the voluntary agreement of an employee to work for their employer, it is difficult for governments to force anyone to accept a particular job.

The other side of the law – either religious or secular – that forbids are the acts of transgression. There is, thus, little choice but to obey or to sin. However, the unacceptable is located in the grey zone between the two and circulates between regimes of power and economies of desire and pleasure. Thus, it is hard to imagine a notion of the unacceptable that does not imply a contestation of what is or is not acceptable, with the forces at stake not simply rational social and economic struggles, but those of pleasure and desire. The unacceptable is not the breaking of a taboo but the eliciting of power, desire and pleasure that circulates around that taboo.

My thesis here is that speech about and representation of aspects of power, particularly those concerned with domination and submission, and violence and coercion, has entered the grey zone of the unacceptable. I first provide some recent examples of this concerning speech about fascism and then use Michel Foucault's concept of 'saying the true' or 'veridiction' to address the conditions of acceptability or not of speaking about and representing fascism and speaking about and representing power. I argue that there are two alternatives to a juridical-theological proscription of certain kinds of speech that seek to remain acceptable: first, an ethico-political one, which examines desire and pleasure around power as an element of working on and governing individual and collective conduct; and, second, a visual-aesthetic one, which allows unexamined images of masochistic pleasure to circulate as a form of consumption and capital. I further suggest that eroticism acts as a 'signature' that moves power from the ethico-political domain, in which speech maintains a central position, to that of the relatively silent language of the visual-aesthetic domain.

Unacceptable speech

In a press conference at the Cannes Film Festival in May 2011, the Danish director, Lars von Trier, enunciated a view that, despite later apologies and reframing as a joke, would prove unacceptable to the festival's board. In response to a question concerning his German roots, and his interest in Nazi aesthetics, he rambled:

> I really wanted to be a Jew... and then I found out that I was really a Nazi, you know because my family was German, Hartmann, which also gave me some pleasure...
>
> What can I say? I understand Hitler. But I think he did some wrong things, yes absolutely, but I can see him sitting in his bunker in the end... [*turning to actor, Kirsten Dunst, seated at his left*] There will come a point at the end of this...
>
> No, I'm just saying I think I understand the man. He is not what you would call a good guy but I understand the man. I sympathise with him a little bit, yes.[1]

There was more to come as he sought to extricate himself from his own strange verbal cul-de-sac. It included a straightforward endorsement of Albert Speer, Hitler's architect, and ironic comments about his Jewish colleague, director Susanne Bier. He called Israel a 'pain in the ass', and at the end muttered a joke, if that could ever be the right word, about 'the Final Solution with journalists'. It is hard to provide the cadence of von Trier's English with its characteristic Danish inflection and accent, his hesitations and self-mocking laughter. However, these comments came after others that also played within the grey zone of unacceptability. He had said that his film in the main competition, *Melancholia*, 'maybe was crap' and not worth seeing. He had joked that Dunst demanded a 'beaver shot' in the film, a slang expression for an unintended picture of a vagina, and that women wanted more 'once they get started'. He talked about wishing to make a hard-core film of 'unpleasant sex'. All of these earlier comments, including the misogyny, were received as jokes and had provoked laughter by the assembled journalists. By the end of the Nazi rave, however, the laughter had dissipated. At the conclusion, Dunst can be heard whispering to him: 'Lars, *that* was intense.'

There was undoubtedly an element of humour through self-exposure and public self-analysis in von Trier's discussion. In a display that is embarrassing to watch and even appalling, we see him drowning under the waves of a simultaneous recognition, rejection and justification of its own desire. Within a day, he had been banned from the festival and declared 'persona non grata' by its board of directors, with effect immediately. They said:

> We profoundly regret that this forum has been used by Lars von Trier to express comments that are unacceptable, intolerable and contrary to the ideals of humanity and generosity that preside over the very existence of this festival.[2]

In doing so, the festival drew a line between its own humanism and von Trier's comments and, by proxy, between humanism and fascism.

The possibilities of interpretation of this minor event are almost endless, as contemporary blogs revealed. Irrespective of the motives, genre and degree of coherence or conviction of his comments, the Danish director had stumbled in his excursus on the terrain of the unacceptable. Or, rather, the unacceptable had found a way to leave its subject in disarray. He would pay a certain price for it, including missed opportunities for awards at Cannes and elsewhere (his film, *Melancholia*, received no Academy Award nominations, despite receiving much critical praise and a number of critics' prizes), although he surely generated enormous additional publicity for his film in the process. The comments *are*, without doubt, unacceptable, not least their trivialisation of the

Holocaust as a topic for humour and making light of anti-Semitism. Whether they placed von Trier outside the ideals of humanity and generosity, which paradoxically would no longer be extended to him by the Cannes committee, is another question.

One hypothesis worth considering, however, is that what is unacceptable here is not so much the express contents of his remarks but his performative relation to them. After all, the 2004 film *Downfall* and historians such as Ian Kershaw had previously sought to understand Hitler as a monstrously flawed but, nonetheless, human figure.[3] Moreover, no member of the assembled audience would regard von Trier as actually a Nazi or anti-Semite. What perhaps was most unacceptable about the Lars von Trier press conference was an eminent artist performing a revaluation of his personal relationship, including that of pleasure, to fascism and fascist aesthetics and linking that to a former, and to some extent ongoing, Jewish identification. In so doing, he had reopened, perhaps unintentionally and by way of these aesthetics, a political problematic of the 1970s. This had approached fascism as less a historically bounded event and more a continuing part of European, if not Western, culture and identity. This was a problematic of the fascist elements of desire, and the desire for power, which had been addressed by Gilles Deleuze and Felix Guattari in their book, *Anti-Oedipus*. Foucault, invoking Saint Frances de Sales, had famously prefaced their book as a possible 'Introduction to a Non-fascist Life'.[4] If one of the first elements of such a life was the willingness to make an ethical examination of the fascism within one's self and one's cultural identifications, rather than viewing it as a historically delimited phenomenon, then it would appear that von Trier had at least begun, if not resolved, his own self-examination. One response to von Trier's comments would be that they belong in a psychoanalytical rather than public context.

For Deleuze and Guattari, his statement, 'I wanted to be a Jew...but now I am a Nazi', illustrated a kind of delirium or oscillation in which desire can be invested alternatively as revolutionary or fascist, as 'schizoid' or 'paranoiac'. They wrote, in an extraordinary anticipation of von Trier's comments[5]:

> We contrasted [...] two major types of equally social investments: the one sedentary and biunivocalizing, and of a reactionary or fascist tendency; the other nomadic and polyvocal, and of a revolutionary tendency. In fact, in the schizoid declaration – 'I am of a race inferior for all eternity', 'I am a beast, a black', 'We are all German Jews' – the historico-social field is no less invested than in the paranoiac formula:

'I am one of your kind, from the same place as you, I am a pure Aryan, of a superior race for all time.'

Deleuze and Guattari have clearly identified not a psychopathology here but the complexity of the 'molecular' investments of desire in particular social fields. In the sense that von Trier's statements included both these investments, which they would characterise as schizoid, as nomadic and above all polyvocal – there is more than one voice here. The press conference was not the first time von Trier expressed the oscillations of his aesthetic-political investments. In a 2005 interview,[6] the questioner asks him about his mother's death-bed revelation that his biological father was not the Jewish father who had raised him but a man who was a descendant of the Danish composer, J.P.E. Hartmann, and that this had been a way of securing a creative genetic makeup for her child. Here, he used the same formulation: 'Until that point I thought I had a Jewish background. But I'm really more of a Nazi.' Of his mother, he says, 'If I'd known my mother has this plan. I would have become something else. I would have shown her. The slut!'

According to this evidence, there appears a closer relationship between the misogyny and the Jew/Nazi oscillation than might have been first apparent. Von Trier had described his parents in the same interview as 'communist nudists' but had now found out that his mother practised a kind of positive eugenics to beget a creative child. In one event, then, he had been deprived of his Jewish identification and become not only of German heritage but the result of the kind of genetic model that had founded Nazi racial policies.

It is clear that what happened at Cannes was more than a publicity stunt and certainly neither an expression of political commitment nor a form of hate speech. In the 2005 interview, he discussed his view of the inseparability of the political and the sexual and his use of 'Nazis, slaves and slave owners':

> These are extreme images which I use to examine the categories that have left their mark on me. My family had a very clear idea of good and evil, of kitsch and good art. In my work, I try to throw all this into question. I don't just provoke others. I declare war on myself, on the way I was brought up, on my values the entire time. And I attack the good-people philosophy which prevailed in my family.

In his 1991 film, *Europa* (called *Zentropa* in the United States), set in immediate post-war Germany, a young idealist American train conductor falls in love with a *femme fatale* with the name of Katharina Hartmann, who later turns out to be a pro-Nazi conspirator. Her father, Max, a railroad industrialist, commits suicide by self-laceration in a bathtub. In this film, we see dream-like sequences of the conductor moving through the cars of the train, from the private compartments of the owners, through crowded corridors and including cars full of Holocaust victims in the characteristic striped clothing of the death camps. The naming of the family makes explicit reference to his own biography and Von Trier appears briefly in the film, credited only as 'Jew'.

The Cannes comments, then, however offensive at a press conference, are consistent with a long-term self-examination. This self-examination is biographical and familial and hence open to coding in terms of a kind of Freudian model. However, von Trier uses it to question aesthetic judgment, moral categories of good and evil, and his own political certainties. In *Europa*, the American, Leopold Kessler, is played as naïve, imagining that because the war was over, Nazism had been expunged from German society, and this is reflected in his love for Katharina. The movement beyond naïveté is then the same movement in which Von Trier's calls into question the very 'good-people philosophy', the humanism, that at Cannes, would place him outside of what was acceptable. In the same 2005 interview, contrary to the express view of being a Nazi, von Trier discussed his own political action of funding an advertising campaign against the anti-immigrant, far right, Danish People's Party. If Walter Benjamin once suggested that fascism was an aestheticisation of politics, Lars von Trier appears to work at the edge of the politicisation of aesthetics.

Von Trier's comments came two months after the British fashion designer, John Galliano, had been sacked by the fashion house, Christian Dior, for blatant and ugly anti-Semitic rants in a Paris bar, some captured on a mobile telephone, for which he was later convicted and fined. There are, no doubt, complex personal issues at stake here and, however vile his comments, it would be a mistake to place Galliano beyond the ideals of humanity and generosity. Where Galliano's rants were not only intolerable but illegal in France, von Trier's stood at the much lower threshold provided by unacceptability, although it has been reported that he was later questioned by police for a possible violation of French law regarding the justification of war crimes.[7]

In a strange coincidence, at almost the same time as the Galliano affair, and only weeks before Cannes, the American designer Marc Jacobs presented his fall/winter 2011 collection in Paris for Louis Vuitton.[8] This undoubtedly beautiful and dramatic collection and its show took inspiration from the 1974 film *The Night Porter*, directed by Liliana Cavani, in which a young concentration camp survivor, Lucia, played by Charlotte Rampling, meets and recommences a masochistic love relationship, after the war, with her former torturer, an SS officer turned hotel porter, Max, played by Dirk Bogarde. The set for the fashion show, like the film, was a hotel, with hotel porters in uniform opening the doors of the metal elevator cages, through which the models entered the catwalk.[9] One commentator of the show stated that Jacobs had 'nailed the mood' of 'dark and disturbing visions' on that season's Paris catwalk. Another gestured to an elision of 'the meaning of the word, fashion... with the meaning of the word fetish'. The collection included S&M toys, such as gold handcuffs and lock-key bags chained to the wrist, and a range of references to SS uniforms, knee-high boots, faux leather belts and bondage items, military pants and coats, and a cap worn often with a mask suitable for a masquerade ball sitting on its peak. The latter references the mask and the SS 'death's-head' badged caps worn by Rampling in the film, and visible in most of its posters. Jacobs's see-through blouses with wide black seams recalls Lucia's topless dance in military pants, braces and cap, as a deadly Salome for the SS officers, while the hand-cuffs, and cuffing to the bags, recalls her chaining in Max's apartment in Vienna in 1957.

It is doubtless salient that all three almost synchronous events occurred in France, a country with its difficult relation, of collaboration and resistance, with fascism, during a time of economic and financial crisis and the passing of a law that bans Islamic veils in public. However, all three principals were not French and this hard-to-delimit relationship with fascism persists throughout not only Europe but the Western world. Somehow, though, the Louis Vuitton collection was not only acceptable but praiseworthy. It escaped the strictures of unacceptability through mediated reference to film, through fetish and eroticisation and entered into the great doxology of the mass and digital media. In contrast to the voluble rave of Lars von Trier and his need to work out a biographical relation with German culture and to Nazism, Marc Jacobs offered the sphinx-like comment: 'I don't know why I love what I love, but I love that I don't know, I just love that I have a primitive connection to the things that give me pleasure... It's not who we are. It's just how we dress.'

In these last two sentences, Jacobs disavows the truth of the subject and the truth of identity. Wearing clothes, like the Paris show, is a performance but it does not define identity. His refusal of specification of inspiration acts as prevention of a von Trier-like moment and as a form of insurance for his employer, a long-established reputable designer in leather goods, especially bags. His performance thus enacts reserve, classiness and tastefulness in contrast to Galliano's vileness and von Trier's tastelessness and offensiveness. Jacobs's speech protects and augments a form of cultural and economic capital; von Trier diminishes both.

Yet, questions remain. How is it acceptable for a major corporation to seek to profit and augment its capital from unexamined references to Nazi uniforms and their sado-masochistic representation in a 1970s film without any reflection on either the filmic or historical objects? The cap, the braces and other parts of the uniform are metonyms for fascism and the unfettered domination manifest in its concentration camps in which the extermination of Jews and other groups took place. Moreover, just as fashion is associated with fetish, and so danger with pleasure and desire, fascism is present as an unspoken and 'naughty' third term. There is a language here that is, however, not rendered into speech, but that associates pleasure and glamour with masochistic submission to fascist domination or, at the least, to that domination in its film version. In contrast, why does the 'generosity' of the humanism of the Cannes festival not extend to a director publicly working out difficult political implications of elements of his own biography and his subsequent aesthetic and intellectual positioning? Is this something to do with the nature of speech itself?

Conditions of acceptability

Perhaps one could approach the entirety of Michel Foucault's work as a concern with the production of the unacceptable. The Great Confinement, the logic of discipline and normalisation, the confession, and the care of the self, are all so many ways of excluding and sequestrating, correcting and even eliciting, selecting and controlling, what is unacceptable at any given moment. The unacceptable might be a collective (lepers, vagabonds, the mad), a quality (idleness, licentiousness, obscenity), an act (infidelity, masturbation, kinds of dress, a form of protest), a style of speech or representation (blasphemy, pornography, hate speech, slang, sarcasm), or even an identity (the terrorist, the child molester, the dangerous individual, the abnormal). Eliciting what one finds distasteful and abhorrent in one's past, memories, fantasies and desires is a component of the therapeutic technique for the production of truth about oneself. It is an example of what Foucault later called practices of 'veridiction', that is, ways of speaking the true.

In a roundtable discussion with a group of historians first published in 1977, Foucault spoke of his work as aiming to grasp the conditions that make practices acceptable.[10] These conditions are found in the interplay of what he called their 'regimes of veridiction' and 'regimes of jurisdiction'. The latter are concerned with governing how we do things, act or behave, and thus anticipate what he was soon to call 'techniques of governmentality'; the former with the production of the truth according to which this governing operates, its objects are formed and its aims are specified. What he called political rationalities and, more specifically, 'programmes of conduct', operate in the interstices of these two regimes.

We might suppose, then, that not only does the intersection of these regimes provide the conditions that make certain practices acceptable but also those that make them unacceptable. The same 'programme of conduct' which specifies the nutritional needs for the development of the human body can both make acceptable the necessary provision of healthy meals in schools and render unacceptable the provision or sponsorship of those meals by fast-food multinationals. Conversely, different programmes of conduct, or different rationalities, might fight it out over their right to make practices acceptable. Thus, the institution of the prison is justified alternatively as a site of rehabilitation of the individual so that he or she might return to society and one of the proper punishment of the criminal and the removal of his or her risk and danger to society. Each of these programmes provides different versions of the unacceptable: judges and courts who deliver insufficient sentences and do not take into account the victim; or, poor and overcrowded prisons that foment criminal activity and forge criminal networks and ties.

The acceptable and the unacceptable are not, therefore, so much a binary as two poles of this intersection of 'what is said and what is done, rules imposed and reasons given, the planned and the taken for granted'.[11] Given that what counts as true and false and what should be done are often contested by different parties and change from time to time, the relationship between what is acceptable and what is unacceptable is often blurred, a twilight in which shapes and forms merge and separate.

The 1977 interview appeared before Foucault's famous ethical turn and thus ignored the third dimension of his concern with the conditions of acceptability of practices. In a 1982 lecture, in a recapitulation of his work, he spoke of organising his research around three dimensions or focal points of an 'experience' such as madness or sexuality. The first dimension seeks to shift analysis from the contents of knowledge to its forms of veridiction.[12] The second operates a shift from the exercise of power to its procedures of governmentality. (In both these respects, we are very close to the 1977 interview.) Finally, however, he spoke of a third 'shift from the question of the subject... to the analysis of these forms of subjectivation through the techniques/technologies of the relation to self, or if you like through what could be called a pragmatics of the self'. This latter dimension is necessary to understand Foucault as a philosopher of the acceptable. The intensive attention we give to what we are, to what we should be, to what part of ourselves we should act upon, of what to include and exclude in ourselves, and what we hope to achieve, is here indexed to the production of the truth about who we are and the governing and self-governing of our conduct.

In the course of investigating this third dimension, Foucault explored the 'culture of the self' in ancient Greek and Roman societies. Within this culture, he identified a figure that is a key exemplar of speaking the truth, the 'parrhesiast'.[13] While this figure and its form of speech, parrhesia, later appears as a partner of another individual's practice of the care of the self, it first appears as a political figure. Parrhesia is a form of speech that tells the truth without reserve and in which there is a bond between speaker and the truth. However, in this commitment to saying the true, the parrhesia puts at risk, to the point of violence, the relationship between speaker and his auditors, between the parrhesiast and the political community. Parrhesia thus requires courage on the part of the speaker. In exercising this courage, we might say, the parrhesiast risks speaking the unacceptable.

Now this might cast some light on what we have been addressing here, the problem of speaking about or representing fascism. From a juridical-theological perspective, certain types of speech are against the law: Holocaust denial, the justification of war crimes and engaging in hate speech and racial vilification. Fascism and Nazism come to embody pure evil, juxtaposed not only to the good of their victims and those who resisted them, but the actions of the Allies, and, by association, the operations of post-war liberal-democratic states. Certain kinds of speech acts transgress not only the law but are presented as evil by association, and outside the boundaries of humanity.

There are rules of veridiction about fascism from this perspective. First, in general, fascism must be produced as an historical object, delimited to two or three regimes, and not associated with the policies or actions of contemporary liberal-democratic governments, or with aspects of an enlightened and humanist culture. Thus, in 2004, a conservative columnist defended Australia's federal government, with its anti-refugee policies, including the mandatory detention of illegal arrivals, against the charge of being 'pre-fascist' by arguing that there have only been two fascist regimes (in Italy and Germany); and that in Australia, like Britain and the United States, leaders need to worry about facing regular elections.[14] If the suggestion that such policies are part of a slippery slope to fascism is 'just nuts', as he put it, then it would be completely unacceptable to interrogate aspects of those countries' avowed liberal policies and Enlightenment cultures, or even one's own subjectivities, for 'fascist' elements, tendencies or desires.

If a juridical-theological approach defines an essential historical truth about fascism and seeks to define what can or cannot be said about it, what might be called an ethico-political one is more concerned with how individuals and societies might govern their own conduct by addressing a fascism within, including within their humanist-Enlightenment culture, their liberal-democratic polities and their own selves. Yet this is clearly a risky business that threatens to break the bonds between speaker and his or her community and to lead to ostracism from that community or worse. Speaking about fascism would take the form of a parrhesia.

Lars von Trier's press conference had some of the hallmarks of the form of veridiction of the patient in psychotherapy: free association, revealing inner truths, the linking of libidinal investments to family history. Yet it also had an element of parrhesia. This is perhaps not an entirely proper parrhesia, but more like the parrhesiast who becomes and appears as 'an impenitent chatterbox who cannot restrain himself'.[15] However, his Jew/Nazi statement was neither a form of hate speech, which sets out to vilify and provoke acts of violence against a group, nor an expression of political commitment but a kind of frank-speaking, without reserve, about himself. In its speaking of the truth about himself in this way, the statement became unacceptable to the film community at Cannes and results in ostracism and risked legal penalty.

Another alternative approach to fascism might be called a visual-aesthetic one instanced by the Louis Vuitton *Night Porter* fashion show of Marc Jacobs. It tacitly acknowledges fascist desire, and the presence of fascism within the iconography of contemporary culture and aesthetics, but turns it into a matter of consumption, nostalgia and glamour, rather than politics and subjectivity. This approach leaves such desire in play and produces and augments pleasure without rendering it into speech. Jacobs, himself, adopted the relative silence of the sage who, according to Foucault, adopts an enigmatic discourse and 'keeps his wisdom in a state of essential withdrawal'.[16] Fashion can be like a silent movie without any dialogue cards.

Power and unacceptability

Is it possible that power, particularly political power, or at least aspects of it, much more broadly has entered into this domain of the unacceptable? Of course, power has not disappeared from our discussion nor is it no longer exercised. However, it is possible that the discussion of power has become, in contemporary liberal democracies, at the least somewhat distasteful, and for some, like Bruno Latour,[17] a useless term of explanation and critique. We might wish then to examine the conditions of acceptability and unacceptability of power.

One could say that there are rules of veridiction that define the conditions of the production of truth about power. Three of these might be stated bluntly. The first concern the proliferation of binaries: collective power versus power over or domination by an individual or group, hard power and soft power, power as the capacity to achieve one's will by whatever means and power as right or legitimate, juridical-sovereign models of power and power as governance, networks and so on.[18] The second concerns the character of modern or liberal-democratic power, which transforms these binaries into a narrative concerning the diminishing import of hierarchical forms of power grounded in force and coercion and the increasing salience of relatively flatter networks working through active cooperation, or even the freedom, of those over whom they are exercised or with whom they enter into partnership. Finally, power can be approached as an outcome or a resultant of these networks rather than as a form of explanation. In terms of political thought, Barry Hindess argued forcefully that the idea of power as right and the notion of legitimate power is the central notion of power in modern Western political thought.[19] One might say that the discourse of legitimate power forms a set of dense and massive rules of veridiction about power in our societies.

A second condition of acceptability of power is found in its procedures and techniques of governmentality, that is, of the way we should govern and be governed.[20] Here, power can only be exercised as a transaction, which, at its most basic, is that of the consent of the governed, but which, more actively, involves and elicits their agency. Some of the techniques concern the promotion of the agency of the governed, the building of their self-esteem, the unleashing of their enterprise and empowering them. Others concern the monitoring and shaping of their performance, building their capacities for planning and achieving their agreed goals. Management is the name of a particular relation of power that concerns the shaping, facilitating, monitoring and securing the agency of those who are managed. Leadership, far from an exercise of 'power over', domination or even legitimate authority, becomes a matter of vision, strategy, team-building and goal-setting that inspires those who are thus led to best realise their own goals, aligned of course to that of the organisation.

Finally, the conditions of acceptability of power relations entail a certain pragmatics of the self. To lead and to be led involves work on oneself: to cultivate capacities for inspiration, strategy and communication, on the part of the leader; and self-motivation, enterprise and effectiveness, on the part of those led. Power can be connected to desire, but only the desire to achieve collective and organisational goals, or to become an empowered individual or active and enterprising subject, one who is effective in the development of his or her own plan and in the achievement of individual or communal goals. In fact, as Stewart Clegg strikingly argues, recent organisational theory goes so far as to propose that power exists only where there is irrationality in the organisation and is associated not with reason, rule or authority but with irrationality, chaos and illegitimacy.[21] Power, in short, becomes a kind of pathology, rather than the normal functioning of systems and organisations.

All of this begins to define what is unacceptable about speaking about and discussing power. We must aver what is spectacular and glorious and embrace what is discrete and quiet; the former qualities, while they still exist in constitutional monarchies and in republics, should be regarded as a mere ceremonial residue that accompanies what is legal, rational and collectively beneficial. We must reject speech that too easily links power to coercion and to violence and talk about the augmentation of power through discussion, agreement, deliberation and consensus-building. We must view violence as the unfortunate and unavoidable limit point of power, applied to those who put themselves outside of humanity such as dictators and terrorists, and not intrinsic to the form exercised in our society. We must regard as archaic that which is grounded in symbol and myth and grasp the rationality and calculability of contemporary power. We must view that which is caught in the will to dominate or the desire to submit as a pathology outside the healthy normality of power in liberal democracies.

There are doubtless many reasons for this. The first is the contraction of the sphere of political contestation in the post-World War II and especially the post-Cold War period. One indication of how little liberal-democratic societies have to fear from radical alternatives is that the recent series of financial crises (2007–2012) have been greeted by a discussion of the limits and legitimacy of capitalism and inequality, not only by the relatively limited protests of the Occupy movements but also by the financial press itself.[22]

While 'extreme' kinds of politics have been largely absent *within* liberal-democracies, there has been an attempt to remove 'power politics' from the manner in which states conduct their external affairs. Partially stemming from the post-World War II settlements, and the principles of universal human rights, the exercise of external power in its various forms, up to and including war, can no longer be justified on the traditional grounds of the defence, expansion and promotion of national sovereignty. War, at least from the perspective of liberal democracies, is a collective action against tyrants and dictators and is justified in the defence of the populations abused and persecuted by them. The existence of states who would wage war for national purposes, or because they view the global order as one of oppressive or imperial rule, is from this point of view indeed unacceptable, and a symptom of the existence of parts of the globe yet to move beyond a barbaric 'pre-modern' statelessness or a Hobbesian modern statist one.[23] The very idea that one would give one's life for a political cause (as in the case of suicide bombers or the 9/11 hijackers) is viewed as a *religious* atavism and a misguided affront to common humanity. It cannot be viewed as a *political* act.

The contraction of the political and the concepts of power are thus accompanied by a moralisation of politics in international and in domestic matters. But, there is also an ambiguous eroticisation of power. This is manifest most superficially in the telegenic glamour of good-looking US presidential candidates. But it is more deeply manifest in the way in which now archaic versions of political power in capitalist societies are viewed as the product of a pathological sexuality. While the Soviet Union and its former satellites have become examples of repressive, dull regimes that are either sexless or anti-sex, without the vitality and variety of consumer capitalism, fascism has become a sexual pathology, and identified with fetishes, sado-masochism, the *femme fatale* and repressed homosexuality.

Giorgio Agamben has raised the methodological issue of what he calls a signature. A signature is not merely, he argues, a semiotic relation between a sign and what is signified, but 'it is what – insisting on this relation without coinciding with it – displaces and moves it into another domain, thus positioning it in a new network of pragmatic and hermeneutical relations'.[24] We might forward the case for the identification of a signature here. Eroticism is the signature that shifts the experience of power from the political into a visual-aesthetic one. From John F. Kennedy's hair and toothpaste smile (which became the essential requisites for generations of candidates) to, more recently, the 'viral' video clip of Barack Obama's singing the opening lines of Al Green's 'Let's Stay Together',[25] we witness attempts to make political power something else. They allow us to consume it, participate in it and take pleasure in it, and render it acceptable and even glorify it, in what we imagine is a perfectly innocent way.

If erotics moves acceptable power into healthy consumer aesthetics, it also identifies unacceptable power with sexual degeneracy. Osama bin Laden's porn collection and Muammar Gaddafi's female praetorian guard (called 'the Amazons') are recent examples. The revelation of the former was certainly a conscious attempt to deprive bin Laden of posthumous charisma among Muslims.[26] But it is fascism, with its arrogation of total domination and demand for total submission, that most marks what is unacceptable about power and what must therefore be approached as a form of sexual degeneracy. Fascism, its uniforms, symbols, acclamations and rallies, all become visual signs of an unacceptable power that led to the unspeakable in the concentration camps. But as the paradigm of the unacceptability of power, it has become, in our visual culture, a form of sexual perversion or degeneracy.

Fascism and film revisited

In a 1974 discussion with the members of the *Cahiers du Cinema* editorial staff, Foucault asked the following question:

> Power has an erotic charge. There's an historical problem involved here. How is it that Nazism – which was represented by shabby, pathetic puritanical characters, laughably Victorian old maids, or at best smutty individuals – how has it managed to become, in France, in Germany, in the United States, in all pornographic literature throughout, the ultimate symbol of eroticism?[27]

This is an interesting historical question, even if Foucault is engaging in a certain degree of caricature of Nazism's sexual politics. Yet the identification of fascism and earlier ideas, derived from psychoanalysis, sexology and eugenics, of sexual degeneracy in popular visual iconography, is intriguing. One response is that there is nothing especially erotic in the fascist exercise of power but that fascism has become associated, in the visual culture of the post-World War II period, with recurrent decadent images, many of which predate fascism and Nazism. In an insightful analysis of fascism in post-war European cinema, Kriss Ravetto lists these pre-fascist images which now stand for fascism as 'the femme fatale, the transvestite, the sexual pervert, the *Untermensch*, of feminine disease circulating at the turn of the century'.[28]

At issue in the discussion in the *Cahiers* were a number of films, including *The Night Porter*, a film generally regarded as distasteful by critics then and now, given its portrayal of a sado-masochistic love relationship between a former concentration camp victim and her former torturer.[29] Foucault's own response to the film, however, is by contrast positive. He argues that it shows the delegation and distribution of power within the population under Nazism, given its depiction of a post-war Nazi secret society and its mock trials as a kind of group psychotherapy.[30] He also applauds the way in which power and desire are entwined in it: the way in which the excess of power is converted to love, while love is reconverted to a kind of surplus power, which in turn is converted to an absence of power. Perhaps the most disturbing aspect of the film is not the representation of 'fascist' sado-masochistic practices, but the way in which the young victim actively participates in the erotics of Nazi power, both while in flashback memories of the camp and later in post-war life. Ravetto has argued that by venturing onto this unacceptable terrain, in which victim and victimiser are blurred, and in which the female victim assumes an agency in her own desire, particularly after the war, the films open up for interrogation the standard representation of the relationship between eroticism and fascist power.[31] As the flashback and memory structure of the film suggest, it deals not so much with the closed history of fascism but its historiography in post-war popular culture. Such a critical potentiality of the film has not only largely bypassed professional critics but has been effectively nullified by the way in which its imagery has been appropriated, not only, as we have seen, by the Louis Vuitton show, but recurrently in the fashion industry.[32]

The Night Porter is one of quite a number of films, particularly from Italian directors, that sought to explore this relations between fascist power and erotics: Luchino Visconti's *The Damned* (1969), Bernardo Bertolucci's *The Conformist* (1970), Lina Wertmuller's *Seven Beauties* (1975) and, perhaps most scandalously, Pier Paolo Pasolini's *Salo or 120 Days of Sodom* (1975).

Not all these films have the same valences and effects, to be sure. However, their point of departure is a kind of displacement of the intelligibility of fascism and the most terrible events associated with it – the Holocaust, World War II – from an analysis of political movements with definite ideologies, and their relationship to capitalism and bourgeois morality, onto a kind of pathological sexuality. Rather than understanding the political content of fascism and the events associated with it, fascism appears as a kind of fetish and access to its essence is given through knowledge of these fetishes. Partially through the legacy of these films, fascism came to be known and experienced in popular memory through a lens similar to the psycho-political writings of the Frankfurt School. There, as Andrew Hewitt put it, sexuality was 'pathologized as a potentially fascistic fascination with the erotics of power, and that fascism, in turn, is presented as a psychosocial manifestation of homosexual narcissism'.[33]

The Conformist, today universally acclaimed as a classic,[34] with its brilliant cinematography by Vittorio Storare, and the fine period evocation in its costumes and set design, presents the best filmic encapsulation of that thesis derived from 1960s Freudo-Marxism. Here, the main protagonist (Marcello Clerici, played by Jean-Luis Tringinant) desires to conform by assisting a fascist assassin to track down and murder his old professor (Quadri), now living in Paris. He journeys to Paris on his honeymoon with his sensitive but vacuous wife, Guilia, and becomes attracted to Quadri's own young, sexually ambiguous and alluring wife, Anna (Dominque Sanda), who, in turn seeks an intimacy with Guilia. Anna had already appeared twice in the film in sexual liaisons with fascist officials. Marcello's own conformism is explained by his repressed guilt at having been approached (shown in flashback) by a homosexual transvestite chauffer, Lino, as a young boy and believing he had killed him. In a final scene, after the fall of fascism in Rome, discovering that he had not in fact killed Lino, and after wildly denouncing him as the fascist who killed Quadri and his wife to the demonstrating crowds, he is seen sitting outside the cell of a young boy, the camera panning over the latter's naked buttocks, with the suggestion of the fulfilment of his long-repressed desire.

We might today wish to re-evaluate this particular film with its identification of the *femme fatale* (Anna) and the repressed homosexual (Marcello) with fascism. We can see that it maintains a clear-cut distinction between good, in the form of Professor Quadri organising the resistance in exile in Paris and benignly tolerating his wife's sexual exploration and Guilia's drunken foibles, and evil located in the desire for bourgeois conformity of Marcello manifested in his marriage to a petit bourgeois wife as a retreat from his latent homosexuality. Confronted many years later with the suggestion that the identification of fascism with repressed homosexual desire might be homophobic, Bertolucci responded: 'With all my old movies I feel I am no more responsible – read: guilty – for them. The person who made these films is so distant from me.'[35]

While Bertolucci's film remains one of the most critically acclaimed of all time, it reproduced the typology of sexual pathology and degeneracy that had been a hallmark of fascism itself. What is unacceptable today is not the identification of fascism with decadent and pathological sexuality, which entered into the iconography of popular visual culture in the 1970s, but the attempt to understand fascism, and the terrible events associated with it, including the Holocaust, in terms of the exercise of certain kinds and aspects of political power that might or might not be continuous with those exercised in liberal democracies. Instead, and under the signature of erotics, fascist political power is understood in terms of aesthetic tropes of camp and kitsch, of *femme fatales* and feminised males, of the perversions of the libido and fetishes.

It is not possible to understand political power in all its forms and manifestations without an examination of the actually existing fascism of the twentieth century and the events associated with it. Conversely, to try to understand fascism it is necessary to have a conception of the place of power in post-Enlightenment liberal culture and society. If, however, we turn to eroticism in the post-war iconography of fascism, we are dealing less with a historically bounded event and more with the way that erotics has come to mark, and to act as a signature, for our reception and understanding of power today.

Conclusion

To summarise the results of the above investigation in a series of more general propositions:

1. The unacceptable is located in a grey zone of power, pleasure and desire, rather than in the black and white logics of law and religion, of the ban and the transgression.
2. Speaking about and representing power, particularly the will to domination and the pleasure of submission, has entered the grey zone of the unacceptable. In this sense, fascism is a paradigm for those kinds

and aspects of power that liberal humanism wishes to exclude from speech about power in liberal-democracies.
3. The juridical-theological approach defines an essential historical truth and morality about fascism and seeks to prescribe what can or cannot be said about it and to ban certain forms of speech and action. It preserves the binary of good and evil, and the privileged distinction between liberal-democracies and totalitarian regimes.
4. An ethico-political approach is concerned with how individuals and cultures might govern their own conduct by addressing fascism within, including within the continuities in the operations of power, politics and culture, and in the will to domination and the desire and pleasure of submission.
5. A visual-aesthetic approach recognises fascist desire but leaves it, without speech, in play in the visual language of pleasure, nostalgia and glamour. While saying the true, in the manner not unlike the ancient form of parrhesia, risks the unacceptable, the visual-aesthetic approach maintains a depthless acceptability in the domain of consumer desire and pleasure and the augmentation of capital.
6. Erotics acts as a signature of power, that is, as something that moves it into another domain particularly in respect of visual culture. In so doing, it displaces the political onto the binaries of healthy vitality and sexual degeneracy, precisely the categories of fascism itself.
7. The conditions of acceptability of our discourse and experience of power can be analysed through its rules of veridiction, its techniques of governmentality and its pragmatics of the self. There is a tension here between rules of veridiction that disqualify a relation to 'extreme' forms of power and domination and a pragmatics of the self that can constitute fascist desire as an ethical substance to be worked on and through with the objective of creating a non-fascist life.

The question of 'frank-speaking' about fascism remains fraught with risk and danger, as Lars von Trier with his own clumsy and unacceptable speech, part misplaced therapy and part poor parrhesia, found out at Cannes. But the very fact of the persistence of visual images that make unexamined reference to fascism and its metonyms, or to its filmic representation, with the objective of generating pleasure, glamour and profit, indicates that some, much more considered and reflective, form of frank-speaking might be all the more necessary. The question is not about how power can be purified of all the unacceptable elements, tendencies and desires that are manifest in fascism. Rather, it is how we can examine the relations, substantive forms and representations of power characteristic of our societies, and our relationship to them, with the courage to speak about that which, within them and ourselves, once made fascism actual and continues to make it a possibility.

Notes

1. The full press conference is available at: http://www.festival-cannes.com/en/mediaPlayer/11391.html (accessed 3 February 2012).
2. Catherine Shoard, 'Cannes festival bans Lars von Trier', *The Guardian*, 19 May 2011. Available at: http://www.guardian.co.uk/film/2011/may/19/cannes-film-festival-2011-lars-von-trier-banned (accessed 24 January 2012).
3. Ian Kershaw, *Hitler: 1889–1936 Hubris*, London: Penguin, 1999. *Downfall* ('Der Untergang') was directed by Oliver Hirschbiegel.
4. Michel Foucault, 'Preface, to G. Deleuze and F. Guattari', *Anti-Oedipus: Capitalism and Schizophrenia*, p. xiii.
5. Deleuze and Guattari, op. cit., p. 340.
6. Katja Nicodemus, 'I am an American woman: interview with Lars von Trier', 17 November 2005. Available at: www.signandsight.com/features/465.html (accessed 29 January 2012). An excellent interview of Lars von Trier by Ib Bondebjerg covering mainly aesthetic themes is found in Hjort and Bondebjerg, *The Danish Directors*, Bristol: Intellect, 2001. In it, von Trier makes repeated reference to his family and once to his position that he would like to see all sorts of films, '...including Nazi films, as long as they have something to say...I believe that it's very important that Nazis be allowed to demonstrate in Denmark. That was also my parents' position' (p. 217).
7. Catherine Shoard, 'Lars von Trier makes a vow of silence after Cannes furore', *The Guardian*, 5 October 2011. Available at: http://www.guardian.co.uk/film/2011/oct/05/lars-von-trier-cannes (accessed 25 January 2012).
8. For a poster of the film, *The Night Porter*, and a video of the collection, including an interview with Marc Jacobs and others cited below, see http://www.kenwerks.com/2011/03/night-porter-louis-vuitton-fw2011.html (accessed 24 January 2012).
9. The full video of the show is available at 'Louis Vuitton Paris Fall 2011/Winter 2012', http://www.youtube.com/watch?v=obEhabcKHkg (accessed 31 January 2012).
10. Foucault, 'Questions of method', pp. 73–86.
11. Ibid., p. 75.
12. Foucault, *The Government of Self and Others*, pp. 4–5.
13. I am drawing upon the summary exposition found in Foucault, *The Courage of Truth: The Government of Self and Others II*, pp. 8–13.
14. Henderson, Gerard, 'It's hardly the death of democracy', *Sydney Morning Herald*, 24 August 2004. Available at: http://www.smh.com.au/articles/2004/08/23/1093246444499.html (accessed 3 February 2012).
15. Foucault, *Courage of Truth*, op. cit., p. 10.

16. Ibid., p. 17.
17. Bruno Latour, *Reassembling the Social: An Introduction to Actor-Network Theory*, pp. 260–261.
18. Mitchell Dean, 'The signature of power', *Journal of Political Power*, 2012, 5 (1), 101–117.
19. Barry Hindess, *Discourses of Power: From Hobbes to Foucault*.
20. From a vast literature see: Rose and Miller, *Governing the Present: Administering Social, Economic and Personal Life* (2008) and Michael Power, *Audit Society: Rituals of Verification* (1999).
21. Stewart Clegg, 'Foundations of Organization Power', 2012.
22. As of January 2012, the *Financial Times* website was running an 'in-depth' series of articles and videos entitled 'Capitalism in Crisis'. Available at: http://www.ft.com/intl/indepth/capitalism-in-crisis (accessed 18 January 2012).
23. To use the language of a senior British diplomat: Robert Cooper, *The Breaking of Nations: Order and Chaos in the Twenty-First Century* (2003).
24. Giorgio Agamben, *The Signature of All Things: On Method*, p. 40.
25. 'Obama sings Al Green's "Let's Stay Together" at the Apollo Theater in Harlem', *The Huffington Post*, 20 January 2012. Available at: http://www.huffingtonpost.com/2012/01/20/obama-al-green-apollo-theater_n_1218070.html (accessed 6 February 2012).
26. The discovery of pornography in bin Laden's compound by the Navy SEALs who had killed him was promoted as a propaganda victory for the USA in diminishing his charismatic legacy among Muslims. See, for example, Asra Q. Nomani, 'Osama's Dirty Mind', *The Daily Beast*, 14 May 2011. Available at: http://www.thedailybeast.com/articles/2011/05/14/osama-bin-ladens-porn-and-muslim-hypocrisy-on-sex.html (accessed 7 February 2011).
27. Foucault, 'Film and Popular Memory', in *Foucault Live*, p. 97.
28. Kriss Ravetto, *The Unmaking of Fascist Aesthetics*, p. 6.
29. Ibid., pp. 150–151.
30. Foucault, 'Film and Popular Memory', pp. 100–101.
31. Ravetto, pp. 180–185.
32. See, for example, the actor Keira Knightly, in the Coco perfume magazine advertisement for Chanel at: http://www.mimifroufrou.com/scentedsalamander/2009/08/keira_knightley_plays_it_the_n.html (accessed 6 February 2012).
33. Quoted by Ravetto, op. cit., p. 12.
34. As a recent example, it was named 13th of all time best drama and arthouse film by *The Guardian*, 20 October 2010. Available at: http://www.guardian.co.uk/film/2010/oct/20/drama-arthouse-25 (accessed 11 February 2012).
35. Stuart Jeffries, 'Films are a way to kill my father: interview with Bernardo Bertolucci', *The Guardian*, 22 February 2008. Available at: http://www.guardian.co.uk/film/2008/feb/22/1 (accessed 31 January 2012).

References

Agamben, Giorgio, *The Signature of All Things: On Method*, New York: Zone Books, 2009.

Clegg, Stewart, 'Foundations of Organization Power', in *Power: State of the Art* (edited by Mark Haugaard and Kevin Ryan), International Political Science Association World of Political Science series, Leverkusen: Barbara Budrich, 2012.

Cooper, Robert, *The Breaking of Nations: Order and Chaos in the Twenty-First Century*, New York: Grove Press, 2003.

Dean, Mitchell, 'The signature of power', *Journal of Political Power*, 2012, 5 (1), 101–117.

Deleuze, Gilles, and Guattari, Felix, *Anti-Oedipus: Capitalism and Schizophrenia*, Minneapolis, MN: University of Minnesota Press, 1983.

Foucault, Michel, 'Preface' to G. Deleuze and F. Guattari, *Anti-Oedipus: Capitalism and Schizophrenia*, Minneapolis, MN: University of Minnesota Press, 1983, pp. xiii–xvi.

Foucault, Michel, 'Film and Popular Memory', in *Foucault Live*, New York: Semiotext(e), 1989.

Foucault, Michel, 'Questions of Method', in *The Foucault Effect: Studies in Governmentality* (edited by Graham Burchell et al.), Hemel Hempstead: Harvester Wheatsheaf, 1991, pp. 87–104.

Foucault, Michel, *The Government of Self and Others*, Basingstoke: Palgrave, 2010.

Foucault, Michel, *The Courage of Truth: The Government of Self and Others II*, Basingstoke: Palgrave, 2011.

Hindess, Barry, *Discourses of Power: From Hobbes to Foucault*, Oxford: Blackwells, 1996.

Hjort, Mette, and Bondebjerg, Ib, *The Danish Directors*, Bristol: Intellect, 2001.

Kershaw, Ian, *Hitler: 1889–1936 Hubris*, London: Penguin, 1999.

Latour, Bruno, *Reassembling the Social: An Introduction to Actor-Network Theory*, Oxford: Oxford University Press, 2005.

Power, Michael, *Audit Society: Rituals of Verification*, Oxford: Oxford University Press, 1999.

Ravetto, Kriss, *The Unmaking of Fascist Aesthetics*, Minneapolis, MN: University of Minnesota Press, 2001.

Rose, Nikolas, and Miller, Peter, *Governing the Present: Administering Social, Economic and Personal Life*, Cambridge: Polity Press, 2008.

2
'Schooling Scandals!': Exploring the Necessity of Cultural Disgust

Chris Haywood

Over the past 30 years, sexuality and schooling has been subject to increasing media coverage that has been central to activating political, educational and popular concerns. Such concerns have circulated through a number of 'sex scandals' that include sex education, pupil sexual relations, technology and pornography, sexual relations between teachers and pupils, and teen pregnancies. Such scandals reveal the moral fault-lines that underpin the boundaries between the acceptable and the unacceptable. Hence, educational researchers have tended to explain such scandals by applying the sociological concept of moral panic.[1]

Generally underpinned by a classic labelling approach in the tradition of Stanley Cohen,[2] researchers have argued that moral panics are a means of generating a shared ideology, often through the amalgamation of disparate moral forces that effect a manufacturing of sexual norms and values. As a consequence, it has been argued that media accounts of sexuality and schooling serve to mislead audiences and secure the continuation of naturalised (hetero-) sexual ideologies of patriarchy and compulsory heterosexuality.[3] At the same time, while recognising that media scandals may indeed consolidate hegemonic narratives of the 'acceptable' through the reconstruction of 'ideal' teachers, pupils and schools, it is argued that sex scandals not only threaten the imaginary and reinforce the boundaries of acceptability, they also create a cultural disgust that is desirable and *necessary*.

To explore the necessity of cultural disgust, this chapter draws upon UK news reporting of school sex scandals from the last 10 years. Media reports of sexuality and schooling cover a diverse range of issues that range from concern over institutional practices such as teaching and learning strategies, to stories that focus on sexual practice and professional identity. Within this range, there is a diversity of sub-issues. For example, stories that focus on professional identities of teachers include: teachers who have been wrongly dismissed for inappropriate sexual advances; teachers who systematically abused pupils over a number of years; teachers having relationships with other teachers; teachers and pupils falling in love with each other; teachers being sexually abused and raped by pupils.

Much contemporary educational research draws on a concept of moral panic theories that has been developed in relation to post-war consumerism, class conflict and racial politics.[4] Rather than class conflict, researchers have suggested that media reports of sexuality and schooling are primarily about the control and regulation of sexuality divisions.[5] As a result, researchers have argued that the media sensationalise the actions of marginal groups or deviant behaviours in order to maintain a sexual hegemony.[6] Epstein[7] provided a good example of this in her discussion of primary school head teacher Jane Brown. The media focused on Jane Brown's decision to decline free invitations for children of her school to watch a ballet performance of Romeo and Juliet. A media-led furore erupted with speculation centring on Brown's alleged suggestion that Romeo and Juliet was a 'blatantly heterosexual' love story. Epstein argued that the coverage of the Jane Brown affair connected with, and was used to support, a homophobic position adopted by most of the tabloid papers. As a result, she demonstrated how the supposed refusal of the tickets on heterosexist grounds becomes re-coded as a concern about the head teacher's sexuality. Thus, the media moral panic 'reconstructs' a popular sexual common-sense and polices heterosexuality by warning of the consequences of taking on alternative sexual identities/practices in the schooling arena. Importantly, moral panics and the accompanying sexual folk devils that are constructed result in tangible 'social, political and economic outcomes'[8] that 'recuperate normative heterosexist relations in schools'.[9]

Kehily's[10] work elaborated on the notion of disproportionality by exploring teenage girls magazines. She suggested that such magazines have been given visibility via a broader state-led moral panic towards a politically orientated conservative agenda. Her emphasis, through ethnographic research methods, was to outline how young men and women 'read' these magazines. In doing so, a juxtaposition between how magazines are represented in the media and the meanings that young people attach to them was established. Similarly, Luschen and Bogad[11] argued that an important aspect of media analysis is to 'collect the facts'.

In their discussion of Dana Rivers, a transgendered teacher working in Sacramento, California, they explored the powerful sexual normativity that the media cultivated through the deployment of representations of professional identities. In their 'media event', professional identities were constituted through a rigid division of public and private space. The transgendered teacher disrupts this division and thus activates the institutional insistence of a normative heterosexual school context. The emphasis in the above approaches is that the reactions of the moral guardians are inappropriate because they ascribe disproportionality to the actual practices that are labelled as deviant. Thus, a characteristic of mainstream approaches to schooling scandals is that they seek to establish 'what really happened'. For example, Pat Sikes[12] has recently highlighted how the press can sensationalise relations between teachers and students. She argued that:

> ...the press, in Britain at least, frequently carries titillating and salacious accounts of sexual attraction and activity between school teachers and their students. Although tales of this type undoubtedly tell us something about, and may even feed, common fantasies around sex and power, they make little contribution to understandings of what is a real and ubiquitous aspect of life in schools.[13]

Sikes suggested that media sensationalism obscures the complexity of teacher–student interactions, resulting in a failure to acknowledge the complexity of the lived experiences of such relationships. Therefore, Sikes implored educational researchers to capture the reality behind media representations to avoid sensationalising what are in reality 'uncontroversial issues'.

Despite the enduring appeal of moral panic theory, a number of critiques have been levelled at the approach. These include the suggestion of the unity of 'state' responses to controversial issues,[14] lack of precision over definitions of 'panic' and risk,[15] the neglect of real social threats rather than simplistic notions of social perceptions,[16] and questions surrounding who defines/judges what is a social threat.[17] Alongside this, Miller et al.[18] also suggested a limitation with the analytical approach of those who use the concept of moral panic. They argued: 'It seems to us that "homophobia", "racism", "sexism" or "backlash" offer a starting point for analysis rather than "the answer".' The shift here is describing what is of cultural significance to why such stories are culturally significant. Thompson[19] has aptly suggested that although: '...moral panics about sex are increasingly the most frequent and have the most serious repercussions in modern society', there continues to be relatively little explanation of *why* sex has an increased media profile. In response, it appears that schools have emerged as a significant space where 'acceptability' can be re-stabilised. As Kincaid pointed out in relation to the excising of sexuality and childhood, 'The irony is not hard to miss: defining something entirely as a negation brings irresistibly before us that which we're trying to banish.'[20] Thus the intensification of sexual scandals in schooling articulates broader issues of political, economic and social cohesion where the reporting of sex scandals in schools initiates a series of dynamic processes of cultural recuperation. However, the recuperation of acceptability is not simply the excision of the unwanted; it is also part of the incitement of such instability. The following sections unpack this complexity by focusing on the cultural anxiety surrounding 'normal' masculinities, the sexualisation of female teachers and precocious boys, and the media eroticisation of child sexual abuse in schools.

Methodology

As indicated above, the research was based on the collection of print news reports (excluding letters, editorials and commentaries) from 1 January 2000 to 1 January 2010 from three national editions of the UK newspapers the *Daily Mirror* (as a tabloid[21]), the *Daily Mail* (a more conservative midmarket newspaper[22]) and the *Guardian* (a liberal broadsheet[23]). This diachronic approach to the research reveals that what is identified as significant and important can change over time.[24] For example, between 2000 and 2001, in the context of the lowering of the age of consent, homosexuality and schooling was one of the most frequent topics discussed in news reports. In subsequent years, homosexuality and schooling became more specialised in terms of sex education or sexual health priorities. In contrast, adult/child sexual activities within school contexts were continually part of the news agenda across the decade.

LexisNexis was employed to profile the amount and scope of the coverage. Matches were produced through a range of search string and keyword combinations: for example, sexual – schooling/sexuality – education/sexual pupil. Reports were then selected based on relevance to the focus of study and involved institutions providing compulsory education to 5–18 year olds. The difficulty of this approach is that 'school' and 'pupil' appear to be highly popular cultural motifs for stories on broader issues of sexuality and have at times very little to do with schooling. For example, we found that news reports on court cases that involved sexual offences with adults often used school history, school teachers' comments and school friendships to provide context. Reports where schooling was the spatial or pedagogical context through which the activity took place were then used inductively and were coded according to the nature of the story. Inter-coder reliability was tested and refined with the two authors by independently double-coding a sub-sample of reports (N: 250, 10%).

Results, analysis and discussion

The news reports identified a number of themes in the news reporting of schooling and sexuality. Table 2.1 shows the range of stories and their frequency within each newspaper. The items in Table 2.1 indicate what subjects were covered by the news reports, their total number and the percentage of the sample. From this, we can see that between 2000 and 2010, sexual activity in schools between adults and pupils was the most frequently reported news item.

However, the category of adult sex with child covers a range of scenarios and this was further broken down into the following categories outlined in Table 2.2.

The data suggests that male teacher and female pupils was the most reported item within adult–pupil sexual activity in schools. However, school auxiliaries were the second most frequent category. Auxiliaries are school workers who support the functioning of the pedagogical relationship between teachers and pupils. This includes classroom assistants, cleaners, caretakers, administration staff, school bus drivers, taxi drivers. However, the results in a quantitative nature only identify the various cultural fault-lines through which sexual issues area distributed. The following sections provide a more in-depth cultural analysis of how the unacceptable is articulated through a number of emblematic representations that included the 'predatory paedophile', 'voracious teachers' and 'precocious children'.

'Predatory paedophiles': desire, anxiety and 'normal' masculinities

In the early 1990s, concern about child sexual abuse gained increasing press attention. Media accounts tended to locate abusers within 'paedophile rings' that targeted vulnerable young people, especially those in state care. The press often linked such attacks to the professional

Table 2.1 Frequency of themes in news reporting of schooling and sexuality

	Adult sex with child	Sexual health	Sex education	Sex outsider risk	Pupil – pupil sex	Teacher porn	Teacher sex with teacher	Young people sexual experiences	School policy and sex	
Daily Mail	369	181	183	51	105	17	11	34	55	1006
The Mirror	347	54	71	52	90	25	7	19	22	687
The Guardian	173	110	117	30	48	0	4	28	15	525
	889	345	371	133	243	42	22	81	92	2218

Table 2.2 Frequency of reports of sexual activity in schools between adults and pupils

	Male teacher–female pupil	Male teacher–male pupil	Female teacher–male pupil	Female teacher–female pupil	Auxiliaries	Other
Daily Mail	168	42	58	11	85	5	369
The Mirror	118	56	84	7	83	6	347
The Guardian	27	66	30	4	40	6	173
	313	164	172	22	208	17	889

incompetence of those with a duty of care. In contrast, social workers were seen as ineffective because of their over-zealousness.[25] However, media reports began to shift from reporting the facilitation of sexual abuse by negligent professionals, to the identification of the professionals *as* paedophiles. For example, paedophiles are often represented as gaining employment to satisfy their paedophilic urges: 'Child sex beast hired to drive school buses; "Piggy back" pervert caged for 15 months.'[26] In effect, institutions were no longer seen as vulnerable to outsiders, children were at risk from those who were there to protect them. The global concern with the Catholic church, as well as more localised anxiety over residential care, foster care and boarding schools, moved danger and risk from outside the school gates, to within them. Thus, in 2002, the murder of two girls in Soham by their school caretaker Ian Huntley generated intense political and media scrutiny. There was consternation towards the system that enabled Huntley, who had a history of sexual offences against underage girls, to gain employment in schools. The incident proved a catalyst for criminal record checks of over 250,000 educational workers and an enduring media epithetic of classic paedophile who sought out employment in order to satisfy his desire for pre-adolescent girls. The destabilising of the safe protective space by outsiders through their 'devious' incursion generates a particular form of predatory paedophilia.

Importantly, the move to create records for educational workers highlights the ambiguity of the paedophile. News reports tend to focus on the innocuous bus driver, caretaker or librarian who harbours secret paedophilic desires. Cowburn and Dominelli suggested that media reports usually position the paedophile as devious and conniving: 'The paedophile, usually but not always, operates within the spaces and protection offered by public agencies and is construed as cunning because he manages to fool his so-called professional co-workers and employers.'[27] The impact is that a culturally imagined safe and protective space is destabilised through outsiders' 'devious' incursions, resulting in schools as places where paedophiles could work and prey undetected.[28] In her discussion of school safety and fear, Lindle[29] highlighted how popular expectations of care are often troubled by the everyday 'realities of institutional security and safety'. She argued[30]:

> Parents assume that the 6 to 8 daily hours when schools house their children offer greater protection than before or after school hours. Safety and security of pupils are foregone conclusions for public educational institutions; thus, episode incursions of safety and security shock and horrify.

The destabilising of the safe protective space by outsiders through their 'devious' incursion highlights the complex nature of the unacceptable. Without an ontological substance, the paedophile as phantasm highlights not only the ambiguity of the cultural form, but also the potential that it could be anyone; thus predatory paedophiles have emerged as ghostly spectres involved in the haunting of cultural consciousness. They could be revealed at any time, as their form remains unknowable. Importantly, like ghosts, they are virtually undetectable, only knowable through various traces.[31] Ohi[32] suggested that this is precisely why the paedophile is so culturally desirable. He said:

> To sustain a stable picture of the paedophile, it is thus paradoxically necessary to assert that paedophilia cannot be detected, that a paedophile cannot be pictured at all. The same gesture that renders him locatable and quarantined makes him unlocatable, omnipresent, and dangerously at large: just the way we like him.

Foucault[33] highlighted that in Victorian times there was an intensified adult surveillance of children who masturbated. In the twenty-first century, the emphasis has changed, with the surveying gaze upon adults themselves carrying out sexual practices on the child. Foucault also suggested that the sexual child was sustained by the very practices that sought to eradicate it. It is argued here that a similar process is taking place, as there is a new 'truth of sex' being written onto strangers. Such truth is articulated through the very practices that seek to identify them. As a result, the procedures designed to capture the paedophiles simultaneously materialise them.

It is ironic that the very surveillance techniques that sustain the child abusers as strangers, unlocatable and unknowable, ignore empirical evidence that appears to show that child abusers are more than likely to be family members. According to Kitzinger,[34] a main reason for this is that:

> The concept of the 'paedophile' locates dangerousness in a few aberrant individuals who can be metaphorically (if not literally) excluded from society and it focuses attention on stranger danger in ways which ignore the scale and nature of sexual violence throughout society and, especially within families.

Therefore, the paedophile becomes a cultural necessity in that it links unacceptable behaviour with paedophilia creating: '...a crucial distance between ordinary men who are deemed not to commit sexual offences from those who do, and thereby contribute to sustaining hegemonic masculinity as an unproblematic entity.'[35] Work by Brown[36] pertinently argued that the intense focus on sex offending is an anxiety-driven need to differentiate the paedophile from normal men. More specifically, the sex offender operates as the 'magnifying model of all the irregularities and perturbations to be found within ordinary men's sexuality'.[37] This resonates with Angelides'[38] claim that the paedophile identity category deflects attention away from 'the fact that child sexual abuse had been exposed by feminism as a problem congruous with dominant and not marginal forms of male sexuality'. Furthermore, such distancing is reinforced by a gender system that affirms a 'normalised' masculinity through the juxtaposition of the *predatory* paedophile to the *protective* 'normal' masculinity.

This distancing also provides the dynamics of the unacceptable in this context. It is argued that news reports on school auxiliaries represent desire as operating outside sexual normative categories of heterosexual/homosexual binaries, creating the gendered ambiguity of the paedophile. As news reports focus on 'age' as the central dynamic of sexual desire, normative gender identities secured through a system of compulsory heterosexuality become destabilised. Thus the paedophile is constituted outside of the sexual and gendered binaries that constitute the parameters of normative Western masculinity. Importantly, as Creed suggested, the abject is found not simply as an opposition between borders, for example in terms of the subject/object divide, but both within and outside the border that defines such difference. As a consequence, the abject – in this case the 'paedophile' – becomes a transfer-point of ambiguous signification:

> Abjection here is a response to an ambiguous form of signification, a signification that does not refer to culturally accepted gender norms, but that through its very ambiguity of performance throws these culturally cherished norms into question. Abjection is dangerous because it is always ambiguous, and is therefore seen as (merely) transitional.[39]

Therefore, it is such ambiguous signification that characterises the unacceptable sexual behaviours of the school auxiliary. Kristeva[40] suggested that the abject does not 'respect borders, positions, rules' and as a result 'disturbs identity, system, order'. Thus the paedophile's abject masculinity, necessarily it consolidates normative social bonds. More specifically, as Butler[41] suggests: 'Identities operate [...] through the discursive construction of a constitutive outside [...] of abjected and marginalized subjects [...] which return to trouble and unsettle the foreclosures which we prematurely call identities.' Thus, in this way, the foreclosures that constitute identities 'are phantasmatic efforts at alignment.'[42] Phantasmatic in this sense becomes the imagined scene where the object is repudiated and where difference is reconstructed. As a consequence, media reports of the predatory paedophile in schools reinforce a cultural imaginary that positions dangerous sexualities outside of the normal masculinities.

Dangerously voracious: the case of Amy Gehring

News reports also have similar functions to Foucault's[43] notion of the reverse discourse, with the media materialising otherness in order to sustain the centrality of the normal. Not only is it argued that the media materialises otherness, but it presents otherness as a sexual alternative. Where the unacceptable is not simply oppositional, it produces the possibility and legitimacy of transgressive sexual subjectivity. We draw upon news reports based upon allegations by three pupils that they were indecently assaulted by their teacher. Working as a supply teacher in November 2000, Amy Gehring befriended a number of pupils at comprehensive school in Surrey. She met the pupils both inside and outside the school. During her time at the school, it was alleged that she had sexual intercourse a number of times with one of the boys and that at other times had sex with his brother and another boy at a New Year's party. The prosecution's grounds for a conviction were based on the claim that 'In essence she became too close, behaving like one of the pupils and ignoring the boundaries of the teacher-pupil relationship.'[44] This closeness was conveyed through the sharing of youthful practices. Instances of drinking and smoking and stories about drug-taking were combined in the context of shopping, sleepovers and parties. The pinnacle of these youthful ascribed practices was exemplified by a shopping trip with the students where she had her navel pierced. The prosecution alleged that such practices demonstrated that there was parity, too much parity, between Amy and her students. The prosecution claimed that Amy removed social and professional boundaries necessary to teaching. Sexual intercourse with these pupils was not so much a transgression as a logical extension of a lifestyle.

Interestingly, the prosecution did not present Amy Gehring as a pathological child abuser. Rather, she was represented as a teacher who was inexperienced and immature. Thus, both the prosecution and the defence concentrated on minimalising the age difference between the teacher and the pupils. This minimalisation became a means to demonstrate the ambivalence of her professional teacher identity. This theme of inexperience was a key feature of the trial primarily because this was the dynamic that had placed her in proximity to the pupils. From the defence, such proximity made her an easy victim to 'playground gossip'. The case for both the defence and prosecution was built upon substantiating whether such inexperience would lead to sexual intercourse with the boys. A main feature of sexual scandals is the susceptibility of those involved.[45] Young female teachers carry such susceptibility as do men,[46] but female teachers also have to face a cultural representation of teachers that identifies them as sexually repressed.[47] The media reports highlight the cultural imagination shaping the sexual landscape of schooling: 'A young biology mistress seduced three teenage boys within weeks of her appointment as a supply teacher, a jury heard.'[48]

Returning to the headline, professionalism is not substituted for the erotic but rather is used to substantiate the erotic. Therefore, it is in the exaggerated codes of (un) professionalism through which the sexual teacher is made visible. Such media accounts generate a version of the female teacher as possessing a powerful insatiability of desire that disregarded the moral, professional and legal codes of conduct. She stands outside the normal, simply by making female sexuality visible. In the post-1945 English cultural context, female sexuality has tended to occupy a positive cultural space through the practice of mothering.[49]

Therefore, in English society, sexuality and femininity are elided, and as a consequence, socially marginal femininities are often re-coded as a cause of deviant sexualities.[50]

In the twenty-first century, rather than re-establishing such traditional understandings of female sexuality, a new form of representation is taking place. The media creates a female sexuality that is fascinating, repulsive and spectacular. In this case, such a spectacle was often reinforced by the news concentrating on the account of the teenage boys. This was the claim that the teacher had sex with one of them only a few minutes after the other. Various testimonies were used by the prosecution to convey this voraciousness. One of these was from a 15-year old boy who suggested that the teacher took his virginity from him. This 'shameless' sexuality was also reinforced by the testimony of a 16-year old girl. It was reported that the girl claimed to have warned Amy Gehring to discontinue the relationship. The girl claimed that Amy ignored the advice and claimed further that the teacher had suggested lesbian sex to another pupil. This led to a report in the paper about another girl from the school who claimed that the teacher had propositioned to have sex with her.[51]

Although the reports recode female sexuality within a patriarchal fantasy, they simultaneously trouble the attempted recuperation of acceptable femininity. Thus, in this case, rather than establish traditional norms and values and reflect them, the reports generate ambivalence due to a syncretism of desirability and danger. The day after the clearing of Gehring of all counts of indecent sexual assault, the *Daily Mail* ran the headline, 'How she lured me to bed, by previous pupil.'[52] This was based on an interview with a pupil at a previous school who claimed that Gehring had sex with him. The language of 'lured' has the connotation of alluring, enticing and capturing, and the main focus of the story was on how the teacher had taken the boys' virginity. This story was supplemented by others: 'Miss seducer; boozy teacher had alley sex with two underage boys and bedded a third'[53]; 'Boy, 15, "saw his teacher lover seducing his little brother"'[54]; 'Too drunk to know; Teacher told police she couldn't recall what happened at sex party.'[55] As a result, such deviancy is conveyed through a particular form of sexualised language.

Such a salacious titillation of the case was evidenced by the following: 'The sex scandal teacher: my story; the 16-year virgin schoolboy; a class of lustful teenagers; they loved my detentions.'[56] The mood of the papers was captured by the judge's claim that the jury should not be misled that this is a 'school boy fantasy' and that the gender of the defendant should be irrelevant. As Miller[57] suggested, the 'school mistress' has a 'gartered and saucy ring'. In this context 'mistress' connects with an older traditional form of teaching that can be associated with discipline. However, a notion of discipline carries a sexualised cultural image of the dominatrix. As Dillabough[58] pointed out, women teachers are viewed in different ways from their male counterparts, and that a woman *as* teacher activates cultural understandings of a natural femininity that is based upon nurturance and care. Furthermore, it is also argued that female teachers have their identities naturalised: 'This position ultimately leads to women's exclusion from the formal language of teacher professionalism, yet [...] defines her inclusion on the basis of female subordination.'[59]

Women teachers who have sex with their pupils, therefore, not only break codes of professionalism, they threaten naturalised notions of female identity. Thus, news reports on female teachers and male pupils signal an immediate transgression of femininity that in turn challenges the social and cultural foundations that underpin their legitimacy as teachers. Using psychoanalysis, Cavanagh[60] neatly identified how news reports have to focus in on the danger of female sexuality as the 'teacher-as mother who adopts a position of power over the male student (coded as son) threatens normative masculine identity development'. Thus, according to Cavanagh, the media's fascination with the unacceptable is premised on a Freudian castration anxiety and the taboo of incest. The violation of heterosexual normativity through the rejection of reproductive bound sexuality is replaced by a phallic sexuality of the lustful and shameless teacher.

In summary, the media accounts of the case draw heavily on the activation of fantasy. Thus the media does not produce sexual otherness to be simplistically vilified; rather, media accounts produce *desirable* otherness. Butler[61] suggested that the use of fantasy describes how individuals psychically recover loss through an imagined scene that reunites them with the lost (never to be attained) object. So, the fantasy allows the reunification with those objects that are inaccessible. It is argued that the above case is an example of the fantasy imbricated in the English cultural imagination.

Obscenely desirable reading

The final dynamic through which unacceptability is activated is through an emphasis on the cultural imaginary of childhood. The majority of news reports focus not only on children as the object of desire but the defilement of childhood itself. According to Beck,[62] 'The child is the source of the last remaining, irrevocable, inexchangeable primary relationship.' Much work has been undertaken on the importance of childhood to contemporary social and cultural arrangements,[63] captured in Meyer's[64] suggestion that the media promotes a discourse about childhood innocence that reinforces solid and secure identities:

> Through this discourse of innocence, children are reproduced as possessing an essentially virtuous and innocent nature. This nature makes them naive and vulnerable, and turns them into helpless victims in constant need of adult protection.

There may also be an added complexity surrounding media accounts of sexuality and schooling that requires further explanation. Not only is there a collapse in the ontological certainty surrounding childhood that can be reflected in education; the organisation of schooling itself is seen as *generating* sexual possibilities. With childhood as a central axiom of the educational process, schools persistently generate the possibilities through which the cultural imaginary can be made. Schools have historically insisted on the formal excision of sex, sexuality and desire from its institutional structures.[65] As Burman[66] suggested: 'A happy cosy childhood is now synonymous with stability and tradition.' It is argued that this semantic juxtaposition is the very dynamic that according to Kincaid[67] *eroticises* childhood. He argued: 'We protect against eroticising the child and thereby write a shadowy story of child eroticism.'[68] Therefore, the sexualness of childhood is not so much contained within erotic practices, it is produced through the ways that sexuality is forcefully projected and denied in the prescription of asexuality where a 'subversive echo' of sexual knowledge and experience is conveyed. In this context, the violation of an imagined childhood innocence is in the process of eroticising the unacceptable. Furthermore, in a productive rethinking of innocence and childhood, Archard[69] argued that innocence may not simply convey protection and vulnerability, but its iteration may expose that which is deemed worth protecting. Innocence 'connotes a purity, virginity, freshness and immaculateness which excites by the possibilities of possession and defilement'.

As a consequence, in much research on sexuality, schooling and moral panics, an important element has been overlooked. More specifically, the analysis of these representations helps us to understand how the shock and horror of media accounts is not simply about the closure or the repression of the unacceptable, but rather the mobilisation of abject and subjunctive sexual subjectivities.[70] Therefore, rather than news reports simplistically operating through notions of lack and closure, Derrida's notion of circularity enables us to consider that the identification and projection of the moral is dependant and constitutive of that which the moral ordering wishes to expel. The complexity of 'what starts as a simple repulsion or rejection of symbolic matter foreign to the self inaugurates a process of introjection and negation',[71] creating a haunting speculative possibility of that which is expelled.[72]

Furthermore, when media accounts identify a collapse in moral boundaries, it is depicted as a collapse precisely *because* of moral certainty. Thus a depreciation of morality is not simply generated through ambivalence or ambiguity of status and identity; rather such a collapse is deemed to be occurring because right and wrong/good and bad/acceptable/unacceptable is clearly defined within the social imaginary.[73] For example, news reports on sexuality and schooling, in particular male teachers and female pupils, contain an erotic charge often represented in stories that focus on the forbidden, highlighting desires that are both culturally prohibited and celebrated. Whereas in the case of the sexual auxiliary there is a suggested pathology, with male teachers and female pupils the stories fall into a classic eroticised genre of illicit lust. This is especially the case with married male teachers. With school auxiliaries, sexual activities are represented as *abuse*; with married male teachers and female pupils, a theme to emerge is that the relationship is described as an *affair*. For example, a teacher who had relationships with a pupils aged 13 and 14 was described as embarking on 'affairs' with the girls.[74] The media is in some ways articulating what Hubbard[75] calls 'scary heterosexualities'. Similar to the female teachers, heterosexual desire that stands outside the normative contours of desire that tends to be marked by marriage and reproduction, is also about the forbidden (but exciting) intergenerational sex. Such sexual identities also stand outside the normative nuclear family and its attendant mothering and fathering practices that are often embedded in pedagogical practices.

Alongside this, Ania Wilczynski and Kate Sinclair[76] suggested that when dealing with sex abuse in authority positions, the tabloids produce sexual titillation. Or, as Sothhill and Walby[77] have suggested, sex stories have a similar iterative function as the tabloid display of naked woman. As a consequence, the sexual desire represented in news reports is less about violence and domination and much more about pleasure, seduction and sex. For example, stories such as, 'I want to cover you in ice cream, PE teacher told girl, 14',[78] 'Spanking teacher sent for re-training'[79] and 'Play xylophone as we have sex'[80] highlights how the male teacher's sexual desire is often played against the eroticised trope of the innocent schoolgirl. Pupils are often reconstructed as sexual objects and are eroticised within the framework of male teacher desire.

It could be argued, therefore, that news stories re-enact an imagined sexual scene that incites the reader to emotionally engage. At the same time, the reported desire for the young female pupil has a monomythical resonance[81] with temptation and lust causing Man's downfall. As a result, the female pupil is subject to blame rather than the teacher. Stories such as 'Jailed, teacher who was seduced by a girl of 15',[82] or in the case of a 14-year old pupil, 'That girl did it all to get him into bed, now he's been punished with jail because he is a school teacher'[83]; 'Girl agreed to cover up affair with teacher'.[84] A theme of the forbidden contextualises how the story is read.

In a discussion of the media narratives embedded in stories of the gender-based violence by Australian rules football players, Toffoletti (2007) provided a useful framework for understanding the dynamics of media representations. She argued that women who demonstrate sexual desire challenge common-sense notions of sexuality, where men are dominant and females are passive. Thus, in such cases, blame is often attributed to females. In English culture, the innocent schoolgirl is a sexualised narrative that can be found in pre-marriage parties, fashion, advertising, television and film. As Ennew[85] suggested, the eroticisation of children is not too far away from the cultural imagination that draws upon teachers being seduced or tempted into relationships with their female pupils. As such, men become victims and through the use of their sexuality, female pupils are seen as 'disempowering men'. New reports often make allusions to a Lolita effect whereby the teacher becomes infatuated with a sexually precocious young girl. It could be argued, therefore, that the newspaper actually metonymically re-enacts the sexual scene where the account makes the teacher fascinating, exciting and enjoyable.

Conclusion

One of the functions of this chapter is to reflect on the dynamics that underpin the unacceptable within the cultural imaginary. In each section, the unacceptable has been articulated through a number of popular epithets including 'the predatory paedophile', 'the voracious female teacher' and the 'precocious pupil'. Importantly, the unacceptable has its own dynamics within the context of schooling with particular practices. In other words, the school is not simply the location for the sex scandal; the school provides the parameters through which notions of the unacceptable are articulated. For example, schools erase the possibility of children engaging in sexual relations and yet, as we have argued, those 'controlling the phantasmatic end up reproducing and proliferating the phantasmatic in advertent ways, indeed, in ways that contradict the intended purposes of the restriction itself'.[86]

At the same time, it is important to locate these episodes within a broader cultural moment where revelation has become an epistemology of truth. Foucault argued: 'We belong to a society which has ordered sex's difficult knowledge, not according to the transmission of secrets, but around the slow surfacing of confidential statements.'[87] The revelation is part of a broader cultural regimen of media reports, talk shows, biographies, blogging and social networks. These popular technologies have displaced the moral centrifugal force traditionally located within religion, the family and community. In the context of such shifts in how the cultural imaginary is made, the negotiation of the boundaries between what is acceptable and unacceptable will intensify.

Finally, as Lianos and Douglas[88] suggested, contemporary society is marked by new emerging ways of asserting difference. They argued that the collapse or the representation of the collapse of key forms of discrimination in terms of gender, ethnicity and class has shifted to an emphasis on dangerousness being a key constituent of social identities. Within the context of sex scandals and schooling, such dangerousness does not preclude fantasy and desire.

Notes

1. Epstein, D. 1997; Epstein, D. and Johnson, R. 1998; Luschen K.V. and Bogad, L. 2003; Sikes, P. 2006; Sikes, P. and Piper, H. 2010.
2. Cohen, S. 1972.
3. Surtees, N. 2005; Plummer, D. and McCann, P.D. 2007.
4. Young, J. 1971; Hall, S., Critcher, C., Jefferson, T., Clarke, J. and Roberts, B. 1978; Hall, S. 1990.
5. Holly, L. 1989; Lees, S. 1994; Mclaren, P. 1994; Haywood, C. 1996; Epstein, D. and Johnson, R. 1998.
6. Sikes, P. 2006.
7. Epstein, D. 1997.
8. Scraton, P. 2002; See also, Cooper, D. 1997.
9. Luschen, K.V. and Bogad, L. 2003, p. 147.
10. Kehily, M. 1999; Kehily, 2002.
11. Luschen K.V. and Bogad, L. 2003.
12. Sikes, P. 2006.
13. Ibid., p. 262.
14. Watney, S. 1988.
15. Cornwell, B. and Linders, A. 2002.

16. Ungar, S. 2001.
17. McRobbie, A. and Thornton, S. 1995; Critcher, C. 2002.
18. Miller, D., Kitzinger, J., Williams, K. and Beharrell, P. 1998, p. 11.
19. Thompson, K. 1998, p. 72.
20. Kincaid, J.R. 1992, pp. 54–55.
21. Hilton, S., Hunt, K., Langan, M., Bedford, H. and Petticrew M. 2010.
22. Harcup, T. and O'Neil, D. 2001; Vincent, J., Imwold, C., Masemann, V. and Johnson, J.T. 2002.
23. Meyer, A. 2007.
24. Harcup, T. and O'Neil, D. 2001.
25. Kitzinger, J. 1998; Houston, S. 2001.
26. *The Mirror*, p. 23, 22 May 2003.
27. Cowburn, M. and Dominelli, L. 2001, p. 12.
28. Carvel, J. 1998; Lawson, T. and Comber, C. 2000; Sandwell, B. 2006.
29. Lindle, J.C. 2008.
30. Ibid., p. 29.
31. Derrida, J. 1978.
32. Ohi, K.J.H. 2001, p. 204.
33. Foucault, M. 1981.
34. Kitzinger, J. 1999, p. 207.
35. Cowburn, M. and Dominelli, L. 2001, p. 6.
36. Brown, M. 2010.
37. Ibid., p. 51.
38. Angelides, S. 2005, p. 126.
39. Schwaiger, L. 2006, p. 28.
40. Kristeva, J. 1982, p. 4.
41. Butler, J. 1993, p. 22.
42. Ibid., p. 22.
43. Foucault, M. 1981.
44. *Daily Mail*, p. 7, 22 January 2002.
45. Lull, J. and Hinerman, S. 1997.
46. Collier, R. 1998.
47. Grumet, M. 1988.
48. *Daily Mail*, p. 7, 22 January 2002.
49. Grumet, M. 1988.
50. Lees, S. 1994; Hey, V. 1997.
51. *The Mirror*, p. 27, 24 January 2002.
52. *Daily Mail*, p. 9, 5 February.
53. *The Mirror*, p. 7, 22 January 2002.
54. *Daily Mail*, p. 29, 25 January 2002.
55. *Daily Mail*, p. 19, 29 January 2002.
56. *The Mirror*, p. 17, 9 February 2002.
57. Miller, J. 1996, p. 6.
58. Dillabough, J. 1999.
59. Ibid., p. 381.
60. Cavanagh, S. L. 2004, p. 76.
61. Butler, J. 1993.
62. Beck, U. 1992, p. 118.
63. James, A. and Prout, A. 1999; Buckingham, D. 2000; Mayall, B. 2002.

64. Meyer, A. 2007, p. 89.
65. Fine, M. 1988; Mac an Ghaill, M. 1996; Ellis, V. and High, S. 2004.
66. Burman, E. 1995, p. 59.
67. Kincaid, J. 1992.
68. Ibid., p. 360.
69. Archard, D. 1993, p. 40.
70. Talburt, S. 2010.
71. Stalybrass, P. and White, A. 1986, p. 193.
72. Colebrook, C. 2000.
73. Lull, J. and Hinerman, S. 1997.
74. *Daily Mail*, p. 5, 14 August 2006.
75. Hubbard, P. 2001.
76. Wilczynski, A. and Sinclair, K. 1999.
77. Soothhill, K. and Walby, S. 1991.
78. *Daily Mail*, p. 23, 14 March 2000.
79. *Daily Mail*, p. 39, 16 October 2008.
80. *The Mirror*, p. 19, 10 May 2007.
81. Campbell, J. 1949.
82. *Daily Mail*, p. 7, 12 March 2004.
83. *Daily Mail*, p. 5, 29 August 2001.
84. *Daily Mail*, p. 28, 31 January 2007.
85. Ennew, J. 1994.
86. Butler, J. 1990, p. 108.
87. Foucault, 1981, p. 63.
88. Lianos, M. and Douglas, M. 2000.

References

Angelides, S., 'The emergence of the paedophile in late twentieth century', *Australian Historical Studies*, 36 (126), pp. 272–295, 2005.

Archard, D., *Children: Rights and Childhood*, London: Routledge, 1993.

Beck, U., *Risk Society: Towards a New Modernity*, London: Sage, 1992.

Brown, M., 'Theorising Dangerousness', in: M. Nash and A. Williams (Eds) *Handbook of Public Protection*, pp. 40–60, Oxon: Taylor and Francis, 2010.

Buckingham, D., *After the Death of Childhood: Growing Up in the Age of Electronic Media*, Cambridge: Polity Press, 2000.

Burman, E., 'What Is It? Masculinity and Femininity and the Cultural Representation of Childhood', in: S. Wilkinson and C. Kitzinger (Eds) *Feminism and Discourse*, pp. 49–67, London: Sage, 1995.

Butler, J., 'The force of fantasy: feminism, mapplethorpe, and discursive excess', *Differences*, 2 (2), pp. 105–125, 1990.

Butler, J., *Bodies That Matter: On the Discursive Limits of 'Sex'*, New York: Routledge, 1993.

Campbell, J., *The Hero with a Thousand Faces*, New York: Pantheon Books, 1949.

Carvel, J., 'Pupils "at risk" of Internet porn', *Guardian*, p. 4, 10 April, 1998.

Cavanagh, S. L., *Sexing the Teacher: School Sex Scandals and Queer Pedagogies*, Vancouver: UBC Press, 2004.

Cohen, S., *Folk Devils and Moral Panics: The Creation of the Mods and Rockers*, London: MacGibbon and Kee, 1972.

Colebrook, C. 'From radical representations to corporeal becomings: the feminist philosophy of Lloyd, Grosz, and Gatens', *Hypatia*, 15 (2), pp. 76–79, 2000.

Collier, R., *Masculinities, Crime and Criminology: Men, Corporeality and the Criminal(ised) Body*, London: Sage, 1998.

Cooper, D., 'Governing troubles: authority, sexuality and space', *British Journal of Sociology of Education*, 18, pp. 501–518, 1997.

Cornwell, B. and Linders, A., 'The myth of "moral panic": an alternative account of LSD Prohibition', *Deviant Behavior: An Interdisciplinary Journal*, 23, pp. 307–330, 2002.

Cowburn, M. and Dominelli, L., 'Masking hegemonic masculinity: reconstructing the paedophile as the dangerous stranger', *British Journal of Social Work*, 31, pp. 399–415, 2001.

Critcher, C., 'Media, Government and moral panic: the politics of paedophilia in Britain 2000–1', *Journalism Studies*, 3 (4), pp. 521–535, 2002.

Daily Mail, 'I want to cover you in ice cream, PE teacher told girl 14', p. 23, 14 March 2000.

Daily Mail, 'That girl did it all to get him into bed, now he's been punished with jail because he is a school teacher', p. 5, 29 August 2001.

Daily Mail, 'Lessons in lust; Biology teacher had sex with three underage pupils, jury told', p. 7, 22 January 2002.

Daily Mail, 'Boy, 15, "saw his teacher lover seducing his little brother"; Schoolmistress, 26, was found in "compromising position"', p. 29, 25 January 2002.

Daily Mail, 'Too drunk to know; Teacher told police she couldn't recall what happened at sex party', p. 19, 29 January 2002.

Daily Mail, 'How she lured me to bed, by previous pupil', p. 9, 5 February 2002.

Daily Mail, 'Jailed, teacher who was seduced by a girl of 15', p. 7, 12 March 2004.

Daily Mail, 'Deputy Head who seduced two pupils is jailed for life', p. 5, 14 August 2006.

Daily Mail, 'Girl agreed to cover up affair with teacher', p. 28, 31 January 2007.

Daily Mail, 'Spanking teacher sent for re-training', p. 39, 16 October 2008.

Derrida, J., *Writing and Difference*, Chicago: University of Chicago Press, 1978.

Dillabough, J., 'Gender politics and conceptions of the modern teacher: women, identity and professionalism', *British Journal of Sociology of Education*, 20 (3), pp. 373–392, 1999.

Ellis, V. and High, S., 'Something more to tell you: gay, lesbian or bisexual young people's experiences of secondary schooling', *British Educational Research Journal*, 30 (2), pp. 213–225, 2004.

Ennew, J., 'Time for Children or Time for Adults', in: J. Qvortrup et al. (Eds) *Childhood Matters: Social Theory, Practice and Politics*, pp. 125–143, Aldershot: Avebury, 1994.

Epstein, D., 'What's in a Ban? The Popular Media, Romeo and Juliet and Compulsory Heterosexuality', in: D. L. Steinberg, D. Epstein and R. Johnson (Eds) *Border Patrols: Policing the Boundaries of Heterosexuality*, pp. 183–203, London: Cassell, 1997.

Epstein, D. and Johnson, R., *Schooling Sexualities*, Buckingham: Open University, 1998.
Fine, M., 'Sexuality, schooling, and adolescent females: the missing discourse of desire', *Harvard Educational Review*, 58 (1), pp. 54–63, 1988.
Foucault, M., *The History of Sexuality, Volume 1: An Introduction*, Harmondsworth: Penguin, 1981.
Grumet, M., *Bitter Milk: Women and Teaching*, Amherst, MA: The University of Massachusetts Press, 1988.
Hall, S., 'The Whites of their Eyes. Racist Ideologies and the Media', in: M. Alvarado and J. O. Thompson (Eds) *The Media Reader*, pp. 7–23, London: BFI Publishing, 1990.
Hall, S., Critcher, C., Jefferson, T., Clarke, J. and Roberts, B., *Policing the Crisis: Mugging, the State and Law and Order*, London: Macmillan, 1978.
Harcup, T. and O'Neill, D., 'What is news? Galtung and Ruge revisited', *Journalism Studies*, 2 (2), pp. 261–280, 2002.
Haywood, C., 'Sex Education and the regulation of young people's sexual practice', *Educational Review*, 48, pp. 121–129, 1996.
Hey, V., *The Company She Keeps: An Ethnography of Girls' Friendships*, Buckingham: Open University Press, 1997.
Hilton, S., Hunt, K., Langan, M., Bedford, H. and Petticrew, M., 'Newsprint media representations of the introduction of the HPV vaccination programme for cervical cancer prevention in the UK (2005–2008)', *Social Science and Medicine*, 70 (6), pp. 942–950, 2010.
Holly, L., 'Introduction: The Sexual Agenda of Schools', in: L. Holly (Ed) *Girls and Sexuality: Teaching and Learning*, pp. 1–10, Milton Keynes: Open University Press, 1989.
Houston, S., 'Beyond social constructionism: critical realism and social work', *British Journal of Social Work*, 31, pp. 845–61, 2001.
Hubbard, P., 'Sex zones: intimacy, citizenship and public space', *Sexualities*, 4 (1), pp. 51–71, 2001.
James, A. and Prout, A. (Eds) (1999) *Constructing and Reconstructing Childhood*, London: Falmer Press, 1999.
Kehily, M. J., 'More sugar? Teenage magazines, gender displays and sexual learning', *European Journal of Cultural Studies*, 2, pp. 65–89, 1999.
Kehily, M. J., *Sexuality, Gender and Schooling: Shifting Agendas in Social Learning*, London: Routledge Falmer, 2002.
Kincaid, J. R., *Child-Loving: The Erotic Child and Victorian Culture*, New York: Routledge, 1992.
Kitzinger, J., 'Defending innocence: ideologies of childhood', *Feminist Rev*iew, 28, pp. 77–87, 1998.
Kitzinger, J., 'The Ultimate Neighbour from Hell?: Stranger Danger and the Media Representation of "Paedophilia" ', in: B. Franklin (Ed) *Social Policy, the Media and Misrepresentation*, pp. 207–221, London: Routledge, 1999.
Kristeva, J., *Powers of Horror. An Essay on Abjection*. Translated by Leon S. Roudiez, New York: Columbia University Press, 1982.
Lawson, T. and Comber, C., 'Censorship, the internet and schools: a new moral panic?' *The Curriculum Journal*, 11 (2), pp. 273–285, 2000.
Lees, S., *Sugar and Spice: Sexuality and Adolescent Girls*, Harmondsworth: Penguin, 1994.

Lianos, M. and Douglas, M., 'Dangerization and the end of deviance: the institutional Environment', *British Journal of Criminology*, 40; reprinted in: D. Garland and R. Sparks (Eds) *Criminology and Social Theory*, pp. 261–278, Oxford: Oxford University Press, 2000.

Lindle, J. C., 'School safety: real or imagined fear?' *Educational Policy*, 22, pp. 28–44, 2008.

Lull, J. and Hinerman, S., 'The Search for Scandal', in: J. Lull and S. Hinerman (Eds) *Media Scandals: Morality and Desire in the Popular Culture Marketplace*, pp. 1–33, Cambridge: Polity Press, 1997.

Luschen, K. V. and Bogad. L., 'Bodies that matter: transgenderism, innocence and the politics of "unprofessional" pedagogy', *Sex Education*, 3, pp. 145–155, 2003.

Mac an Ghaill, M., 'Deconstructing heterosexualities within school arenas', *Curriculum Studies*, 4 (2), pp. 191–209, 1996.

Mayall, B., *Towards a Sociology for Childhood. Thinking from Children's Lives*, Maidenhead: Open University Press, 2002.

McLaren, P., 'Moral panic, schooling, and gay identity: critical pedagogy and the politics of resistance', *High School Journal*, 77 (1–2), 157–168, 1994.

McRobbie, A. and Thornton, S., 'Rethinking moral panic for multimediated social worlds', *British Journal of Sociology*, 46 (4), pp. 559–574, 1995.

Meyer, A., 'The Moral Rhetoric of Childhood', *Childhood*, 14 (1), pp. 85–104, 2007.

Miller, D., Kitzinger, J., Williams, K. and Beharrell, P., *The Circuit of Mass Communication*, London: Sage, 1998.

Miller, J., *School for Women*, London: Virago Press, 1996.

Ohi, K. J. H., *Innocence and Rapture: The Erotics of Childhood in Aestheticism*. Unpublished PhD Thesis, Cornell University, 2001.

Plummer, D. and McCann, P. D., 'Girls' germs: sexuality, gender, health and metaphors of contagion', *Health Sociology Review*, 16 (1), pp. 43–52, 2007.

Sandwell, B., 'Monsters in cyberspace: cyberphobia and cultural panic in the information age', *Information, Communication & Society*, 9 (1), pp. 39–61, 2006.

Schwaiger, L., 'To be forever young? Towards reframing corporeal subjectivity in maturity', *International Journal of Ageing and Later Life*, 1 (1), pp. 11–41, 2006.

Scraton, P., 'The Demonisation, Exclusion and Regulation of Children: From Moral Panic to Moral Renewal', in: A. Boran and D. Balsamo (Eds) *Crime: Fear or Fascination?* pp. 9–39, Chester: Chester Academic Press, 2002.

Sikes, P., 'Scandalous stories and dangerous liaisons: when male teachers and female pupils fall in love', *Sex Education*, 6, pp. 265–280, 2006.

Sikes, P. and Piper, H., *Researching Sex and Lies in the Classroom: Allegations of Sexual Misconduct in Schools*, London: Routledge, 2010.

Skidmore, P., 'Telling Tales; Media Power, Ideology and the Reporting of Child Sexual Abuse in Britain', in: D. Kidd-Hewitt and R. Osborne (Eds) *Crime and the Media*, pp. 78–106, London: Pluto, 1995.

Soothhill, K. and Walby, S., *Sex Crime in the News*, London: Routledge, 1991.

Stalybrass, P. and White, A., *The Politics and Poetics of Transgression*, London: Methuen, 1986.

Surtees, N., 'Teacher talk about and around sexuality in early childhood education: deciphering an unwritten code', *Contemporary Issues in Early Childhood*, 6 (1), pp. 19–29, 2005.

Talburt, S., 'After-queer: subjunctive pedagogies', *International Journal of Qualitative Studies in Education*, 23 (1), pp. 49–64, 2010.

The Mirror, 'Miss seducer; boozy teacher had alley sex with two underage boys and bedded a third, court told she kissed me. We just started snogging. I thought what am I doing…I haven't a clue – alleged victim, boy A', p. 7, 2 January 2002.

The Mirror, 'Schoolgirl, 16: miss asked me to make out with her; pupil tells jury of sex proposal', p. 27, 24 January 2002.

The Mirror, 'The sex scandal teacher: my story; the 16-year virgin schoolboy a class of lustful teenagers they loved my detentions', p. 17, 9 February 2002.

The Mirror, 'Child sex beast hired to drive school buses; "piggy-back" pervert caged for 15 months', p. 23, 22 May 2003.

The Mirror, 'Play xylophone as we have sex', p. 19, 10 May 2007.

Thompson, K., *Moral Panics*, London: Routledge, 1998.

Ungar, S., 'Moral panic versus the risk society: the implications of the changing sites of social anxiety', *British Journal of Sociology*, 52, pp. 271–292, 2001.

Vincent, J., Imwold, C., Masemann, V. and Johnson, J. T, 'A comparison of selected "serious" and "popular" British, Canadian, and United States newspaper coverage of female and male athletes competing in the Centennial Olympic Games', *International Review for the Sociology of Sport*, 3 (3–4), pp. 319–335, 2002.

Watney, S., 'AIDS, Moral Panic Theory and Homophobia', in: P. Aggleton and H. Homans (Eds) *Social Aspects of AIDS*, pp. 52–64, London: Falmer, 1988.

Wilczynski, A. and Sinclair, K., 'Moral tales: representations of child abuse in the quality and tabloid media', *Australian & New Zealand Journal of Criminology*, 32, pp. 262–283, 1999.

Wise, S., 'New right or backlash? Section 28, moral panic and promoting homosexuality', *Sociological Research Online*, 5 (1), pp. 1–13, 2000.

Young, J., *The Drugtakers*, London: MacGibbon and Kee, 1971.

3
Presumed Innocent: Picturing Childhood

Catharine Lumby

A painting by Australian artist Cherry Hood hangs in the hallway of my home. It depicts a young girl, aged six or seven, her head half turned to gaze back at the viewer. The left side of her face is illuminated by a silvery unseen light source. The other half is washed with a shadow that gathers into darkness below her neck. Her body is obscured. The child is beautiful: full-lipped, with large almond-shaped eyes. It's not her beauty, however, which makes the portrait so compelling; it's the ambiguous nature of her gaze. She fixes the viewer with a look that can be read as fear or defiance, depending on what the observer is inclined to see. Hood's capacity to capture the ambiguity of children's gazes – to make that ambiguity visible – is the hallmark of her extraordinary talent. The more I've studied the painting in my hallway, though, the less I see it as a portrait of a child and the more I'm inclined to see it as a portrait of myself or, indeed, of any other adult viewer.

Pictures of children are currently the source of widespread anxiety across much of the Western world. Testament to this is a framed newspaper banner also hanging in my hallway that reads 'Teen Porn Uproar – Artist To Be Charged'. It was printed in May 2008 at the height of frenzied public debate about the Australian photographer Bill Henson whose image of a nude 13-year-old girl sparked calls for his prosecution under child pornography laws.

The controversy began when an invitation to Henson's Sydney exhibition featuring a photograph of the girl caught the attention of conservative media commentators. Despite the fact that Henson is an internationally acclaimed artist who has been exhibiting images of nude teenagers for decades, the then Australian Prime Minister Kevin Rudd felt compelled to denounce Henson's images as 'absolutely revolting' on breakfast television. His remark poured fuel on a fire that was already being stoked by radio 'shock jocks' and led to Henson being accused of being a paedophile masquerading as an artist.[1] These public commentators claimed that the exhibition of Henson's works was unacceptable. Thirty-two photographs were seized by police from the Roslyn Oxley Gallery in Sydney but were ultimately returned after the Australian Classification Board declared the images 'mild' and safe for viewing by children as well as adults.[2]

The Henson case is a dramatic illustration of the pervasive anxiety provoked by images of children.[3] It was preceded in Australia by the launch of an inflammatory, if empirically thin, report by a left-wing think tank, the Australia Institute, titled *Corporate Paedophilia*.[4] The authors of the *Corporate Paedophilia* report based their evidence on a set of general observations about an extremely small sample of advertisements and marketing material (14 advertising images in total) and what they dubbed a 'content analysis' of three single issues of three different tween magazines. The Australia Institute report also employed content coding categories – beauty, fashion, celebrity, crush – that were so broad they had no empirical validity. 'Fashion', for instance, could denote anything from a T-shirt to stiletto shoes. 'Beauty', could refer to lip-gloss or plastic surgery. Despite this reliance on a small and apparently randomly selected sample, the authors felt confident to state that 'Images of sexualised children are becoming increasingly common in advertising and marketing material.'[5] Their assertion mirrors a claim that has become so widely accepted that to interrogate it is to run the risk of being accused of actively promoting child abuse – as a Professor of English at the University of California discovered. On the publication of his book *Child-Loving: The Erotic Child and Victorian Culture*,[6] James Kincaid was described in the British press as a 'passionate champion of paedophilia'.[7] Kincaid is one of a number of scholars examining the question of what is animating debates about the sexualisation of children and why we invest representations of children with so much cultural weight.[8] It's a topic that has become so fraught that questioning the investment that many adults have in child 'protection' and its relationship to child control is an invitation to accusations of a desire to actually harm children.

In this chapter I want to unpack the modern cultural history of representations of children in order to shed light on the question of how we have come to a pass where even the most innocuous images are subject to scrutiny. I want to understand what it is we seek in images of childhood and why we are simultaneously fascinated and repelled by what hovers beneath the surface.

Family photographs of children are rarely just snapped and automatically displayed. We choose these images with great care. Family albums of our own childhood and our own children are just as involved in framing our notion of what it means to be a child as any media image is. The question of what a child looks like in an acceptable photo varies widely from family to family. Some family albums are festooned with images of children whose faces are smeared with vegemite or hummus. Others feature orderly children smiling for the camera. The 'natural' child is always the socialised child – the child viewed from particular social and cultural ideals of how children should behave or look.

Regardless of these differences, there are still strong social and cultural norms that govern the way we show and understand images of children. We rarely show them expressing ideas or feelings that suggest they have lost their innocence, as adults imagine it. How many photos do any of us have of ourselves as children, or of our own children or grandchildren showing the infant in an uncontrollable fury? The less-than-ideal moments are quietly shredded. Even in families that celebrate the chaos of family life, it's something amusing or winsome which is in the frame – not true resistance to adults, not raw fury, not the rampant boiling Freudian Id that characterises so much of our youth. The Kodak moments picture children as we want to see them. They don't simply picture childhood – they frame it. Images of children carry enormous symbolic weight for adults – they determine how we see ourselves. If we think there is something amiss with childhood then we are prone to think that there is something deeply wrong with our society as a whole.

Picturing innocence

In her visual history of the representation of children in art and photography, art historian Anne Higonnet wrote:

> Pictures of children are at once the most common, the most sacred, and the most controversial images of our time. They guard the cherished ideal of childhood innocence, yet they contain within them the potential to undo that ideal[9]

As Higonnet demonstrated, the eighteenth century saw an important shift in representations of children and in ideas about childhood. Earlier portraits show children posed as little adults. The portraits are necessarily of children born to the aristocracy and were painted to demonstrate their future social status. They are dressed in adult clothing and they are posed against a background of family estates, houses and hounds. They are posed to suggest adult authority: hands on hips, imperious gazes.

Late eighteenth-century European portraiture ushered in a new age. British portraitists, in particular, began showing children in a way that we now understand as childlike. Thomas Lawrence, for instance, painted the Calmady children in 1823 at the dawn of the era of the Romantic child, an era which continues to dominate the way we see children even two centuries later. The images from this era began to radically separate the experience of children and adults. The children in these images are innocent in every way of the adult world: they have no knowledge of class, race, sexuality, gender or religion. Ironically, almost all the children who were painted in this period were children from a very particular background: they were the wealthy progeny of the aristocracy and the growing middle class. In the nineteenth century, the Romantic ideal of childhood innocence can be found in popular chocolate box representations of children: John Everett Millais's painting, *A Child's World*, later retitled *Bubbles* (1886) was purchased and used in a Pear's soap advertisement of the time. Images, in this sense, not only represent a given idea of childhood, they tutor their audience in those ideals.

There is also a very different and more ambiguous side to Victorian images of children. Most infamous are the photographs of Charles Dodgson, who wrote *Alice in Wonderland* under the pseudonym Lewis Carroll. Dodgson was known for the intense friendships he struck up with the children of friends. The Alice character was modelled on a real child, Alice Liddell, whom he also photographed. In a well-known image, Alice poses as a street urchin begging in rags. Despite the contrived nature of the mise-en-scène, it's not the implied narrative that holds the contemporary viewer's attention. It's her pose: hand on hip, one leg thrust slightly forward with a sideways glance at someone off camera. It's a knowing look that prompts the question: what does she know?[10]

Images like this are simply ones that bring a deeper question to the surface: a question that lies dormant in all contemporary images of children today. It's the question of what it is that children understand about the adult world and of how much they don't tell us about what this knowledge entails. We reconstruct our own childhood through memory, through utopian or dystopian stories that we tell ourselves and our children. Yet the truth of childhood – the memory of what it was *really* like – remains both elusive and repressed. We express indignation when our children defy us – our own memories of resenting adult authority instantly banished. We grow alarmed if children are found engaging in sex play and suspect that their aberrant behaviour is prompted by hidden abuse. We worry that the adult world is too available because of new technologies and forget those afternoons when our parents went out and we hunted through their drawers searching for signs of something private and disreputable.

Higonnet made the provocative argument that the innocence depicted in images of the Romantic child 'entails adult sexual knowledge'. She wrote:

> A polar opposition of values is also a binary opposition. If one value is defined mainly as the opposite of something else, then perceiving one value always entails thinking of the other value... Romantic innocence puts all children at a kind of risk[11]

In a similar vein, James Kincaid wrote:

> Childhood in our culture has come to be largely a coordinate set of *have nots*: the child is that which *does not have*. Its liberty, however much prized, is a negative attribute, as is its innocence and purity [...] The construction of the modern 'child' is very largely an evacuation, the ruthless sending out of eviction notices. Correspondingly, the instructions we receive on what to regard as sexually arousing tell us to look for (and often create) this emptiness, to discover the erotic in what is most susceptible to inscription, the blank page.[12]

In his book, *Eroticising Innocence*, Kincaid made a powerful case for the interdependence of our need to see children as innocent and our fear that adults are secretly sexualising them. Victorian images of children 'playing' at being adult resonate with more contemporary images of child models and participating in beauty pageants. The question both Higonnet and Kincaid posed was: Why are we drawn to images of innocence on the verge of corruption by allegedly foreign and adult forces? What lies beneath this fascination with a liminal zone between childhood and adulthood? And what does this fascination with images have to do with actually protecting children at risk of poverty and abuse?

The knowing gaze

Of all the supermodels who rose to prominence in the late twentieth century, UK model Kate Moss fuelled the greatest public debate. Moss became famous because she *looked* as though she was transgressing the boundary between childlike 'innocence' and adult 'knowing', a position that produced a very interesting reading of her in the popular media. If looked at as a *child*, then she was too knowing and was accused of encouraging paedophilia; if looked at as a *woman*, then she was unnaturally thin and androgenous, and was accused of encouraging anorexia.[13] Popular anxieties over images of young or young-looking models frequently turn on questions of knowledge, on questions of what they know: of the adult world, of adult pleasures, of adult desires.

In her book, *The Importance of Being Innocent*, philosopher Joanne Faulkner asked why we have become so consumed with fears that children are being corrupted and why we cling to an understanding of childhood as 'unworldly, incapable and pure'.[14] At the heart of this insistence on children's fundamental and necessary estrangement from the adult world, she argued, is a submerged investment in our identity as adults, grounded on the vulnerability of children because they are 'proxies for our vulnerability'.[15]

It's a complex question that Australian media studies scholar Kate Crawford unpacked in her book *Adult Themes*.[16] Crawford argued that the status of adulthood is dependent on the anxious policing of what constitutes childhood and youth. She asked why buying a home is seen as a sign of maturity, while purchasing a smart phone (unless for professional purposes) is seen as a sign of frivolous consumption and an inability to 'grow up'. The ex-nominated status of adulthood is the flip side of the intense scrutiny focused on children and adolescents – or to be more precise, the anxious scrutiny that middle-class children and adolescents receive. As Faulkner noted:

> A barely hidden resentment of teenagers and underprivileged children is directly proportional to the overvaluation of innocence. The importance of innocence permits ignorance of, for instance, the mortality rates of adolescents, which are today fourfold that of small children.[17]

Faulkner drew our attention to the high, if obscured, dividend adults receive from an investment in the alleged purity of children, which underpins a host of naturalised beliefs: the value of family, the authority of adults, the need to control children under the guise of protecting them. The sting in the tail of her argument is the evidence she offered of how abjectly we turn the same anxious gaze away from children and adolescents who are perceived to have fallen from grace. There are many explanations for this dissonance, including fictions of national identity and a pervasive denial of social inequity.

Control disguised as protection was an inherent feature of the conservative Howard government's 2007 'intervention' programme into indigenous communities in the Northern Territory of Australia. The programme supported radical measures – medical, social and legal – introduced to prevent and repair child abuse. The initiative was underwritten by a report titled *Little Children Are Sacred*.[18] This highly controversial intervention was preceded by decades of government policy which saw Indigenous children taken from their parents and put into institutional care.

When a young child dies in horrific circumstances, media attention inevitably scripts the story as one of aberrant parenting. The inadequate mother or the dysfunctional step-father is put on public trial for their failure to live up to ideal family values. It's rare to see commentary that asks why some parents were so unprepared to parent. An area that requires deeper exploration, however, is the question of how new media technologies are reshaping the domestic environment, parental authority and children's access to knowledge.

The print media era was grounded in a gatekeeping approach to knowledge. Walk into any library and the traces of this approach are still evident. Children's books are carefully separated from adult texts. In newsagents, magazines intended for women and men are filed separately. It's still the case. The print media era is a remnant of an era in which gender and age were marked by clear and visible boundaries. Librarians required a card. Newsagents vetted the age of the buyer. It was an era in which adults' capacity to control children's access to information was far higher than it is today. Images and information are now not only online but mobile. Parents can pull the plug on every electronic device in the house but the moment their child gets on the school bus or goes to a friend's place, their denied access is lifted. The anxiety that we can no longer control what children know or don't know is undoubtedly contributing to our general anxiety about children. Yet, it's important to understand this anxiety as equally connected to contemporary anxieties about what it means to be an adult – and about where the boundaries lie between the two states.

There's no question that online, social and mobile media do expose children and teenagers to higher risk of access to information and images that can cause them harm compared with the days when kids stumbled across porn magazines in the local park. Yet, as research has repeatedly shown, it's not what children encounter but how parents have prepared them for what they encounter that matters the most.[19] The issue for many parents, however, isn't risk – it's the perception of risk underpinned by the way that media debate tends to collapse the relationship between risk and harm. In a survey of 400 Australian children and their families conducted in 2004, which was modelled on data gathered in 25 European countries, 30 per cent of children reported being bothered or upset by something they had encountered online. To be more specific, 24 per cent of 11–16 year olds said they had seen sexually explicit images and 6 per cent said they had seen violent sexual images. Yet the survey also shows that Australian parents and teachers are extremely active in engaging children and teenagers about their use of the online world. Regardless of the actual risks and potential harm posed to children, what the online and mobile media world does, however, is remove a large degree of control over access to knowledge, information and images from parents and other adults.

Fit to be seen?

Class is a barely submerged issue in the sexualisation of children debate. While middle-class children are routinely coached in extra-curricular time by expensive tutors in maths, sport and music, the children of parents with fewer resources are often under scrutiny for being coached to perform in beauty pageants and talent contests. As the death of North American child Jon-Benet Ramsey illustrated, performing kids have a particular fascination hold on the public mind – a grip that is equal parts fear and loathing. Received wisdom has it that girls are at risk of being sexualised by the early marketing of adult clothing and ideas. In reality, it is white middle-class girls who are perceived as under threat from working and minority class culture. This threat is portrayed in popular debate as a recent one spawned by the internet and MTV. It has, however, a longer history, which is rooted in a gender politics.

In her book, *Pink Think*, Lynn Peril traces a US cultural history of media, toys and advice marketed to young girls and their parents. She cites a very popular US pamphlet titled 'What is a girl?' published in 1950. The author, Alan Beck, notes that little girls love 'new shoes, party dresses [...] dolls, make-believe, dancing lessons. Kitchens [...] make-up [...] and tea-parties'. Somewhat alarmingly, he also describes them as a delightful combination of 'Eve, Salome and Florence Nightingale'.[20] This pamphlet was so admired that it was read into the Congressional record. A 1952 ad marketed the Miss Saucy Walker doll to girls: the ad claimed that the doll 'Does everything!' – particularly, it seems, walking and flirting.

In 1954, Lawrence K. and Mary Frank wrote their booklet *How To Be A Woman* in which they told parents to encourage young girls to practise their womanly wiles on their father. 'You have probably seen little girls of 2 or 3 playing up to their fathers. They flirt. They coax,' they wrote admiringly.[21] In 1956, *Parents* magazine published an article that typified contemporary advice on rearing girls of the time. The article was titled 'Raise Your Girl To Be A Wife'. The author told parents that there was 'a lot they can do from the moment of birth to lay the groundwork' for their newborn daughter's happy marriage by developing inner patterns of femininity. She recommended that mothers help their daughter understand that the kitchen is 'as important a room as the boudoir' and fathers were encouraged to rave over their offspring's first attempts at cake-making and doll-dressing. Fathers, it must be said, play a rather alarming role throughout 1950s and 1960s parental advice literature: they are surrogate husbands on whom the daughter practises her domestic and erotic arts. 1960s-era toy ads and catalogues in Australia and the US feature housework toys – some of them fully functional – designed to educate girls in their future role as wives and mothers. Australian magazines, department store catalogues and sewing and knitting patterns of this period also show numerous images of children dressed to imitate adult fashion, as well as ads marketing toys that encourage them to 'dress up like mummy' or 'go to the moon like Daddy', as one knitwear catalogue of the era suggests.

The tutelage of girls in their gender roles clearly extended to explicit invitations to see themselves as potential sexual partners for their future boyfriends and husbands. The invitation was, of course, veiled – the focus was on encouraging girls to think about fashion, beauty and comportment. But there's no question that these lessons started young. In the early 1960s, the *Mystery Date* game was marketed to Australian girls and young teens. The object was to collect all the right cards that left you ready for your dream date. When you landed on the 'Open the door' square, you got to open the three-dimensional plastic Mystery Door in the centre of the board. The dates included: a Beach Date, a Ski Date, a Formal Date, a Bowling Date and The Pest (the guy with no money). Woe betide the girl who opened the door to Hunky Mr Ski Instructor only to discover she was holding a bikini, a bowling bag and high heels.

Until the eighteenth century, even very young children were portrayed and treated as young adults and, in Christian terms, as persons born into sin and in need of strict discipline and corporal punishment. In the nineteenth and even early twentieth century, the experience of childhood was strongly divided along class lines.[22] Upper-class and, increasingly, middle-class children had access to education and leisure, while their working-class counterparts frequently had little or no education and were sent out to work from the age of eight on farms, in mines, in domestic labour and in factories. The late nineteenth century saw a major political movement that raised and aimed to address the human rights abuses of children, which included child labour and child prostitution. In Australia, the age of consent was 10 in the nineteenth century and 12 in the early part of the twentieth century. Furthermore, it was common for much of the twentieth century for girls to marry as young as sixteen. The teenage fertility rate has significantly decreased over the last three decades from 55.5 births per 1000 women in 1971 compared to 16 births per 1000 women in 2005.[23]

Contemporary Australian ideas about childhood, which include a strong belief in the importance of educating all children and protecting them from participating in the adult worlds of work and sexuality, represent important human rights advances. It is, however, important to bear in mind that these social and economic advances have only been extended to many Australian children and teenagers relatively recently, and that we still live in a society in which the most vulnerable young people remain at risk of child sexual abuse, domestic violence, poverty and inadequate access to education and health care. Improving the social and economic well-being of all Australian children should begin with an evidenced-based recognition of which children are most at risk, and of what social, economic and cultural factors are at play in that risk.

The historical perspective is important when it comes to assessing claims that contemporary popular culture is impinging on a once universal and ideal experience of childhood. Historical evidence of how differently other groups of children in our past lived reminds us that when we make decisions about how resources are spent, we should pay careful attention to the constraints of socio-economic background, family environment and community. If we focus the majority of our resources on children who already have willing advocates, what happens to the children whose parents are not advocating for them?

Images have a capacity to remind us as much of what we can't see as what we do. Foucault described this as the 'positive unconscious' of vision, a concept John Rachjman developed by noting that 'there is much more regularity, much more *constraint*, in what we can see than we suppose'.[24] To return to the artists I began this chapter by discussing – Cherry Hood and Bill Henson – it is important to note that visual images of children bring us an awareness of something that adults find particularly hard to acknowledge – that the state of being a child is a state of liminality. And the state of being liminal is something we find hard to accept.

Notes

1. David Marr, *The Henson Case*.
2. David Marr, 'Henson photo not porn, says censor', *The Sydney Morning Herald*, 6 June 2008. http://www.smh.com.au/news/arts/henson-photo-not-porn/2008/06/05/1212259014096.html. Accessed 10 February 2012.
3. For an extended discussion of the Henson case and of the Corporate Paedophilia report see Lumby, Catharine and Albury, Kath, 'Too Much?: Too Young?: The Sexualisation of Children Debate', *Media International Australia, Incorporating Culture & Policy*, May 2010, Vol. 135, pp. 141–152.
4. Emma Rush, and Andrea La Nauze, *Corporate Paedophilia: Sexualisation of Children in Australia*.
5. Ibid., p. 3.
6. James Kincaid, *Child-Loving: The Erotic Child and Victorian Culture*, New York: Routledge, 1990.
7. James Dalrymple, *Sunday Times*, London, 7 March 1993, n.p.
8. See for example Anne Higonnet, *Pictures of Innocence: The History and Crisis of Ideal Childhood*; Henry Jenkins, 'Childhood Innocence and Other Modern Myths', *The Children's Culture Reader*, pp. 1–40; Judith Levine, *Harmful to Minors: The Perils of Protecting Children from Sex*.
9. Higonnet, p. 7.
10. For an extended discussion of Victorian child photography and the adult gaze see Lumby, Catharine. 'Ambiguity, Children, Representation, and Sexuality', *CLCWeb: Comparative Literature and Culture* 12.4, Purdue University Press, 2010. http://docs.lib.purdue.edu/clcweb/vol12/iss4/5.
11. Ibid., pp. 37–38.
12. *The Children's Culture Reader*, op. cit., p. 247.
13. For an extended analysis of the semiotics of modelling see Hartley and Lumby, 'Working Girls or Drop Dead Gorgeous? Young Girls in Fashion and News', pp. 47–68.
14. Joanne Faulkner, *The Importance of Being Innocent*, p. 2.
15. Ibid., p. 3.
16. Kate Crawford, *Adult Themes: Rewriting the Rules of Adulthood*, Sydney: Pan Macmillan, 2006.
17. Faulkner, p. 3.
18. Wild and Anderson, *Ampe Akeyerename Meke Mekale (Little Children Are Sacred)* report of the Northern Territory Board into the Protection of Aboriginal Children from Sexual Abuse (2007). As Joanne Faulkner notes, the authors of this report were 'devastated' to discover that their work was used to justify the 'intervention' as recorded in Sarah Maddison's 2009 book *Black Politics*.
19. Lumby, Green and Hartley, *Risks and Safety Report*, 2010.

20. Lynn Peril, *Pink Think: Becoming a Woman in Many Uneasy Lessons*, p. 26.
21. Ibid., p. 32.
22. Philippe Aries, *Centuries of Childhood: A Social History of Family Life*; Anne Higonnet, *Pictures of Innocence: The History and Crisis of Ideal Childhood*.
23. Australian Bureau of Statistics, *Births Australia*, Canberra: ABS 2005, p. 15.
24. John Rachjman, 'Foucault's Art of Seeing', *October*, Vol. 44, Spring 1988, pp. 88–117.

References

Aries, Philippe, *Centuries of Childhood: A Social History of Family Life*, trans. Robert Baldick, New York: Knopf, 1962.

Crawford, Kate, *Adult Themes: Rewriting the Rules of Adulthood*, Sydney, NSW: Pan Macmillan, 2006.

Faulkner, Joanne, *The Importance of Being Innocent: Why We Worry About Children*, Melbourne, VIC: Cambridge University Press, 2011.

Hartley, John and Lumby, Catharine, 'Working Girls or Drop Dead Gorgeous? Young Girls in Fashion and News', *Youth Cultures: Texts, Images and Identities*, eds. Mallan, Kerry and Pearce, Sharyn, Westport, CT: Praeger, 2003, pp. 47–68.

Higonnet, Anne, *Pictures of Innocence: The History and Crisis of Ideal Childhood*, London: Thames and Hudson, 1998.

Jenkins, Henry, 'Childhood Innocence and Other Modern Myths', *The Children's Culture Reader*, ed. Jenkins, Henry, New York: New York University Press, 1998, pp. 1–37.

Kincaid, James, *Child-Loving: The Erotic Child and Victorian Culture*, New York: Routledge, 1990.

Levine, Judith, *Harmful to Minors: The Perils of Protecting Children from Sex*, Minneapolis, MN: University of Minnesota Press, 2002.

Lumby, Catharine and Albury, Kath, 'Too Much?: Too Young?: The Sexualisation of Children Debate', *Media International Australia, Incorporating Culture & Policy*, Vol. 135, May 2010, pp. 141–152.

Marr, David, *The Henson Case*, Melbourne, VIC: Text Publishing, 2008.

Peril, Lynn, *Pink Think: Becoming a Woman in Many Uneasy Lessons*, New York: W. W. Norton, 2002.

Rachjman, John, 'Foucault's Art of Seeing', *October*, Vol. 44, Spring 1988, pp. 88–117.

Rush, Emma and La Nauze, Andrea, *Corporate Paedophilia: Sexualisation of Children in Australia*, Discussion Paper Number 90, Canberra, ACT: The Australia Institute, 2006.

Wild, R. and Anderson, P., *Ampe Akeyerename Meke Mekale (Little Children Are Sacred)* report of the Northern Territory Board into the Protection of Aboriginal Children from Sexual Abuse (2007).

4
The Sombrero Comes Out of the Closet: Gay Marriage in Mexico City and a Nation's Struggle for Identity

Santiago Ballina

The issue of gay marriage has come to symbolise better than any other boundaries of what is considered as unacceptable in modern societies. It not only forces them to make explicit and confront their deepest fears and prejudices, but in the process it also reveals their inner contradictions. Looking at how a particular society deals with homosexuality is, therefore, akin to placing it in front of a mirror.

This chapter focuses on the approval in 2009 of same-sex marriage in Mexico City and the debate surrounding it, with a particular interest in the responses of the most reluctant sectors of society and the arguments put forward by them to hinder such development. This work has a special interest in the responses of the opposing factions because, as it will be repeatedly pointed out, they allow us to discover the nuances of what is considered unacceptable in contemporary Mexican society. This permits us to have a deeper look at the way that conservative stakeholders have had to frame their contentions to fit intolerance within the framework of a democratic society. Furthermore, the purpose of this exploration is to highlight a much deeper, underlying debate surrounding same-sex marriage: that of Mexican identity. Trapped between modernity and traditional canons, between democratic values and religious precepts, the debate on this particular nuance of the unacceptable reveals a nation's quest of character in a way that few other issues have done in the past. As this work will insist, this is a struggle that has long-reaching historical roots and that remains undecided in contemporary Mexico. It did not start with, and will certainly not end, with whatever is the outcome of the debate on same-sex marriage. However, the contradictions that arise in this national pursuit of modernity are best highlighted by looking at a debate surrounding the 'unacceptable' case of gay marriage.

This research will start by outlining the exceptional social and cultural character of Mexico City within a broader national context as one of the factors that enabled the same-sex marriage reforms in 2009. It will be followed by a detailed analysis of the process that culminated with their approval, including the passage in 2006 of the law on civil unions, the immediate antecedent of gay marriage. The political stances of both their proponents and foes will be described as to glimpse into the contradictions and disruptions that can be found in them, and the way they reflect the main issues at stake in the discussion of the reforms.

A third section will focus on the reactions of the main opponents of same-sex marriage, with a particular emphasis on their discursive and propagandistic elements. For the purposes of this research, the chosen actors are the Catholic church, particular sectors of civil society and the President of Mexico, all of whom expressed their opposition and challenged the reforms at some point. While superficially different, some underlying elements underpinned their arguments and these will be highlighted as well.

Finally, this chapter concludes by examining the claim that the same-sex marriage discussion highlights the difficult transition of Mexico towards modernity. The struggle for identity has contributed to shape what is considered as unacceptable in a society that is undergoing a constant effort to reinvent itself.

Mexico City, the exceptional

Equating Mexico with its capital and vice versa would be a dangerous over-simplification. Serving as the neuralgic centre of the country and concentrating all its dimensions of power, Mexico City possesses a distinctive feeling that is simply absent in any other major city of the country, particularly in its vast and underdeveloped rural areas. However, it is precisely in the microcosm of the capital where the tensions and contradictions that define the Mexican character are more clearly represented. Cosmopolitan and chauvinistic, rich and appallingly unequal, über-Westernised and profoundly conservative, the contrasts that define it are not foreign to other major capital cities of the developing world. Yet it is by walking through its streets that one can best grasp the unique soul of the country and witness firsthand its most pressing concerns.

It is against this backdrop of shade and light that we must interpret the process that began to take form more than a decade ago and that culminated in late 2009 with the approval of the law that legalised same-sex marriage. Mexico City and its exceptional nature have made it an obvious candidate for political experimentation, which over the years has translated into a reputation of social progressivism. It is no coincidence that issues that not long ago were considered taboo in the national political system have been opened to debate in the capital, leading sometimes to the enactment of relevant legislation. Mexico City has the most liberal legislation in the country regarding abortion, and a serious debate on euthanasia has led to the introduction of law initiatives in the Legislative Assembly (Local Congress).

The special character of Mexico City in the national political landscape is a direct result of the democratisation process experienced by Mexico in general during the turn of the century, and it is a remarkable achievement considering the fact that, before 1997, people of Mexico City did not enjoy the right of choosing a *Jefe de Gobierno* (chief of government, roughly equivalent to the position of city mayor), which until then had remained a prerogative of the president. In that regard, the arrival of democracy to the capital predated the end of the era of dominance of the ruling party, the *Partido Revolucionario Institucional* (Institutional Revolutionary Party or PRI). Three years after the first local elections were carried out in Mexico City, the PRI suffered its first defeat in a presidential election in 70 years, a major step in the political transformation of the country.

Yet within the broader trend of democratisation, the city still enjoys a more peculiar character. Ever since the introduction of free elections, the leftist *Partido de la Revolución Democrática* (Party of the Democratic Revolution or PRD) has held both the position of chief of government and a comfortable majority in the local law-making organism – the Legislative Assembly – a fact that allowed the latter to sponsor and ultimately approve the same-sex marriage reform.

That such a reform was carried out under the tenure of a left-wing government will seem familiar to the experience of other liberal democracies. Yet we should be careful not to draw too many parallels, for the relationship between the political left and homosexuality in Mexico is far from cosy, and in a way reflects the difficult transition that the country has experienced in its goal of becoming a stable democracy and a more equal society. The Mexican left resists any clear-cut comparisons with its homologues in developed nations. To an outside observer, it will appear orthodox, ultra-nationalistic and quite frequently infused with an aura of Marxism. As a result, its interaction with the gay rights movement has tested over the course of the years, as expressed by Dehesa, 'just how far party actors are willing to go'.[1] It's worth reminding ourselves that it was precisely a PRD-emanated chief of government and subsequent presidential candidate – Andrés Manuel López Obrador – who operated behind the political scenes to block the approval of the law on civil unions, the immediate antecedent of the gay marriage reform. The road that led to the adoption of gay marriage is less close to the romantic vision of the forces of enlightenment prevailing over backwardness, resembling more a nervous stuttering with occasional victories.

The upward climb (with enemy fire)

In February 2001, one of the first openly lesbians members of parliament serving as deputy in the Legislative Assembly – Enoé Uranga – a member of the PRD, introduced a law proposing civil unions inspired in the French model of 'pacts of solidarity', aiming at the recognition of the legal rights of – among others – same-sex couples, including rights of alimony, inheritance and tenancy. While the law was regarded as a groundbreaking initiative, its supporters were very careful in the way it was framed before the public opinion. A poll conducted by one of Mexico City's leading newspapers revealed that 62 per cent among those surveyed opposed gay marriage, while 54 per cent did not support in any way the legalisation of same-sex unions.[2] Hence, its backers would not lose any chance to remind the general public that their initiative was not in any way an attempt to modify or undermine the institution of marriage and, most importantly, that they were not intending in any way to open the door for adoption by gay couples, an issue that was considered at the time as too controversial and consequently off limits.[3]

The conservative Partido Acción Nacional (National Action Party or PAN) opposed the initiative from the outset, while the PRI received it in a lukewarm manner. While such reactions were perhaps foreseeable, the inconsistent support – when not tacit opposition – of members of the PRD to the civil unions law hindered the discussion process and delayed its approval during six long years. This attitude enraged gay activists and supporters of the proposal, one of which accused the PRD of being 'opportunistic', and failing to meet with its previously stated commitment to support the law 'in order to avoid its high political costs'.[4]

Though PRD deputies rarely expressed their objection in public, they eventually contributed to the success of the dilatory tactics employed by both PRI and PAN, supporting last-minute suspension motions or quite simply abstaining from voting against them. During one particular session, PRD deputies quietly began to abandon the room so that when a vote was called it would meet with a lack of quorum.[5] Knowing that such behaviour was likely to occur, activists waited outside hoping to block the unexpected departure of any deputies. Yet the vote of silence strategy succeeded and the discussion of the law initiative was once again brought to a halt.

The biggest setback in the law approval process would come from the then chief of government, Andrés Manuel López Obrador, a highly renowned member of the PRD, who earned a reputation of leading one of the most socially oriented governments in the history of the city. After a mid-term election that rewarded the PRD with an absolute majority in the Legislative Assembly, conditions appeared optimal. The draft law was voted and approved in the respective committees and was ready to be brought before the floor. However, just one week before that occurred, López Obrador, who until then had refrained from publicly expressing any opinion on the initiative, derailed the process by stating during a press conference in late 2003 that he personally preferred a referendum to be held on the matter. Insisting that the issue was simply too polemic, he said that 'we need to accept the opinion of people on the matter as to avoid misinterpretations', on the basis that his government was 'truly democratic'.[6] The turn of the tide shocked activists and members of the PRD, who were baffled by the amount of friendly fire that was hindering the legalisation of civil unions. Speculation ensued: at the time, it was increasingly clear that López Obrador would make a bid for the upcoming presidential elections in 2006. While representing a left-wing party, it appeared that he could simply not afford to alienate a large sector of conservative voters and the powerful Catholic church, which, while officially banned from involvement in politics, nonetheless remains a key player in Mexican society.

As a result of the implicit rejection by the chief of government of the law on civil unions, during the next three years its discussion was virtually absent from the floor of the Assembly, and many analysts thought of it as a dead letter. An opinion piece in the most important left-wing media outlet of Mexico City labelled Obrador as a 'Pontius Pilate'. Despite the PRD's presenting of itself as heading a democratic revolution, its author concluded, homosexual rights appear not to fit into such a vision.[7]

The initiative on civil unions would have to wait until the uproar over presidential elections had faded and a new chief of government was sworn. In late 2006, the then coordinator of PRD in the Legislative Assembly – Víctor Hugo Círigo – acknowledged that the law on civil unions was a pending commitment, and called on his party to support the law as an act of political congruence. He conceived the initiative as an issue of human rights, and as such 'not subject to the result of any poll'.[8] Hence, he reintroduced it into the legislative agenda. The law was finally passed in November 2006 with the unanimous support of the PRD (minus one abstention), almost six years after the original draft was introduced in the Assembly. Enoé Uranga, the PRD deputy responsible for the original proposal back in 2001, acknowledged that her party was undoing its 'wrong track', and recalled that former chief of government López Obrador turned out to be, paradoxically, the main obstacle for its approval.[9] In the struggle for equality, it became clear that the political left had sometimes become an uncanny ally of the gay rights movement, striving to be portrayed as modern and progressive, yet haunted by its own ghosts.

Marriage, Mexican style

On 21 December 2009, the Legislative Assembly of Mexico City voted in favour of reforming the local Civil Code so as to allow the marriage of same-sex couples, becoming the first city in Latin America to do so. The approved reforms went even further, and in an unexpected turn that was met with shock by the opposition and a large sector of Mexican society, it granted adoption rights, the same issue that was purportedly excluded from the 2001 civil union law because of its controversial nature. Unlike the convulsive process that characterised the debate regarding civil unions, the one that led to the legalisation of gay marriage was expedited and made possible thanks to a more unified party line and, most importantly, because the incumbent chief of government fully endorsed the reforms, as he saw them congruent 'with the spirit of the left-wing movement' that he represented.[10] Considering the sweeping relevance of the changes brought by the reforms, it is noteworthy that little less than a month elapsed between the introduction of the draft bill and the decisive vote. Having in mind the lessons of the civil union conundrum, it is clear that supporters of gay marriage devised an elaborate strategy that would minimise the amount of media exposure and deprive the opposition, particularly the conservative PAN party, of enough time to politicise the issue and reframe it as an attack on the institutions of marriage and family (as it eventually did).

During the discussion of the project, it became apparent that the overall public attitude towards gay marriage had experienced a significant upturn since the approval of the law on civil unions, perhaps as one of its unintended consequences. Evidence of this shift in public opinion was borne out in the 2009 survey conducted by the *El Universal* newspaper which asserted that 50 per cent of the general population actually approved gay marriage, while only 38 per cent was explicitly against it. Among the 18–29 age bracket the rate of support was even higher, and reached an astonishing 67 per cent.[11] Yet, as will be analysed in the following section, it would be false to say that the reforms faced no opposition from large sectors of the Mexican political spectrum and society in general. This was particularly evident in the controversial issue of adoption, a subject that for many seemed a direct attack on the traditional models of society. In a country that is deeply bound by Catholic tradition and that has always found great pride in the closeness of its familiar relations, this was not a minor hurdle. For example, while polls revealed a greater aperture to gay marriage, when adoption was brought into the equation the figures looked less optimistic. In fact, a late 2010 poll – when the Civil Code reforms had already been favourably voted – showed not surprisingly that 67 per cent of Mexicans were opposed to adoption by gay couples.[12] While there is no comparable figure from the civil union discussion in 2001, it is not farfetched to suggest that the subject had – at the very least – the same degree of disapproval back then.

The fact that opposition to adoption remained constant makes its inclusion in the final stage of the reform process even more intriguing. Yet a closer look at the legislative process reveals that the left had to face – once again – the question of just how progressive it wanted to appear before the eyes of its local constituents and a national audience that closely followed the debate occurring in the capital.

In early November, not long before the proposed bill containing the reforms to the Civil Code was introduced in the floor of the Legislative Assembly, PRD deputy David Razú – the primary sponsor of the reform who was backed by a coalition of civil society organisations in drafting the project – offered an interview to outline the most relevant issues of his proposal. A number of technical questions were brought up, such as its recognition under current national welfare laws. Yet when asked about adoption, Razú made it explicit that adoption was not an issue on the table and would not be brought up during the discussion of the reform, effectively closing the door to such a possibility.[13]

According to some analysts, the ban on adoption was imposed as a fundamental precondition by deputies of the PRI and other minor political parties to grant its support to the initiative.[14] Knowing beforehand that PAN legislators would reject it, the support of other parties – however minor – appeared crucial. In late November the initiative was finally introduced in the Legislative Assembly, and an explicit prohibition was drafted into what would become a new article in the Civil Code. It read: 'Adoption shall have no legal basis when spouses belong to the same gender,' in a quiet assurance that the issue to which Mexican society at large showed strong opposition would be fundamentally left out of the field.

While the degree of acceptability towards the explicit prohibition of adoption varied among advocates of the law, particularly gay rights organisations, some nonetheless considered it a guarantee that the proposed reforms would not meet with an insurmountable degree of resistance both in the Legislative Assembly and among the broader public. Once one of the major hurdles was removed, the debate continued in predictable terms. When the initiative was brought to the plenary for its general discussion and eventual vote, members of PAN attacked it on the contention that marriage embodied a 'natural institution developed throughout the course of millennia' and was intrinsically linked to a relationship between a man and a woman, a status that a same-sex union could never achieve. David Razú, the main supporter of the law, reminded deputies that marriage was a social and judicial construction that needed to take into account social realities, thus making the reform a pressing issue of equality.[15]

While the general lines of the debate were perhaps foreseeable, the motion of a single PRD deputy turned the Assembly upside down when the ban on adoption – which seemed set in stone – was challenged. In her view, a law whose spirit was that of expanding rights was not compatible with a prohibition that simultaneously imposed restrictions on them, putting at risk the judicial soundness of the initiative as a whole. She proceeded then to introduce a motion to exclude the ban from the final draft, a development that surprised even its supporters and that would eventually cause four PRD deputies to abstain from the final voting.[16]

The unforeseen move outraged the opposition, which did not shy away in accusing the PRD from backtracking out of its original commitment to drop adoption from the table. Seizing the opportunity that arose from confusion, the motion was put to a vote, and managed to obtain enough support to prevail. Activists and representatives from the gay community who attended the session as observers were in uproar, as PAN deputies abandoned the floor and threatened to exhaust every single legal resource to challenge the recently approved reforms.

While the legalisation of same-sex marriage and adoption rights was considered a historical victory in the name of equality and human rights – and it certainly was – it is nonetheless remarkable how the PRD adopted expediency as a strategy to bypass opposition that existed in both the political arena and its own ranks, profiting as well from its numerical advantage in the Legislative Assembly. Its initial stance on adoption, as well as the unexpected move to include it as part of the reforms – whether part or not of a deliberate legislative strategy – reflects not only how sensitive the issue was deemed by both supporters and detractors, but also the inherent difficulties that adopting a socially and culturally charged subject posed to the Mexican left and civil rights organisations. That the most progressive legislation in the history of the city was fundamentally shaped by a last-minute stroke of technicality, was a reminder that the path to embrace equality and legally redefine what is considered as unacceptable is filled with bittersweet moments.

Observing the battlefield

In the seventeenth century, one of the largest clandestine networks of homosexual men was uncovered in Mexico City by the Spanish authorities. Over 100 men were involved, out of which 19 were put on trial accused of the 'nefarious sin of sodomy'. Of those, 14 were finally burned at the stake in one of the largest homosexuality-related scandals of colonial Mexico. As Mino has asserted, violence against sexual dissidents back then was in fact strongly shaped by misogyny. 'The feminine was associated with weakness, ignorance and sin [...] therefore an effeminate male was consciously renouncing to his human condition', a behaviour deemed utterly unacceptable, and hence worthy of exemplary punishment.[17]

Five centuries later, as the media reproduced the photographs of the first same-sex couples engaged in civil marriage, no calls for public burning or lynching were heard across the streets. Mexico could not appear farther from its colonial past of homosexual prosecution. After all, the legalisation of gay marriage and adoption in Mexico City seemed to place the country in the selective basket of liberal democracies representing the avant-garde on the struggle for equality, such as Sweden,

Norway and Canada. Yet, for all the progress achieved over the course of hundreds of years, Mexico was far from reaching the status of a truly egalitarian and tolerant society, and found itself confronting a reality where claims of progressivism were frequently trumped by intolerance. Hatred and discrimination had not disappeared, but they now presented themselves with a different, almost unrecognisable face, shaped by the same forces of modernisation and progress that made gay marriage a reality in the first place. 'Till DEATH do them Part', read the headline of one of Mexico City's multiple sensationalist tabloids, paired with a photograph of one of the newly wed couples. The fact that the word 'death' had been highlighted in red offered an uncanny reminder of the morbid fascination – when not vocal opposition – that gay marriage spurred in some sectors of Mexican society.

The church: business as usual?

Of all the reactions against gay marriage, the most viral – yet perhaps the most predictable – was that of the church, a voice that is simply too powerful to ignore in a country where, according to the latest census, 82 per cent of the population defines itself as Catholic and where a large share of the political elite is known to have close ties with the church hierarchy.[18]

It is worth noting that, in spite of its ubiquitous influence, national legislation is stringent when it comes to the role of the church as a political player. As a reaction against the immense power and influence it held during five centuries of Spanish colonial rule, a strict separation between state and religion was envisaged by the founders of modern Mexico as a precondition to advance in the construction of an independent country. Among them was Benito Juárez, by far the most revered national figure of the post-colonial era, whose liberal doctrine considered that the rule of law and the benefit of society at large had to prevail over the interest of any particular individual or group (interestingly enough, the tenets of Juarez's political thought would be invoked during the discussion of same-sex marriage by both supporters and detractors).

The legacy of Juárez and other liberal thinkers is still strongly felt in the Mexican Constitution, which expressly forbids religious associations (including the Catholic church) from pursuing political goals, and prohibits them from promoting or attacking 'any candidate, political party or political association', or expressing in any way dissent with the country's laws or institutions.[19] Before 1991 members of religious associations did not enjoy the right to vote, and the church lacked legal personality, effectively curtailing its right to property. It is no overstatement to say that the secular character of Mexico as represented by its legal regime is one of the fundamental pillars that sustains the vision of a modern, Western country that Mexico has built around itself.

In practice, however, the church has never shied away from strongly expressing its view on any issue it considers vital to its interests, and gay marriage was certainly not to be an exception. In a press release issued in late December, after the Legislative Assembly delivered its final vote on the issue, the Mexico City Archdiocese blamed the PRD for staging a deliberate attack against the 'principles and values' valued the most by Mexican families, and for being insensitive to the rights of children that, as a consequence of the law, would be 'exposed to a tutelage that will translate in serious psychological, affective and moral damage'.[20] This would be only a small piece in the aggressive media campaign that Catholic authorities undertook to condemn the legalisation of same-sex marriages and adoption. In turn, the arguments utilised by the religious authorities would harden, to the point where the most prominent Catholic figure in Mexico, Cardinal Norberto Rivera, labelled same-sex marriage as 'abhorrent' and 'intrinsically immoral', further adding that it stripped marriage from its sacred nature and original intent.[21]

The political confrontation between authorities in the church and those representing Mexico City escalated on a par with the legal stakes of the reforms. As the Federal Government brought the legalisation of same-sex marriages and adoption rights before the Supreme Court on the ground of unconstitutionality, only to finally receive a majority endorsement from its justices, Cardinal Sandoval Íñiguez – frequently considered as the spokesperson of the ultra-orthodox wing of the Catholic church – accused the Government of Mexico City of bribing the Supreme Court to obtain a favourable outcome, a scandalous claim lacking substantiation. In an example of how invoking modernity – or denying it – has become central to the debate on same-sex marriage, Mexico City's chief of government – Marcelo Ebrard – dismissed the statements of Cardinal Íñiguez as those of a 'caveman'. Asked to elaborate on this last thought, Ebrard considered that the cardinal's inspiration could be 'traced back to the eleventh century'.[22]

Left-wing politicians and social activists did not hold back in labelling the church as medieval and retrograde, unable to catch up with the spirit of the times. They accused it of disguising a profound repulsion in alleged objectives of a higher moral order, such as safeguarding the psychological integrity of adopted children. That the Catholic church was failing to acknowledge a rapidly changing social reality is perhaps not surprising, and is certainly a feature shared by many other religious institutions. Yet behind the general aura of medievalism, a finer analysis has to recognise that its discourse has certainly not remained static since the times when homosexuals were actively persecuted and set on fire.

In an editorial piece published in early 2010, the church attempted to rebuff its reputation of backwardness. 'We are constantly reminded that this is the twenty-first century and not the Middle Ages, as if our values were contingent upon a specific time and not based on a set of principles [...]' read the text. Along the claims regarding the atemporality of human nature appeared one that exemplifies just how subtle the shapes of the debate can be. It accused those who 'invoke laicism to promote intolerance', further adding that people elected to public posts 'have forgotten that they serve and represent from government a society that holds dear religious values, living them in a natural, free manner'. The piece ended with a quite unexpected call for tolerance and a respectful debate.[23]

Furthermore, the media campaign instigated by the religious hierarchy would not lose any opportunity to remind its followers how the PRD had used its majority in the Legislative Assembly to push forward the debate on same-sex marriage and a last-minute technical move to bring in the subject of adoption, in spite of the fact that it had initially promised not to do so. On repeated occasions, the church accused the PRD of behaving in an authoritarian, 'almost fascist' manner.[24]

It became evident that the church was attempting to reframe the debate in its favour by appropriating the discourse of democracy and tolerance. In accusing the Legislative Assembly and the PRD in particular of overlooking the opinion of a large sector of Mexican society, it was fundamentally attacking its legitimacy and portraying it as a dangerous minority that attempted to impose its own view using undemocratic means.

While it was clear that the spirit of discrimination had not disappeared, to dismiss the opinion of the church as a minority and radical sector of Mexican society would, unfortunately, be erroneous. It had to be acknowledged that its arguments resonated deeply in a number of sectors, notably right-wing civil society organisations and key decision makers, as will be further explored in the following sections.

Civil society: not homophobia, just my opinion

When a popular radio presenter authored an opinion piece in the Mexican press expressing his dissent towards the decision recently taken by the Supreme Court to uphold the legality of same-sex marriage and the rights of same-sex couples to adoption, the tension had already reached its zenith. Accusations of intolerance flowed back and forth, as celebrities, NGOs and academic institutions joined the argument on both sides.

It was not the first time that a public figure contributed to shape the debate. In late December 2009, the host of a breakfast television show stirred controversy upon publicly expressing his view that homosexuality was neither 'normal' not 'natural'. Recordings and videos of his comments were virally spread through the internet, as Facebook and Twitter became a virtual battleground. A Facebook group demanding his resignation gathered in less than one week tens of thousands of followers, as the hapless anchorman insisted that he was not contributing to homophobia, but merely 'expressing my own opinion'.[25]

Baffling as those comments were, they seemed to crystallise the result of an obvious contradiction laying at the heart of the argumentative apparatus invoked by many of those opposing homosexuality and adoption: appealing to the values of democracy and tolerance to encapsulate ideas that were exclusivist by definition; framing traditional prejudices in a modern envelope, a strategy in which the Catholic church seemed to lead the way, and in which other conservative sectors of society would follow suit.

In an attempt to resolve such contradiction, voices against gay marriage often went to great lengths to express their arguments in ways that could appeal to a wider audience, while consciously avoiding the mere broadcasting of the ideas of the church, a move that would have failed in gaining the adherence of more moderate individuals. In that regards, two paths would be followed.

In the first one, arguments on the immorality and unacceptable character of homosexual unions and their right to adopt were presented as the result of a 'logical' chain of thoughts and moral opinions posing as axioms. Many of these were clearly adaptations or plain repetitions of similar ideas expressed by the Christian right in other countries where same-sex marriage has been the subject of discussion, such as the alleged fact that 'very few homosexuals actually want to get married', thus making the need for any reform redundant.[26] A different argument suggests that in fact gay marriage was actually not necessary to bridge the inequality gap, because 'almost all' of the legal benefits that marriage entitled to could be mutually agreed and legally arranged by a homosexual couple.[27]

The attempt to produce logically coherent anti-homosexual statements sometimes produced less than neat results, such as the following argument:

> A homosexual complaining of discrimination because he's not allowed to marry his partner is like a polygamous man that complains of discrimination because he's not allowed to have many wives, even like a promiscuous complaining because he's not allowed to marry many men and women at the same time. There is no discrimination, because the law treats everybody as equals.[28]

Equally enlightened opinions feared that broadening the scope of rights to include homosexuals would eventually benefit other, perhaps more 'perverse' minorities. A federal senator from the ranks of the conservative PAN publicly expressed his concern that such reforms could open the door for 'people who enjoy having sex with seven-year-old girls, or even with cows' to plea against discrimination based on the same laws.[29]

On the other hand, more moderate opponents of same-sex marriage appealed to legal arguments to base their opposition in a way that, in their own words, excluded all traces of morality and religion and framed the issue as a purely judicial one. This legal strategy would not only be pursued by members of civil society, but would in fact be championed by the Federal Government and no other than the president of the Republic himself.

The president: a silent pine

The discussion surrounding same-sex marriage and adoption rights was so sweeping that very few people noticed that the voice of the most prominent political player in the country had been completely absent from it: that of incumbent President Felipe Calderón. Since the beginning of the debate, nothing but silence seemed to emanate from the 'Pine Forest', the informal name by which the official residence of the president in Mexico City is known.

It was clear that the issue was not indifferent to Calderón, a man from the ranks of the right-wing PAN, born in one of the most conservative states of rural Mexico and who attended Catholic schools as a young boy. Two years before the legalisation of same-sex marriage, his government had spearheaded a judicial attempt to overrule the reforms that the Legislative Assembly in Mexico City had passed concerning abortion, and which gave the capital the most liberal regime in the country.[30]

In January 2010, shortly after the final vote had been delivered on the Legislative Assembly, the Office of the Attorney General (PGR) filed before the Supreme Court a lawsuit calling for the abrogation of same-sex marriages and their right to adopt on the grounds of unconstitutionality. It was clear for everybody that it was a signal coming from the presidential house, for it is worth remembering that the federal attorney under Mexican law is a direct appointee of the president. The central argument advanced by the PGR (equivalent to a Department of Justice) was that same-sex unions were 'fundamentally incompatible' with the juridical nature of civil marriage, whose ultimate purpose 'is that of protecting and defining the rights and obligations that stem as a consequence of the spouses bearing progeny'. Yet somehow the PGR insisted that the call for unconstitutionality was 'not equivalent in any way to stigmatising, discrimination or denying the right of raising a family, much less a call for violence'.[31] Furthermore, it accused the law of turning a blind eye to the 'supremacy of the best interest of the child, a right superior to any other one',[32] overtly implying that a household composed by two persons of the same sex could not provide an adequate familial environment.

The confirmation that this was part of a legal strategy devised from the Presidential Office came a month later, as President Calderón publicly spoke for the first time on the matter on a press conference in Japan, where he was fulfilling a state visit. While he backed the legal action undertaken by the PGR he refrained from offering further detail on the motivations of such course of action, or even from fixing a personal stance on the matter. Interrogated by journalists, Calderón offered a laconic, almost nihilistic response: 'This is merely a legal debate that has to be addressed by the Supreme Court, it is not politically motivated and does not stem from any prejudice.'[33] Furthermore, he declared that he was fully respectful of 'the sexual preferences of any person and of same sex couples'.

Left-wing civil society and gay activists were not convinced of the alleged 'merely judicial' nature of the legal resource promoted from the Presidential Office. For them, this seemed to represent yet one more example of how the political elite had succumbed to the pressure of the powerful Catholic church. The call for unconstitutionality had, no doubt, a highly symbolic force, yet what they failed to acknowledge was how remarkably low-key had been the public stance of President

Calderón regarding an issue that was clearly at odds with his mindset and that of the right-wing government which he leads.

A number of possible reasons can be offered to explain the seemingly inconspicuous reaction of the president against the immense social changes that were taking place in Mexico. It seems reasonable to suggest that, once the legal resource had been filed before the Supreme Court, he intended to shy away from making any statement that could be interpreted as an attempt to coerce the judicial branch into a particular course of action. Yet this would fail to explain why his government chose to remain silent during the process that led to the legalisation of same-sex marriage, when the political costs associated with fixing a public posture would have been offset by the benefits of reasserting himself before the conservative voting base of Mexican society.

An alternative view would have to take into account the role of Calderón and his conservative party in the life of a democratic Mexico. While the spectre of repression and censorship has been hard to cast away in a country where traditional power structures still favour a strong centralisation of power, Calderon's National Action Party's arrival to power was effectively made possible because PRI failed to acknowledge that social plurality had no chances of being suppressed. As a general principle, PAN has embraced press and speech freedom as a way to set itself apart from the authoritarian ways of its predecessor, and boasts its reputation as the party that allowed a democratic transition towards a more diverse and open society. Furthermore, and with the arrival of democracy, it has become increasingly unacceptable to frame moral issues as denial of rights, and Calderón, as the head of government of a democratic country, was certainly aware of that. His silence was far from a tacit approval, and fits better as an attempt to play by the rules of a liberal, Western democracy.

Mexico: the uncomfortable verge of modernity

Elements of the debate surrounding homosexuality and same-sex marriage in Mexico will appear familiar to other Western, democratic societies where the issue has been openly addressed and/or legislated. However, it is important to frame the problem in culturally specific terms. It is only through the prism of cultural specificity that we can understand the behaviour, discourses and images that define the key actors in our case study, some of which – such as the political left, the president, the Catholic church and civil society – have been discussed at length.

It is my contention that the gay marriage conundrum in the context under analysis is embedded in a broader, more general quest for identity of Mexican society as a whole. In this debate about what constitutes the essence of our nation and how we perceive ourselves vis-à-vis a rapidly changing and unpredictable world, the fundamental dichotomy of modern versus traditional is ubiquitous, and is constantly redefining the boundaries of what is considered as unacceptable.

This is hardly an original claim in the sense that Mexico is certainly not the first country – nor the last – to face social and cultural issues that put into question its willingness to infringe the borders of its traditional values in order to accommodate a changing reality. More interesting is, perhaps, the way in which individual societies react to such pressing matters and the momentum that they are able to elicit at any particular time: Where the drive to reinvent themselves and transform their realities has prompted other nations to quickly take sides in the dichotomy, in Mexico it has met with astonishment and indecision, and any move in either side is often paired with many others running in the opposite direction. The Mexican case is peculiar if one is to consider for how long the quest for national identity has been in progress and the acuteness of its contradictions.

Ever since Nobel Laureate Octavio Paz opened a Pandora's box by depicting the underlying contradictions of Mexican identity, attempts to grasp and define how Mexico deals with 'the modern' have eluded even the brightest minds. In his seminal work *The Labyrinth of Solitude*, Paz frequently draws from the examples of other nations, particularly developed democracies, to contrast them with the case of Mexico. Referring to the differences between Mexican and American societies, for example, he states:

> It seems to me that North Americans consider the world to be something that can be perfected; for us, it is something that can be redeemed. *They are modern.* We, just like their Puritan ancestors, believe that sin and death constitute the ultimate basis of human nature [...][34]
>
> (emphasis added)

This inherent difficulty in the process of embracing modernity has far-reaching consequences. In the international arena, Mexico is repeatedly forced to choose between contrasting regional affiliations, sometimes to no avail. While a Free Trade Agreement has bound Canada, the USA and Mexico by strong commercial ties, linguistic and cultural barriers set their societies apart. Even though a shared history, language and cultural traditions make Mexico appear closer to its Latin American neighbours, its deep ties with the USA and its lack of regional leadership has frequently isolated it from broader developments south of its border. Jorge Castañeda, a former foreign minister and a notorious intellectual, has expressed this conundrum as a fundamental indecision regarding 'which postcode Mexico wants to belong to'.[35]

This traditional–modern dichotomy is well reflected in the social fabric of the country. Whereas in 1990, 73 per cent of households could be described as nuclear families, during last year's census this percentage had dropped to 60 per cent.[36] Out of every 100 households, 25 are headed by a woman, and in Mexico City this figure is over 30.[37]

The appreciation that Mexican societal dynamics have quickly evolved was invoked as one of the key arguments during the drafting of the same-sex marriage act, and is commonly acknowledged by large sectors of society. In practice, this has also resulted in a transformation of traditional values, a process that is far from being smooth. In the words of an analyst, 'Mexico has begun to admit its diversity, but it's having a hard time swallowing it'.[38]

A fascinating insight into this universe of contradictions, particularly regarding the role of sexual minorities, is provided by a 2010 government-sponsored survey on discrimination. According to it, 4 out of 10 Mexicans would not be willing to share his or her household with a homosexual. Yet, 42 per cent of those surveyed readily acknowledged that the rights of gay people are frequently infringed. Even more perplexing is the contradictory finding that 67 per cent of those surveyed considered that opposing to same-sex marriages is *not* justifiable.[39]

What could explain such contradictory results? In support for my argument, I rely once again on the competing alternation of traditional and modern values that characterises Mexican society. It is the result of that interaction which defines its rapport against sexual minorities. One could go even further and suggest that this clash of mindsets is nothing new and has always been present in Mexican culture. In his study of representation of homosexuality in the printed media, McKee concluded: 'Mexico has been cited as having fostered the hybrid society par excellence, in which a wide variety of indigenous and migrant cultures have intermingled and changed one another, but without consuming each other completely.'[40] Schuessler further added: 'The construction of homosexuality in Mexico was unique from its very beginning. This is due to the syncretic and dually homophobic nature of Mexican culture and its people, *inheritors of the best and worst* of pre-Hispanic and European Civilisation' (emphasis added).[41]

Regardless of when the beginning of this dilemma is dated, it is clear that it keeps shaping the attitudes of Mexican society. In trying to make sense of the results of the discrimination survey, a respected political pundit concluded: 'There is an enormous gap between the country we believe to be and the country that we really are [...] The faces of discrimination reveal a country that is fundamentally at odds with our notion of a modern, democratic and egalitarian nation.'[42]

The legalisation of same-sex marriage in Mexico City seemed to tilt the balance in favour of modernity and equality in a way that very few other developments during the last decade had seemed to achieve. Yet, the case of Mexico City is a particular one within the broader national context. Furthermore, as the capital seemed determined to go ahead with its progressive agenda, developments in the rest of the country risked transforming Mexico City into a judicial island of enlightenment in a sea of gray shades.

More conservative states in the country closely followed the debate taking place in Mexico City. Soon after its legalisation in the capital, states such as Jalisco and Baja California introduced initiatives to amend their local constitutions as to explicitly define marriage as the 'union between a man and a woman', with others following suit. The effect is similar to the one that followed decriminalisation of abortion in Mexico City in 2007. Ever since those reforms were passed, 17 out of the 31 states in Mexico enacted pro-life reforms, further reinforcing the exceptional status of Mexico City.[43]

Conclusion

In liberal Western societies it has become increasingly unacceptable to overtly express negative moral judgments, prejudices and to publicly state that a certain minority should not be entitled to equal rights. Yet, intolerance and discrimination have not disappeared; they have merely embraced and adopted the language of democracy and modernity. While huge progress has been made, particularly on the rights of sexual minorities, we could ask ourselves whether something has really changed in human nature over the course of the last centuries, or if it is only that we have become so obsessed with political correctness and sanitisation that we have forced our old ghosts to reappear with a more palatable face, while leaving untouched its root causes.

Mexico is certainly not the first country to face social and cultural issues that put into question its willingness to infringe the borders of its traditional values in order to accommodate a changing reality. However, what is unique about the case of Mexico is how the debate on same-sex marriage played along the fault-lines of a society that is fundamentally divided as to where it belongs in the physical, economical and emotional cartography of nations.

It is even more remarkable that this question remained unaddressed for over half a century. In that regard, all the contradictions that the opponents of same-sex marriage and adoption have displayed – an intolerant church calling for tolerance, bigotry disguised in free speech and a secular president appealing to religious arguments – are only one more expression of a fundamental mismatch between Mexico as it is imagined by its citizens and Mexico as it really is.

That is, probably, the most unacceptable contradiction of all.

Notes

1. Dehesa, Rafael de la, *Refracted Modernities: Homosexuality and Party Politics in Brazil and Mexico*, p. 242.
2. Botello, Blanca, et al., 'Propuesta Polémica'.
3. Brito, Alejandro, 'Del derecho de convivencia a la conveniencia de no reconocerlo', pp. 134–157.
4. Ibid.
5. Dehesa, op. cit., p. 249.
6. Sánchez, Raymundo, 'López Obrador le pone hielo a ley de uniones gay; quiere consulta'.
7. Brito, Alejandro, 'Pilatos Obrador'.
8. Cruz González, René, 'Fija PRD plazo para aprobar sociedades de convivencia'.
9. Cuenca, Alberto, 'Ve impulsora de Ley de Convivencia inminente aprobación'.
10. Rivera, Francisco, *Defiende Marcelo Ebrard matrimonio gay y alza de precios*, 2010.
11. El Universal, *Capitalinos avalan matrimonio del mismo sexo*.
12. De Las Heras, María, 'Matrimonio gay en México: con mayoría en contra'.
13. Cabrera, Rafael, 'Hallan fórmula legal para matrimonio gay'.
14. Brito, Alejandro, 'Matrimonio del mismo sexo, una conquista laica', pp. 4–5.
15. Ibid.
16. Díaz, Gloria, *Mayoría perredista aprueba matrimonios gay*.
17. Mino, Fernando, 'La persecución de los perversos en el México novohispano', pp. 4–5.
18. INEGI, *Censo de Población y Vivienda*.
19. *The Political Constitution of the Mexican United States*.
20. SIAME, *La Iglesia lamenta publicación de la Ley de adopción de Menores por parejas gay*.
21. SIAME, *Pronunciamiento por el Emmo. Sr. Cardenal Norberto Rivera Carrera*.
22. Pantoja, Sara, 'Ebrard llama "cavernal" a Sandoval Íñiguez'.

23. SIAME, *Derechos humanos de quién?*
24. SIAME, *La Iglesia Lamenta*....
25. Moreno, Eva Díaz, 'Me vale gorro', Esteban Arce. *Excélsior*.
26. Uno Más Una, *12 argumentos para decir no al matrimonio homosexual* [Online]. Available: http://marchaunomasuna.blogspot.com/2010/06/12-argumentos-para-decir-no-al.html, 13 June 2010 [accessed 1 April 2011].
27. Uno Más Una, Facebook Profile.
28. Ibid.
29. Guerrero, Claudia, 'Frena PAN reforma: teme sexo con vacas'.
30. Otero, Silvia & Alcántara, 'Liliana. Llega a Corte controversia sobre aborto'.
31. Arellano, Silvia, 'Bodas, incompatibles con gays, alega la PGR'.
32. Mosso, Rubén, 'Impugna PGR en la Corte matrimonios gays y derecho a que adopten'.
33. López, Lorena & Arellano, Silvia, 'Calderón se opone a matrimonios gay'.
34. Paz, Octavio, *El laberinto de la soledad*.
35. Castañeda, Jorge. 'Código Postal'. *Reforma*.
36. INEGI, *Censo de Población y Vivienda*; INEGI, *Vivimos en hogares diferentes*; Gómez Quintero, Natalia, 'La familia evolucionó en México antes que las leyes'.
37. INEGI, *Vivimos en Hogares Diferentes*.
38. Merino, José. *México reconoce su diversidad, pero no la termina de digerir*.
39. CONAPRED. *Encuesta Nacional sobre Discriminación en México*.
40. Mckee, Irwin Robert. 'The Famous 41: The Scandalous Birth of Modern Mexican Homosexuality', pp. 353–376.
41. Schuessler, Michael, 'Vestidas, Locas, Mayates and Machos: History and Homosexuality in Mexican Cinema', pp. 132–144.
42. Nassif, Alberto Aziz, 'Los discriminados', p. A11.
43. GIRE, *Leyes sobre el aborto en México*.

References

Arellano, Silvia, 'Bodas, incompatibles con gays, alega la PGR', *Milenio*, 30 January 2010.
Botello, Blanca, et al., 'Propuesta Polémica', *Reforma*, 15 December 2000.
Brito, Alejandro, 'Del derecho de convivencia a la conveniencia de no reconocerlo', *Debate Feminista*, Issue 16, 2005, pp. 134–157.
Brito, Alejandro, 'Matrimonio del mismo sexo, una conquista laica', *Letra S*, Issue 162, 2010, pp. 4–5.
Brito, Alejandro, 'Pilatos Obrador', *La Jornada*, 18 December 2003.
Cabrera, Rafael, 'Hallan fórmula legal para matrimonio gay', *Reforma*, 11 November 2009.
Castañeda, Jorge, 'Código Postal', *Reforma*, 6 August 2009.
'Centro de Opinión Pública, Encuesta: Divide matrimonio gay', *Reforma*, 14 December 2009.
CONAPRED. *Encuesta Nacional sobre Discriminación en México*, Mexico: CONAPRED, 2010.
Cruz González, René, 'Fija PRD plazo para aprobar sociedades de convivencia', *Crónica*, 4 November 2006.

Cuenca, Alberto, 'Ve impulsora de Ley de Convivencia inminente aprobación', *El Universal*, 9 November 2006.
De Las Heras, María, 'Matrimonio gay en México: con mayoría en contra', *El País*, 11 January 2010.
Dehesa, Rafael de la, *Refracted Modernities: Homosexuality and Party Politics in Brazil and Mexico*, Doctor in Philosophy Thesis, Boston, MA: Harvard University, 2005.
Díaz, Gloria, 'Mayoría perredista aprueba matrimonios gay' [Online]. Available: http://www.proceso.com.mx/rv/modHome/detalle Exclusiva/74974, 21 December 2009 [accessed 10 April 2011].
El Universal, 'Capitalinos avalan matrimonio del mismo sexo' [Online]. Available: http://www.eluniversal.com.mx/graficos/pdf09/infografias/encuesta_g. html, 2009 [accessed 1 April 2011].
GIRE, 'Leyes sobre el aborto en México' [Online]. Available: http://www.gire.org. mx/contenido.php?informacion=70, January 2011 [accessed 10 March 2011].
Guerrero, Claudia, 'Frena PAN reforma: teme sexo con vacas', *Reforma*, 24 February 2011.
Gómez Quintero, Natalia, 'La familia evolucionó en México antes que las leyes', *El Universal*, 7 March 2010.
INEGI, *Censo de Población y Vivienda*, Mexico City: INEGI, 1990.
INEGI, *Censo de Población y Vivienda*, Mexico City: INEGI, 2010.
INEGI, 'Vivimos en hogares diferentes' [Online]. Available: http://cuentame. inegi.org.mx/poblacion/hogares.aspx?tema=P#, 2010 [accessed 1 April 2011].
Jiménez, Eugenia, 'Califica Norberto Rivera como aberrantes los matrimonios gays', *Milenio*, 8 August 2010.
López, Lorena & Arellano, Silvia, 'Calderón se opone a matrimonios gay', *Milenio*, 3 February 2010.
Mckee, Irwin Robert, 'The Famous 41: The Scandalous Birth of Modern Mexican Homosexuality', *GLQ: A Journal of Lesbian and Gay Studies*, Issue 6, 2000, pp. 353–376.
Merino, José, 'México reconoce su diversidad, pero no la termina de digerir' [Online]. Available: http://www.animalpolitico.com/2011/04/mexico-reconoce-su-diversidad-pero-no-la-termina-de-digerir/, 14 April 2011 [accessed 15 April 2011].
Mino, Fernando, 'La persecución de los perversos en el México novohispano', *Letra S*, Issue 163, 2010, pp. 4–5.
Moreno, Eva Díaz, 'Me vale gorro', Esteban Arce, *Excélsior*, 6 January 2010.
Mosso, Rubén, 'Impugna PGR en la Corte matrimonios gays y derecho a que adopten' [Online]. Available: http://www.milenio.com/node/369505, 27 January 2010 [accessed 10 March 2011].
Nassif, Alberto Aziz, 'Los discriminados', *El Universal*, 19 April 2011, p. A11.
Otero, Silvia & Alcántara, Liliana, 'Llega a Corte controversia sobre aborto', *El Universal*, 26 May 2007.
Pantoja, Sara, 'Ebrard llama "cavernal" a Sandoval Íñiguez', *El Universal*, 14 October 2010.
Paz, Octavio, *El laberinto de la soledad*, México: Fondo de Cultura Económica, 1950.
Rivera, Francisco, Defiende Marcelo Ebrard matrimonio gay y alza de precios [Online] Terra Noticias. Available: http://www.terra.com.mx/noticias/articulo/

889286/Defiende+Marcelo+Ebrard+matrimonio+gay+y+alza+de+precios. htm, January 15, 2010 [accessed 24 April 2011].

Sánchez, Raymundo, López Obrador le pone hielo a ley de uniones gay; quiere consulta, *Crónica*, 12 August 2003.

Schuessler, Michael, ' "Vestidas, Locas, Mayates" and "Machos"': History and Homosexuality in Mexican Cinema, *Chasqui: Revista de Literatura Latinoamericana*, Issue 34, 2005, pp. 132–144.

SIAME, 'Derechos humanos de quién?' [Online]. Available: http://www.siame.mx/apps/aspxnsmn/templates/?a=613&z=5, 10 January 2010 [accessed 1 April 2011].

SIAME, 'La Iglesia lamenta publicación de la Ley de adopción de Menores por parejas gay' [Online]. Available: http://www.siame.mx/apps/aspxnsmn/templates/?a=450&z=1, 29 December 2009 [accessed 1 April 2011].

SIAME, 'Pronunciamiento por el Emmo. Sr. Cardenal Norberto Rivera Carrera' [Online]. Available: http://www.siame.mx/apps/aspxnsmn/templates/?a=1594&z=1, 8 August 2010 [accessed 1 April 2011].

The Political Constitution of the Mexican United States, Mexico City: UNAM, 2005.

Uno Más Una, '12 argumentos para decir no al matrimonio homosexual' [Online]. Available: http://marchaunomasuna.blogspot.com/2010/06/12-argumentos-para-decir-no-al.html, 13 June 2010 [accessed 1 April 2011].

Uno Más Una, 'Facebook Profile' [Online]. Available: http://www.facebook.com/unomasuna [accessed 1 April 2011].

5
The Drug Cultures in France and the Netherlands (1960s–1980s): Banning or Regulating the 'Unacceptable'

Alexandre Marchant

Western societies at the turning point of the 1960s and 1970s saw a massive and rapid increase of legal and illegal drug consumption, valorised by the counterculture of the period, and disproportionately affecting many youths through disturbing addiction cases. Public drug scenes, that is, gatherings of wandering addicts, with drug transactions and public drug use, appeared in central or peripheral areas of all large Western cities. Drug abuse, including that of cannabis, heroin, LSD, and (later) cocaine and crack and misused legal medicines, was termed an 'epidemic' by the media, designated a 'social plague' by politicians, and conceptualised by intellectuals as a threat to civilisation. In France, for instance, the writer Jean Cau used the metaphor of a contaminant disease to warn public opinion of the arrival of this terrifying wave in a mainstream magazine in 1970:

> Parents, beware! The plague comes to you [...] No one knows where it will stop and how deep it will ravage the American nation. Heroin, morphine, cannabis, hallucinogens have established everywhere their hideous reign. From there, the monster jumped in Britain and Sweden. For two years now, he has put some tentacles on France.[1]

The reaction of moral panic was indeed global, at least as seen by observers based in the West. In 1971, a report from the World Health

Organisation found a new kind of pharmaco-dependence problem, with a less dramatic accent than Jean Cau, but depicting the same phenomenon:

> A decade earlier, the pharmacodependence problem concerned only a few countries and was linked with opium derivatives. Today the problem has the size of a *pandemic*, to which have been added a range of psychotropic substances to which too many young people are addicted.[2]

The same year, US President Richard Nixon designated, in a famous speech in June, drug abuse as the 'public enemy number one in America', and launched the huge rhetoric of the 'drug war'. He was imitated by the other Western politicians; in the meantime, in the USA as well as in Europe, laws were voted or reaffirmed to address this new social and health public problem.

In France and Holland, two Western countries in which the debate was passionate, both displayed emotional public discourses including frenzied media accounts, and shared many negative stereotypes demeaning and denigrating drug addiction as a disease. It was clearly 'unacceptable'. But the question is: why? In October 1969, in France, during an extraordinary session of parliamentary hearings devoted to this new spread of drug use, the conservative deputy Alain Peyrefitte said: 'if drugs were just a fact of civilization, we would just have to recognise it: we can't put crowds in prison'.[3] In saying this, he obviously denied that drugs were a fact of current society. To the contrary, the eminent psychiatrist Claude Olievenstein, one of the pioneers of drug abuse health care in the 1970s, supported policies of recognition of the problem, along with various treatment options, but for him it was a new path of civilisation and society must accept it, by taking into account this new desire of absolute freedom expressed by the young generations. It is therefore meaningful to analyse the cultural and political logics which made a practice – and a subculture linked to it – socially unacceptable, even if this set of practices and subcultures was too massive to be totally abnormal, accidental or ephemeral. This reflection will be divided into two parts. First, it is necessary to present the new drug cultures which were emerging with the rise of massive drug abuse. Second, the policies set up in response to the problem will be examined. This entails identifying some cultural logics explaining how new forms of drug abuse in the 1960s–1980s period were simply termed 'unacceptable'.

The new drug cultures of the period

Since the nineteenth century, the criteria of what had been the stereotype of generic drug abuse were: a practice limited to specific social poles such as writers; an underworld of criminals and mafia; cases of simple addiction; phenomena perceived as a form of perversion; and a quite insignificant problem for politicians. But these characteristics suddenly changed in the 1960s through a tipping point, transforming drug addiction into a young and 'mass phenomenon', valorised by the counterculture, in an anti-authoritarian and entertaining perspective.[4] There was indeed a kind of cultural matrix to this 'drug epidemic'. To define more precisely these cultural frames, we may identify four main components around which the new drug subcultures were structured: counterculture and psychedelics, neo-orientalism of the hippie trail, and later urban subcultures and junky lifestyles.

The first component involved the psychedelic and countercultural movement. One main characteristic of the 1960s drug scenes was actually the existence of a cultural background which gave a sense to the drug use. Initially, before becoming a public drug use problem, the drug scene phenomenon was only a cultural one. French and Dutch drug scenes had intellectual leaders. In Holland, the Provos, young anarchists and protestors – against the monarchy, the consumerist civilisation, American imperialism as exemplified in the Vietnam War – were led by activists and writers like Luud Schimmelpennink, Bernard de Vries or Simon Vinkenoog. But they were recognised by public authorities in spite of a natural mistrust; one example was Luud Schimmelpennink's being seated in February 1967 on the Amsterdam City council. By contrast, the French cultural drug scene was led by an artistic bohemia which expressed a certain dislike of the public; their publications were limited to what they termed the 'underground'. This cultural scene was dominated by authors like Jean-François Bizot, Jean-Jacques Lebel or Alain Dister. An example of their writing is the collective book *Le Dossier LSD* from the group of artists 'Mandala', published in 1967, reprinted in 1974. The idea was to valorise the use of hallucinogens so as to explore unknown dimensions of unconsciousness, alone or in small groups. So, as the Dutch drug scene was an activist and politically minded one, the French scene rather followed the elitist tradition of 'artificial paradises' inherited from authors like Charles Baudelaire or Henri Michaux.

Nevertheless, beyond these differences, in both France and Holland, we find the influences of aspects of the American counterculture through the spread of a huge discontent expressed by young generations, especially through countercultural values, beatnik, hippy or psychedelic movements, with topics such as rebellion against society, Western values, consumerism, capitalism and representative democracy, themes like sexual revolution and of course drug use. The models of the young Europeans hippies were the hippie neighbourhoods of Haight-Ashbury in San Francisco or Venice Beach in Los Angeles. The venerated US authors were the same: Allen Ginsberg, William Burroughs, Timothy Leary. Some books and cultural references circulated between Paris and Amsterdam. A good example was the book of the Dutch poet Simon Vinkenoog: *The Book of Grass*, an anthology of historical texts devoted to an apologetic for the use of Indian hemp throughout history for medical purposes, or sheer daydreams, published in English in the Netherlands in 1967, and translated into French in 1970. There were also some public associations in Amsterdam valorising the use of drugs, such as De Kosmos Meditatie Centrum, founded in 1968. Some members of this structure discussed in their texts the use of cannabis or LSD as a means of exploring the unknown parts of consciousness; they advocated a lifestyle expressing rebellion toward the consumerist society. But, when analysed more closely, these structures and these actors always denounced addiction: neither good nor bad in themselves, drugs were a means for spiritual journeys. In this way, both in France and Holland, cultural drug scenes were overwhelmed by the later spread of 'hard' drugs, that is, opiate abuse within the countercultural youth. Their initial ambiguity about the use of drugs implied perverse effects.

The second cultural component, closely connected to the first, was the neo-orientalism of the 1960s and 1970s. Many hippies, including French and Dutch ones, made the pilgrimage to the Far East to reach the supposed capital of spirituality, Kathmandu, as part of their research of mysticism through drugs. This phenomenon, historically dated, nowadays quite forgotten, was however perceived by the observers at the time as a massive and huge problem reaching the perspective of a civilisation crisis. For instance, the writer Gérard Borg wrote a book devoted to this problem based on his own experience of the 'hippie trail', which he followed for two years: *Lire phonétiquement Dictionnaire – Afficher le dictionnaire*:

> Is the appearance of the drug era the end of Western civilization? [...] When I returned to the West I also witnessed the evidence: actually I had always believed that the problem was below and beyond the drugs which were just an epiphenomenon. Between San Francisco, London and Hong-Kong, thousands of young people are wandering in search of life, being known that their route most often leads them

to the heart of night. They belong to all social classes, their motivations are endless. And they no longer count on us. Not anymore. We are still trying to persuade ourselves that the Beat Generation and brutal upsurge of drugs are just a manifestation of an irrational rejection phenomenon or a juvenile identity crisis more serious than others, but always temporary. Public authorities, when the phenomenon overflows and make anxious, will not understand that until they will integrate the quest for the Absolute and the sense of despair of youth into their calculations and technological forecasting. These factors will add to the mistakes of public authorities.[5]

In 1970, there were about 10,000 young Western people in India and Nepal. These new kinds of traveller were generally young – around 20 years old, on average – mostly students or unemployed. They presented as reasons for their travel the expressed intentions to break with the West and modernity in general. They travelled by backpacking, by hitchhiking, by train to Turkey, Iran, Afghanistan and Pakistan, and then India and Nepal. They formed communities in cities of North India like Varanasi, the holy city, Calcutta, Delhi, Mumbai and Goa, and of course Kathmandu in Nepal. But many of them stopped before reaching this goal due to insufficient money or because they had fallen prey to drug addiction and were unable to leave their static junky lifestyle. An important number of them were repatriated to Europe by their respective embassies. Hippie subcultures had actually reactivated earlier currents in Western philosophy criticising Western rationalism in favour of the so-called mysticism of traditional Oriental religions like Brahmanism or Buddhism. Such topics were developed for instance in the work of René Guénon, *The Crisis of the Modern World*, published in 1946, and reissued in 1969. The book's thesis is that Western civilisation is declining and that the conditions of its rebirth are to be found in Oriental values such as holism versus individualism, or transcendence versus Western empirical science, unfortunately now detached from any metaphysical roots. This reference is, for example, taken by the young Parisian hippie artist Gérard Rutten, who justified the reasons of his runaway to Kathmandu in a famous letter of 1968. This letter was highlighted by journalists at the time as emblematic of the mindset of a generation – 'See the Indies and die' – as shown in the following quotation:

To my parents,

it is better to die by making efforts to be awakened, than to live in sleep.

If anything from the West can be saved, it will be with the help of the Orient, said René Guenon. It seems, indeed, we are at a turning point in which the frames of Western world are miserably falling on the ground. [...] Emerging from LSD, a new generation fights back Reason. [...] It's the end of the world. That of the western, white, pale-face world. A world killed by a science misused by his servants: the technocrats

[...] I must admit that in France we had lost contact with the source of Being. The desire from American, French and English hippies is due to the nostalgia that we have found this source, [...] Humanity is approaching an end, and nobody has better defined that as René Guénon, in *The Crisis in the Modern World*.[6]

Far from the East, the third cultural component, arriving somewhat later, involved a new urban subculture making wandering and drug-taking in marginalised spaces a lifestyle. Indeed, in their development through the 1970s, the initial cultural scenes became more and more structured only around drug addiction, without any countercultural references but with increasing signs of social desperation. The social extension of the drug scene phenomenon brought together people from different social origins: the initial psychedelic groups were joined by people coming from lower-class backgrounds, poorly educated, and generally injecting themselves with heroin. In fact, drug underworlds always functioned actually as 'social interbreeding spaces' between different levels of society, the upper- or middle-class children who wanted to express revolt against their parents or society, and the underworld of traffickers, racketeers or wanderers taking advantage of this opportunity to sell their merchandise.

Later, in the 1980s, drug scenes became mainly composed of extremely marginalised persons, with pauperised immigrant populations such as Northern and Central Africans but also Asian immigrants in France, Asian and Surinamese immigrants in Holland. Some urban districts were directly affected by the extension of visible 'junkie habits': La Goutte d'Or or Belleville in Paris, some main streets of the old city such as De Zeedijk or southern districts such De Pijp in Amsterdam. Sociologist investigations at the time showed that half of the addicts in cities were in the company of other addicts when they had their last heroin injection: a shared 'shooting up' was a common practice in the junkie subculture, in which addicts usually depended on each other to obtain drugs.[7]

The gatherings of junkie populations in certain districts were the sources of the construction of a new urban subculture in which the urban décor is very important and functioned as a series of symbols of social desperation or decadency. These included dirty and dangerous locations, doorways, abandoned buildings or empty warehouses used as heroin shooting galleries, public parks, train stations or toilets. This created public fantasies about the 'drug urban cancers' (an expression from the French magazine *Paris Match* at that time). In Paris, at the beginning of the 1980s, a square of abandoned buildings called the 'Chalon island' (îlot Chalon), designated for destruction and located between the Avenue Dauménil and the Gare de Lyon train station, had become a symbol of the degraded drug scene: drug black market, meeting place for drug addicts, asylum for hobos or immigrants in illegal situation, place of concealment for bandits and traffickers, prostitution area. Suddenly, between February and May 1984, under the pressure of the government, a series of police assaults put an end to this situation causing a lot of debates in the press or TV. For public opinion, images of death, filth, disease and violence would remain for a long time. However, the problem simply moved to another area.

To take another example of the same year, De Zeedijk in Amsterdam was at the heart of a huge debate about the place of drug addicts in the urban landscape. In 1984, municipal authorities decided to put an end to the nuisance resulting from the open concentration of junkies in downtown, by enforcing safety and by extending unrestricted access to methadone distribution stations. Drug addicts and dealers (Chinese selling Asian heroin, Surinamese selling Turkish heroin) were meeting on De Zeedijk, causing problems that were extending into the subway station. In response, the City Council increased the repression, doubling the number of arrests, targeting obviously a foreign population (black Surinamese). This action prompted protests in front of the Town Hall denouncing a supposed will to stigmatise lower-class and immigrant populations. Similarly, the municipality, anxious to preserve the image of downtowns, shut down several health and help centres in the central district (in De Warmoesstraat), but this created a perverse effect, by putting to the street again all the drug users that had been picked up. This was in turn denounced by users' associations such as the Junkie League (*Het Junkiebond*).[8] The local structures of medical care also contributed to delimit and 'institutionalise' the problem, especially in the Netherlands where the choice of harm reduction policies through methadone distribution points contained the problem within particular neighbourhoods in Amsterdam, or in Rotterdam around the 'Perron

Nul' post near the central station, an ambitious experiment involving the use of substitute drugs such as methadone in the 1980s.[9]

The French and Dutch political reactions regarding the drug epidemic

Facing this problem, societies and public authorities were confronted with a choice: to refuse to accept and to fight, or to accept and to regulate, the new widespread use of drugs. This interrogation leads us to the second part of the reflection. Let us examine here the two countries and their different 'drug policy cultures', both deeply inserted in their respective national backgrounds of inherited patterns and cultural values. If policy is a result of political calculations and rational decisions, a state intervention in social life is always a 'moral made policy'. There were several cultural factors justifying these policies, definitively defining drug abuse as unacceptable.

On the one hand, in France, in an atmosphere of moral panic, public authorities set up, in 1970, a prohibitionist logic. Public authorities over-reacted against what they named a 'cancer striking the Youth', a 'contaminant evil', to quote the language of French politicians. Emergency policies in matters of repression, health care and prevention were set up. Instead of using a legal framework inherited from the past – an old law of 1916, until then only weakly enforced – Parliament voted in 1970 for a law giving exceptional powers for the police force. Prison sentences for traffickers were significantly increased (formerly 5, now 20 years of prison, even 40 years for recidivists). Both public and private use of narcotics were criminalised, imposing on the culture the figure of the diseased drug user. In the meantime, the new health policy was oriented toward a curative perspective with an objective of total abstinence per detoxification therapy, thus rejecting the principle of harm reduction policies until the 1990s.

To quote the language of the French politicians, the 1970 law was one of 'public safety', voted in response to public irritation and dramatisation of the danger. It recalled the inherited symbolic tradition of the French Revolution: the Fatherland is in danger, civil society is surrounded by a source of corruption to be fought, and the Jacobin State centralises the use of exceptional means. By doing so, the moral public underlying the law is also connected to typical French Christian roots or later revolutionary conceptions of the 'General Will' (*Volonté générale*) as more important than individual interests. The drug user is a victim; if he or she doesn't want to take the opportunity to choose the free medical care option when he is facing the judge after his arrest (*'injonction thérapeutique'*), then he or she will be sent to prison. Fortunately, things have changed since the 1990s.

For sociologists Henri Bergeron and Alain Ehrenberg, this mental framework is directly connected to the French conception of law: determining norms and interdicts. The State has an educative mission, a 'pedagogic model', with high moral requirements. As drug use is a danger involving a break of the social link so valorised in the Republic, the law must promote abstinence and therefore forbid the private use of drugs.[10] In a way, this constitutes a soft 'drug war model', as in the USA, but tempered by medical considerations and a 'moral philanthropy' toward the drug user, who is not considered entirely as a criminal but still relatively despised. Moreover, the spirit of the law was also conditioned by particular circumstances. Two years after the student riots of May 1968, the conservative and Gaullist Right wanted to reaffirm the authority of state and to control subversive and far-Left groups. Politicians established a connection – quite arbitrary and false – between protestors and the use of drugs. But many observers at the time suggested that, as public authorities couldn't directly attack the protestors, they attacked them for drug use with a new legislation increasing means for police, especially by searches and raids in premises belonging to protestor groups and arbitrarily suspected to be places of drug storage.

On the other hand, by contrast, Dutch authorities were more receptive to countercultural claims and youth protests, and established a model of harm reduction. In the late 1960s, the Dutch policy engaged in a painstaking debate about the merits of greater control versus a more tolerant approach; that debate led to the new *Opiumwet* of 1976. This is a pragmatic and non-moralist drug policy. Problems of deviant drug-taking and drug-selling are deeply and inescapably part of the society in which they occur: social logics are responsible as the drug user has also a right to self-determination. There is in consequence no moral crusade for a 'drug-free society' as in the US model. This response was founded on two key concepts: the 'normalisation' of drug addiction in the way society looks at the problem; and a 'separation' between illegal hard drugs and soft drugs. The latter are decriminalised and tolerated in establishments which are 'borderline' and semi-illegal with regard to the United Nations international conventions in matters of drug control. Examples of these were the famous coffee shops of large Dutch cities. For Dutch researchers like Peter Cohen, the 'junkification' of drug users was in consequence weaker than in other countries: ostracising of drug addicts was simply not dictated by the law.[11]

Here again, this political response seems to be deeply rooted in the Dutch mentality, which consists of the high valorisation of individual liberties and social tolerance in Dutch history, as seen in the experiment of the decentralised Republic in the seventeenth century, a refuge for all the persecuted thinkers of monarchical Europe. Regarding religious background, Protestantism valorised free will and particular institutional legacies, as the historian Maartje de Kort has shown. The *Opium Regie*, which ruled the production and sale of opium at the time of the colonies was very flexible, and a law inherited from this time even allowed Chinese immigrants to smoke opium in their dens until the 1970s.[12] In the second half of the twentieth century, Dutch society also developed a specific social-democrat system in which an immense variety of care and assistance institutions work for a large number of groups.

In addition, Dutch drug policy is also inspired by the principle of *het gedoogbeleid*, 'tolerance policy'. Dutch people and public authorities often consider that, for the balance of society, some social spaces have to be preserved from a strong intervention of social regulation, allowing a certain ambiguity and lack of jurisdiction. An example is the shadow market for supplying drugs to the coffee shops, technically illegal but tolerated by the police. There are no clear rules, no law enforcement, and in addition no means to control the efficiency of policies.[13]

Nevertheless, cannabis or mushrooms are decriminalised, but not liberalised: this nuance is significant. The partial decriminalisation of cannabis through spot fines, that is, only for traffic, possession and personal culture of more than 30 g in that period, 5 g today, still considers drug-taking as not a public good. Otherwise, it would be directly accepted as a 'fact of civilization', without the adoption of restrictive laws or regulation, without any state interventions. We are finally here in a model of 'repressive tolerance', to quote the title and the main ideas of an essay by Herbert Marcuse, 'accepting' certain deviant behaviours for the larger purpose of better overall control.[14] In the same perspective, the ambitious proposal of free heroin distribution for medical purposes – the ultimate step of the harm reduction philosophy – made in 1983 by the Partij van de Arbeid (PvdA, the Dutch Labour party), seated in the City Council, was passionately discussed but never adopted.

This means that, beyond apparent and formal differences, the comparison highlights a common opposition of Christian and conformist societies to drug underworlds which were denying, by their simple existence, the traditional symbolic order. There was also an international context in which contemporary drug abuse was fiercely fought, including pressures from the international arena and 'drug diplomacy', from the United Nations and its conventions of 1961 and 1977, to the USA and presidents such as Nixon and Reagan. The drug war is also an inherited prohibitionist framework, born in 1912 with The Hague International Opium Convention and a host of international treaties targeting drug abuse as a source of corruption to be destroyed.[15] But when a social behaviour is fought, in every policy or official state reaction, the question of defining and imposing norms is always present. There were, therefore, unspoken and unutterable words or logics acting beneath the surface of these events. There were obstacles held successively by a culture, ulterior motives and a taboo.

First, the culture is Western and rationalist. Drug abuse was initially interpreted by the authorities as a subversive threat in the frame of the larger ongoing societal dispute about lifestyles and values in the 1960s. This was especially evident in claims made against young hippies smoking cannabis on the wharves of the Seine, among them many young foreigners, such as British, German or Scandinavian people, importing the hippie or beatnik values. A typical remark of this view is, for instance, that from the French Commissioner Pierre Ottavioli in 1970:

> It was obvious that young foreigners in Saint Germain des Prés and on Seine wharves were drug adepts. Coming from Anglo-Saxon countries, they smoke haschisch and advocated its use, through their pseudo-philosophy based on the negation of traditional values, the refusal of pain, disinterest for tomorrow, and a so-called intellectual research beyond classical ways.[16]

In the first age of the drug scene, when the problem was countercultural, the reaction was based on morality and on a discussion about lifestyles. Beyond that, the eruption of mass drug abuse and underground subcultures was interpreted as a negation of what the Western world had become. In France, in *Le Monde*, Doctor Jacques Escoffier-Lambotte wrote a series of articles about the current drug epidemic. For him, there was no possibility of acceptable long-term outcomes countenancing drug use. He considered drug abuse to be a negation of reason, the sense of reason that Western civilisation has constituted on the basis of Cartesian philosophy and the Enlightenment.[17] For another French doctor, Henri de Couedic, 'Drugs coincide with the denial of all is that is organised, structured and reasonable. With products like amphetamines and hallucinogens, there is a fight engaged against reason, a refusal of all that is constructing our society'.[18] There were the same kinds of reaction in Holland, with the same lexicography.

There were also ulterior motives in the campaigns against drug use. In the 1970s–1980s, as previously mentioned, a pauperisation of drug users and drug scenes occurred. As the hippies became junkies wandering in the cities, sometimes stealing from people for money to buy drugs, drug abuse became, in the main social representations, a sign of criminality. For certain observers, drug use elicited denunciation of what they saw as the deep-rooted social decadence in the 1970s–1980s. Public reactions were sometimes very strong against junkies, particularly if they were foreigners, highlighting ulterior motives, as this Dutch example of people stigmatising, insulting and threatening the Surinamese during a hearing of the Amsterdam's City council in 1977 demonstrates:

> Members of the city council were shocked by the 'fascist remarks' made by residents during a hearing. Some Amsterdam citizens proposed to expel all addicts to labour colonies or an island somewhere in the ocean. Others wanted to transport all people from Surinam back to their own country. Some threatened to stone Surinamese addicts or burn them alive. Two new drop-in centres for Surinamese addicts were in fact burnt to the ground.[19]

This could appear quite surprising from a country known to be so liberal, but clichés have sometimes to be relativised. In France, stigmatisation of social decadence induced by the presence of foreign junkies in city streets was also sometimes very strong, especially when associated with the spread of AIDS, as seen in examples of Far Right propaganda. For instance, in a short film from the National Front dated from the presidential election campaign in 1988, needles presumably used by heroin addicts were projected as darts. This scenography took place on a degraded urban landscape, populated by junkies squatting in streets or doorways. The drug scenes were very cosmopolitan, fed by the drug tourism in the 1960s–1970s, then immigration in the 1970s–1980s; so stigmatisation of foreigners, in a xenophobic or racist way, in societies weakened by the economic and social crisis, is one of the implicit reasons explaining the demonisation of the 'unacceptable'. Drugs had become a symbol of the entry into a period of social uncertainty and urban insecurity that can lead to the release of fantasies about strangers.

Finally, drug abuse was also conceived as unacceptable because it raises a taboo, with anthropological implications: that of the violation of bodily integrity, with physical and mental degradations and often death by overdose. It questions the standards of health versus pathology. Drug abuse is a perversion of the individual, through his or her body. Sometimes, descriptions can lead to very confused and negative portraits, revealing the trouble caused by the drug epidemic in Christian societies, generating a lot of amalgams, resurrecting the images of vice, sin and degeneration. Christian journals in France dealt with drugs as a defilement of human nature. *La France catholique*, for example, defined drug consumption as an 'aggression against mankind', and a monstrosity which will fortunately disappear: 'we just have to know if addicts tend to congregate' and, if so, thanks to mass suicide so orchestrated 'they will disappear by themselves over generations by the same mechanism that created them, bringing an unexpected testimony of laws that ensure the salvation of life'.[20] These words are very harsh, even shocking.

We can find the same religious defence of the integrity of the body by Dutch reformers: a reverend presents drug abuse as a vice and an offence to the body created by God: 'Do you know that homosexuality and drug taking often work together? Our body is a gift from God. Men should know that we must not corrupt the body.'[21] Beyond these passionate public outbursts, we are in the presence of a true obsession with the image of the junkie, disproportionate in regards to the concrete hazards relating to drug consumption (overdoses or social behaviour guided by drugs). The social cost of drug abuse is even less high than alcoholism or road accidents. But, as far as representations are concerned, drug abuse strikes especially at the youth and consequently threatens the future of the nation. French doctor Jean-Marie Sutter, a neuro-psychiatrist from the teaching hospital of Marseille, recognised: 'of course, road kills more often than drugs, but it doesn't multiply wrecks, deprived of any physical or spiritual resources. Ignoring this aspect of the problem is a proof of bad faith'.[22]

Conclusion

When the drug epidemic appeared, with a small shift of a few years between the Netherlands and France (public awareness can be dated around 1965–1966 in Holland, and 1969–1970 in France), we can observe the same wide range of reactions, obsessions, representations, ways of denouncing and stigmatising the problem. We found a structural homology between the two debates concerning public spaces. In both national discourses, we can also find the five historical and anthropological criteria, identified by David Courtwright, defining tipping-points when a strong collective reaction rejecting non-medical use of drugs suddenly emerges. These criteria are: direct harm with the denunciation of contagion and risks related to drug use; social cost with cases of physico-social degradation and deaths; religious or moral disapproval with the Christian or moral condemnation of libertarian values; association of threat with deviant groups such as hippies or young protestors; and finally anxieties about the future of the nation with the idea of a corrupted youth and the 'civilization crisis'.[23] These are among the reasons why drug use and its linked set of subcultures was considered by many political or social actors as fundamentally unacceptable.

In the 1990s, the generalisation of harm reduction policies in European countries changed the main social representations of the problem. Drugs are still criminalised but the time of the moral panic seems to be over, except in the discourses of very conservative or Far-Right movements. Nevertheless, massive drug use is still considered as unacceptable and has remained for 40 years a denied 'fact of civilization'. This conclusion holds even if the price to be paid is a contradiction between, on the one hand, the mission assigned to the modern state, which is, in a liberal democracy, to guarantee individual freedoms and free choice of lifestyles, and, on the other hand, the development of a contemporary individualism. The latter makes increasing demands in terms of enjoyment and willingness to transform the body and the mind, even with the use of drugs.

Notes

1. *Paris-Match*, 11 July 1970. All quotations have been directly translated into English.
2. 24th World Assembly, 14th session, Geneva, 19 May 1971, French Health Ministry archives, CAC 19900545/1.
3. Peyrefitte, Alain, *La Drogue: ce qu'ont vu, ce que proposent juges, médecins, policiers, Ministres*, Paris: Plon, 1970, during audition of Claude Olievenstein.
4. Bachmann, Christian and Coppel, Anne, *Le dragon domestique; Deux siècles de relations étranges entre l'Occident et la drogue*, Paris: Albin Michel, 1989, chapter 30 'La drogue ressuscitée'.
5. Borg, Gérard, *Le voyage à la drogue*, Paris: Le Seuil, 1970, pp. 13–14.
6. Lancelot, Michel, *Je veux regarder Dieu en face; vie, mort et resurrection des hippies*, Paris: Albin Michel, 1968, pp. 233–239.
7. Renn, Heinz, *Urban districts and drug scenes: a comparative study on nuisance caused by 'open' drug scenes in major European cities*, Luxembourg: Office for Official Publications of the European Communities, 1996.
8. MDHG Archives, box 11, International Institute of Social History Amsterdam. See also Rene, Mol, TrautmannFranz, 'The liberal image of

the Dutch drug policy. Amsterdam is singing a different tune', in *The International Journal on Drug Policy*, vol. 2, 1991, pp. 16–21.
9. Hans, Visser, *Perron Nul; opgang en ondergang*, Zoetermeer: Uitgevrij Meinema, 1996.
10. Bergeron, Henri, *L'Etat et la toxicomanie; histoire d'une singularité française*, Paris: PUF, 1995, chapter 1. See also Ehrenberg, Alain, *Drogue, politique et société*, Paris: Descartes, 1992.
11. Cohen, Peter, 'Junky Elend. Some ways of explaining it and dealing with it', in *Wiener Zeitschrift für suchtforschung*, vol. 14, no. 3/4, 1991, pp. 59–64.
12. De Kort, Maartje, *Tussen patient en delinquent. Het geschiedenis van het Nederlandse drugsbeleid*, Rotterdam: Verloren, 1995.
13. Derks Jacks, T.M., Kalmthout (van) Anton, M., 'Facteurs déterminants de la politique néerlandaise en matière de drogues', in *Déviance et société*, 1998, vol. 22, no. 1, pp. 89–100.
14. Marcuse, Herbert, Wolff, Robert Paul and Moore, Barrington, Jr, *A critique of pure tolerance*, Boston, MA: Beacon Press, 1969.
15. McAllister William, B., *Drug diplomacy in the XXth century*, London, New York: Routledge, 1999.
16. Commissaire Ottavioli, Conference on drug abuse, hospital Sainte Anne, January 1970, French Health Ministry archives, CAC 19760224/183.
17. 'La drogue: de l'angoisse à la servitude', *Le Monde*, 20 January 1970.
18. *Ouest France*, 15 August 1971.
19. Blok, Gemma, 'Pampering "needle freaks" or caring for chronic addicts? Early debates on harm reduction policies in Amsterdam, 1972–82', in *Social History of Alcohol and Drugs*, vol. 22, no. 2, Spring 2008, pp. 243–261, testimony of the Dutch criminologist Ed Leuw.
20. 'Eschatologie de la drogue', *La France catholique*, 7 July 1971.
21. Ds. Ploeger from the Christian Geheelonthoudersvereniging (abstainer association), *Algemeen Dagblad*, 18 July 1968.
22. Report 'Les Jeunes et la Drogue', 1971, Youth and Sport Ministry archives, CAC 19840511/1.
23. Courtwright, David, *Forces of habit: drugs and the making of the modern world*, Cambridge, MA: Harvard University Press, 2001, chapter 9 'About face: restriction and prohibition'.

References

Bachmann, Christian and Coppel, Anne, *Le dragon domestique; Deux siècles de relations étranges entre l'Occident et la drogue*, Paris: Albin Michel, 1989.
Bergeron, Henri, *L'Etat et la toxicomanie; histoire d'une singularité française*, Paris: PUF, 1995.
Blok, Gemma, 'Pampering "needle freaks" or caring for chronic addicts? Early debates on harm reduction policies in Amsterdam, 1972–82', in *Social History of Alcohol and Drugs*, vol. 22, no. 2, Spring 2008, pp. 243–261.
Borg, Gérard, *Le voyage à la drogue*, Paris: Le Seuil, 1970.
Cohen, Peter, 'Junky Elend. Some ways of explaining it and dealing with it', in *Wiener Zeitschrift für suchtforschung*, vol. 14, no. 3/4, 1991.

Coppel, Anne, *Peut-on civiliser les drogues? De la guerre à la drogue à la réduction des risques*, Paris: La Découverte, 2002.

Courtwright, David, *Forces of habit: drugs and the making of the modern world*, Cambridge, MA: Harvard University Press, 2001.

De Kort, Maartje, *Tussen patient en delinquent. Het geschiedenis van het Nederlandse drugsbeleid*, Rotterdam: Verloren, 1995.

Ehrenberg, Alain, *Drogue, politique et société*, Paris: Descartes, 1992.

Lancelot, Michel, *Je veux regarder Dieu en face; vie, mort et resurrection des hippies*, Paris: Albin Michel, 1968.

Mandala group (collective book), *Le Dossier LSD*, in *Les cahiers noirs du soleil*, no. 1, Paris, 1967 [éditions Pierre Belfond, 1974].

Marcuse, Herbert, Wolff, Robert Paul and Moore, Barrington, Jr., *A critique of pure tolerance*, Boston, MA: Beacon Press, 1969.

Peyrefitte, Alain, *La Drogue: ce qu'ont vu, ce que proposent juges, médecins, policiers, Ministres*, Paris: Plon, 1970.

Renn, Heinz, *Urban districts and drug scenes: a comparative study on nuisance caused by 'open' drug scenes in major European cities*, Luxembourg: Office for Official Publications of the European Communities, 1996.

Vinkenoog, Simon, *Le Livre du chanvre*, Paris: Fayard, 1970.

6
'When the Smoke Clears': Confronting Smoking Policy

John Scannell

As smoking indoors is now considered unacceptable in vast sections of the world, the next frontier, for certain sections of the anti-smoking lobby at least, is outdoor public space. My own institution, Macquarie University, implemented a campus-wide outdoor smoking ban in 2011, hastily installed without community consultation, yet enacted with little resistance. As indemnification against litigation continues to motivate anti-smoking policy, institutional liability continues to take precedence over advocacy. While such directives are regrettable, they are not an entirely unexpected outcome of the public relations stranglehold that governs campus life these days. Yet, there persists an even more disconcerting dimension to such initiatives: this general rubric of 'health concern' mobilises certain private individuals to feverishly enforce anti-smoking measures on behalf of their institutions. Within this environment, the beleaguered smokers find themselves involuntarily indulged with yet another over-zealous rant, from an uninvited party that walks ten metres to deliver it. While the chastened smokers are becoming used to hostility and derision, that they should also suffer unsolicited displays of sanctimonious remonstration as well, remains a sore point. The question that must be asked is whether it is actually the business of smoking that is truly at the heart of the protestation in question?

It is the contention of this chapter that bans on outdoor smoking not only range among the more superfluous manifestations of anti-smoking policy, but are fundamentally more destructive than they are productive. While many non-smokers may rejoice in the banishment of their smoking peers, this more extreme regulation of the corporeal, is wholly symptomatic of the 'control society' proposed by philosopher, Gilles Deleuze. Taking his cue from Foucault, Deleuze argued that contemporary 'societies of control' are constitutive of those spaces which have emerged in the twentieth century and particularly after World War II, that 'are continuous in form. The various forms of control constitute a network of inseparable variations.'[1] Whereas the individual of the disciplinary society, 'is placed in various "moulds" at different times [...] the individual in a contemporary control society is in a constant state of modulation'.[2] As the care of the self continues to be outsourced to external regulation, it is fair to say that the more extreme forms of anti-smoking regulation are symptomatic of this shift from disciplinary society to the 'societies of control'.

It is not without irony that I utilise the work of Gilles Deleuze in this essay. A victim of smoking himself, it is a habit that is, without doubt, dangerous and lamentable. However, his work has much to offer when reflecting on recent trends of enforced smoking bans in public spaces, in particular the enforced 'encounter' between smoker and assailant that such measures have facilitated. The recent institution of the campus-wide outdoor smoking ban at my own university has allowed me to witness some of the unintended consequences of such institutionally driven directives – in particular, the antipathy that many smokers feel towards the inordinate over-zealousness that drove its implementation and the divisiveness such policy promotes. Smoking might be the target now, but once eradicated, one wonders what might be next?

These inordinately harsh outdoor smoking measures present a more insidious state of affairs, where a rubric of unacceptability is allowed to be indiscriminately applied to any activity deemed unacceptable. As the workplace further encroaches upon individual practice, the influence of neo-liberalist policy in the university sector assures us that it is also just as demanding as any other corporate workplace. As Professor of Public Health at the University of Sydney, Simon Chapman, has discussed in 'Going too far? Exploring the Limits of Smoking Regulations' (2008), smokers can now be denied employment because of their habit.[3] It is a particularly inequitable state of affairs; as such policy is not equally extended to all avoidable causes of death, for example, cancer death from sun exposure.[4]

We are reaching a stage where employers can now impose restrictions not only on what one does at work, but also about what one puts into or onto one's body as well. This is the 'network of inseparable variation' to which Deleuze referred, and the continuous subjection that we need to be wary of. As most of us give enough to our employers already, do we also need to relinquish control over what goes into and out of our bodies as well? This vigilant surveillance of employees, it is fair to say, is less about the public good and more about public relations and fashion.

The encounter

Lest it be said that we all have the right to an equitable public space, sadly there are any number of inconsiderate smokers who do pollute and generally disrespect that arrangement. Yet current trends in enforcing smoking bans in *all* public spaces have cultivated a somewhat over-zealous interpretation of acceptable behaviour. As ongoing smoking bans impel further collisions between habit and policing, such unmitigated encounters have driven the more indignant of the nicotine-addicted to some widely reported incidents of 'smoke rage'-related physical violence. For example, two weeks after the 2004 introduction of smoking ban in bars and restaurants in Ireland, there was an incident at the Speaker Connolly pub in North Dublin when 'a smoker "went berserk" when a barman refused to serve him and his friend unless they stubbed out their cigarettes. After heated words, the man flew into a rage, punching all round him and flinging a bar stool across the room.'[5] While an extreme and unnecessary reaction, the anecdote serves to illustrate the consequences of such expedited behavioural change. As the smoker is forced to withdraw from public space entirely, many more such encounters will undoubtedly ensue.

While the numbers of inconsiderate smokers are many, there are plenty more who are just as mindful of their surrounds, and are generally responsible towards their environment. Despite the widespread view that smoking and responsibility are, by nature, mutually exclusive, it is not always necessarily the case. For the general preponderance of noxious fumes, we, as a society, are collectively responsible, and those very same stone-throwing individuals who protest smoking, will most definitely have cars safely parked in their glass houses (and most likely an SUV or two).

This is not an endorsement of an 'anything goes' attitude towards smoking. I am totally empathic to the bans in enclosed areas, such as those legislated in pubs and clubs in my own state of New South Wales (NSW), Australia and effective since mid-2007,[6] even if this legislation has presented smokers with some prevailing logistical difficulties. For example, the prevalence of open-air sections in hotels and clubs are not only increasingly cramped with smokers, but also the social smokers, and their extended entourages, who arrive to converse with their peers. The inextricable relationship between drinking and smoking is such that smokers will generally remain there for the rest of the evening, whereby the company must come to them. Most of the smoking sections in pubs are cramped, while the smoke-free indoor areas remain half-empty at best. One can observe such similarly cramped conditions at the Macquarie campus, where the newly designated smoking areas seemingly attract more non-smokers than the clientele that they were reserved for. Smokers are left to wonder whether the well-meaning planning committees behind such initiatives actually frequent the types of buildings they design.

Even so, the smokers I know remain vehemently opposed to any form of indoor smoking in public, and their behaviour is now sufficiently regulated and internalised to the extent that the average smoker probably couldn't smoke indoors these days, even if they wanted to. If this segregationist policy continues to work as it should, then perhaps over time, the number of people cramped into smoking sections will lessen. Until then, however, the smoker lights up as he or she basks in the irony. Nevertheless, it is hardly time to be smug, as the biggest victim of all in this struggle over public space, is the very fabric of community itself. As law enforcement takes precedence over camaraderie, we find that the punitive work of our increasingly litigious society is enthusiastically undertaken by private volunteers. It would be understandable if this castigation of smokers came from those non-smokers placed in jeopardy, such as the bar-person forced to contend with slow-poisoning within an enclosed environment. But the most disconcerting thing is the enthusiasm with which some non-smokers have greeted these directives as a means to assert their own personal power. Bolstered by directives such as outdoor smoking bans, there are some rather more pernicious individuals who use this to go out of their way to remonstrate smokers for their activities.

The science

If the recently empowered anti-outdoor-smoking crusaders care to do some research, they will find that science is not actually on their side. This comes from no less an authority than world-renowned leader in anti-smoking policy, Simon Chapman. Celebrated for spearheading successful anti-smoking campaigns the world over, in 1997 Chapman won the World Health Organisation's 'World No Tobacco Day Medal' and in 2003 was awarded the American Cancer Society's Luther Terry Award for outstanding individual leadership in tobacco control. Furthermore, he won the NSW Premier's Cancer Researcher of the Year medal in

2008, the Public Health Association of Australia's Sidney Sax medal, and was a NSW finalist in Australian of the Year. He was deputy editor (1992–1997), then editor (1998–2008) of the British Medical Journal's Tobacco Control and is now its commissioning editor for low- and middle-income countries. His publications on anti-smoking initiatives are legion, including the rather forthright, *Public Health Advocacy and Tobacco Control: Making Smoking History* (2007).[7]

His concerted efforts to curb smoking speak for themselves, yet Chapman has spoken against the excessive nature of outdoor smoking bans, which he perceives to be counter-productive to global anti-smoking policy initiatives: 'the current excesses in secondhand smoke policy [...] risk undermining the much needed case for smoke-free indoor policies in most parts of the world where smoking remains a normal, unremarkable, and unregulated activity'.[8] In fact, the institution of outdoor smoking bans, he says, is an example of when the regulation of second-hand smoke (SHS) goes 'too far':

> To me, 'going too far' in SHS policy means efforts premised on reducing harm to others, which ban smoking in outdoor settings such as ships' decks, parks, golf courses, beaches, outdoor parking lots, hospital gardens, and streets. It is also the introduction of misguided policies allowing employers to refuse to hire smokers, including those who obey proscriptions on smoking indoors while at work.[9]

The reality of the matter, says Chapman, is that for second-hand smoke to be injurious to the non-smoker there needs to be contact within half a metre of 'between 8 and 20 cigarettes smoked sequentially' to provide particle exposure greater than the 24-hour Enivonmental Protection Authority (EPA) health-based standard for fine particles.[10] While this might prove a problem within a confined indoor setting, the exposure to smoke in an outdoor setting is negligible. The intermittent contact one would experience at a university campus, for example, would not constitute a health risk at all. It is perhaps this lack of direct evidence that has driven the university to cite 'environmental damage from cigarette waste' as 'the leading factor behind the institutional change of policy'[11] rather than exposure to second-hand smoke.

Nevertheless, smokers are banned (at present) from 98 per cent of 126 ha (hectares) or 1.2 km of open space on the Macquarie University campus.[12] According to the directive issued by 'Campus Experience', smoking spaces will be reduced each year until completely phased out in 2015.[13] As one can imagine, within such expansive grounds, the intermittent smoke dissipates to the point of inconsequence. While there is certainly a case to be made for spaces within, say, ten metres of buildings, to include the whole campus is overly officious. In fact, the creation of smoking areas has perhaps even exacerbated exposure to passive smoking as non-smokers must now enter a chimney of concentrated smoke so they can converse with their smoking peers.

With a discernible lack of credible scientific evidence to back up such concerns about second-hand smoke in an outdoor environment, the anti-outdoor-smoking lobby presents the counter-argument that its presence can be attractive to children.[14] Given that the university is supposed to be frequented by adults, this should not present much of a problem. In fact, such zealous regulation is reflective of universities' ever-increasing paternalism, which not only fosters the infantilisation of the student body but further contributes to the steady decline of campus life. One wonders how many students actually spend enough time on campus these days to be affected by anything, let alone cigarette smoke. In fact the physical presence of students on campus seems to be an impediment to the bottom line, and with so many virtual provisions made for study at home, they are seemingly actively encouraged to keep away from campus. To quote the art of printmaker Nick Bleasel, 'stay in your homes, you'll only get in the way',[15] advice which seems to be well heeded if concerns over attendance numbers at lectures these days are anything to go by.

In the absence of university life, there is plenty of 'room to breathe', to quote the rather ludicrous anti-smoking campaign used at Macquarie University. If only we could foster an equally dedicated 'room to think' campaign. The only students that I see spending any amount of time around campus, are overwhelmed international students (many from the heavy-smoking south-east Asia region) and the more conscientious locals, two demographics with a much higher than normal percentage of smokers among their constituency. Why does the Macquarie University announcement that it will be the 'healthiest campus by 2015'[16] sound so ominous? What is a healthy student to the university anyway? One that is liquid? One that doesn't waste valuable resources by being on campus to take part in pesky lectures or exams? These days it would appear that the healthy student is the invisible student. Driving the smokers away from campus surely helps to fulfil this brief.

The reality of the matter is that such injustices will only contribute to the smokers' indignation, and with good reason; with the vast tuition fees they are paying, they should not have their legal rights dismissed so easily. However, to frame this discussion as an erosion of legal rights is perhaps too general to be constructive here. A more interesting approach to this study would be to analyse why such over-zealous directives begin in the first place, and how the effects of over-regulation are much worse than the chronic physical ailments that smokers voluntarily bring upon themselves.

Ressentiment

To best situate some of the more egregious examples of reactionary policy, including the over-zealous ban of outdoor smoking at my own institution, we might define its impetus in terms of 'reactive force', which Deleuze has referred to as a 'base way of thinking'[17] and the enemy of thought. Symptomatic of the triumph of public relations over logic, and/or even care, 'reactive force' is driven by a 'ressentiment' that impels the nihilism that infects so much of institutional life. Invoking the work of Nietzsche, Deleuze referred to the development of nihilism as the logical end-point of a Western philosophy driven by the ascetic or the renunciation of desires for the sake of some higher or better world beyond appearances. Our despair or nihilism is borne of a failure to grasp this true world, of which the result is our lingering ressentiment.[18] This ressentiment assumes a reassignment of inferiority onto a third party, as a fabricated cause of such malaise. There are many colloquial terms for this condition: the 'fun police', or the 'little man syndrome' among many others. This sense of inferiority is somehow assuaged by the moral superiority that the victims of ressentiment indulge: 'if only you stopped doing x then everything would be so much better'. It is the cumulative effect of this drive for a better or truer world which has led to the essence of man as the becoming-reactive of all forces as a result of such nihilistic persuasion.[19]

In *Nietzsche and Philosophy* (1962), Deleuze foregrounds that philosopher's diagnosis of:

> a disease (nihilism) by isolating its symptoms (ressentiment, the bad conscience, the ascetic ideal), tracing its etiology in a certain relation of active and reactive forces (the genealogical method), and setting forth both a prognosis (nihilism defeated by itself) and a treatment (the revaluation of values).[20]

While the work of Nietzsche is important to this diagnosis of nihilism, the relationship of forces that Deleuze refers actually comes from the work of Spinoza. As Kenneth Surin writes, 'Deleuze is particularly impressed by Spinoza's philosophical ambition to view all of life as the expression of a fundamental striving or conatus, so that the body becomes an ensemble consisting of those forces that it transmits and those forces that it receives.'[21] Deleuze's anti-transcendental, anti-dialectic philosophy gives prominence to immanence and the physical capabilities of bodies whose relations are governed by, 'dominant and dominated forces'[22] and where 'every relationship of forces constitutes a body – whether it is chemical, biological, social or political'.[23] In short, all of reality consists of 'quantities of force' in mutual 'relations of tension'[24] between active and reactive forces.

Within this metaphysical constitution of life, superior or dominant forces are defined as active, and the inferior or dominated forces as reactive. Active forces are creative and transformative which go 'to the limit of what they can do'.[25] On the other hand, reactive force is separated from what it can do.[26] Instead of embracing the power of creation, reactive forces tend instead towards conservation and adaptation, such as securing 'mechanical and utilitarian accommodations, [as] the regulations which express all the power of inferior and dominated forces'.[27]

Consciousness, then, for Deleuze is the expression of these reactive forces of adaptation, which remain dominated by the unconscious active forces of the body.[28] The important point to keep in mind is that 'the philosophy of consciousness operating within the paradigm of subjectivity thus remains wholly within reactive forces, and as such is powerless to think the active forces of life itself'.[29] Thus, our conscious lives are governed by reactive forces, and for this reason, says Deleuze, 'we do not feel, experience, or know any becoming but becoming-reactive'.[30]

Active and reactive forces are defined in respect to the will-to-power, willing creation as the positive power of difference. In his article, 'Active Slaves and Reactive Masters? Deleuze's Anti-Dialectical Nietzsche', Robert Sinnerbrink told us how, under Deleuze, the Nietzschean will to power is

> a metaphysical concept designating that which wills in the dynamic relations of force that are qualitatively expressed as active and reactive. The will to power is the differential and genetic element of force, from which is derived both the quantitative difference of related forces, and their respective qualities as active or reactive.[31]

These active and reactive forces are primordial qualities of the will to power, and whose affirmation drives the engine of creative difference.

As such, active force is nominally 'good' in that its creative nature affirms the difference of life and its becoming. As Deleuze tells us, 'active force asserts itself, affirms its own difference, and makes this difference an object of enjoyment; reactive force, by contrast, limits active force, imposes restrictions, and remains under the spell of the negative'.[32] However, 'active force' can be problematic too, in the sense that it is dominating and 'acts of its own accord. In doing so, it may impose forms upon lesser forces or otherwise appropriate or subordinate them to its own ends. Active force goes to the limit of what it can do, even to the point of its own destruction and transmutation into something else'.[33]

In terms of Nietzsche's master/slave dialectic, it is active force that is associated with the masters who 'affirm themselves and enjoy their own difference; slaves negate that which differs and resent their own impotence [...] Active force affirms difference, reactive force denies it'.[34] These concepts produce 'a naturalised ontology of "types": the weak, cunning reactive type who triumphs over the strong, creative, active type by inventing powerful ideological and moral fictions that restrict the latter's power to act'.[35] According to Nietzsche, it is the 'weak' who are the most prone to ressentiment, as those who experience insecurity cannot suppress their capacity to react. It is the weak that harbour ressentiment and are prone to the reactive when it comes to regulation. Coercive institutional power provides a sustained engagement with reactive force. Each time I am coerced into a designated smoking area at work, I am inclined to fantasise about the very point when the motion was passed, and the gallery of overly didactic and/or reactionary individuals mumbling about how good it would be if all smokers were quarantined into a handful of spaces. Such a response is also, of course, reactive in nature, which illustrates the contagion of ressentiment.

What goes through the mind of the over-regulated smoker is how such overarching regulation shields us from the encounter (for better or for worse). To inhabit a life of directives at the expense of negotiation equates to a lack of sociality, and the thought that lay behind it. This creates the effect of people thinking less, and reacting more out of ressentiment. Hence we inhabit the nihilism of modernity as a culmination of reactive forces. As Sinnerbrink explained, 'Deleuze depicts culture as having been perverted from its original function of training and selection, and having become diverted instead into nihilistic forms of institutional organisation (Nietzsche's "herds").'[36]

It is the absolutist nature of the outdoor anti-smoking edict that demonstrates those 'mechanical and utilitarian accommodations, the regulations which express all the power of inferior and dominated forces' which effect such a dramatic impact on our lives. Those institutional organisations, the culmination of Nietzsche's 'herds', are imbued with increasingly greater powers to regulate our lives. One would like to think that, of all places, universities would be the most tolerant of difference, but this is sadly not the case. The concentration on fiscal responsibilities seemingly takes precedence over common consensus. Reflected in Deleuze's comment that today, 'the factory has given way to the corporation',[37] the contemporary university is run by public relations at the expense of actual negotiation and thought. Educational institutions have been forced to co-exist as corporations grappling for yet another selling point: 'Marketing. We are taught that corporations have a soul, which is the most terrifying news in the world. The operation of markets is now the instrument of social control and forms the impudent breed of our masters.'[38] Such is the climate of the contemporary university.

Over-zealous public relations exercises, including banning smoking campus-wide, present a strategic deflection from more pressing concerns about the actual decline of the educational environment. None of these campus directives comes from the actual academics, who are generally overwhelmed with pedagogical inclination. As Nietzsche might contend, the more active, 'strong-willed' individuals are occupied with more creative concerns. In fact, the people who have had everything to say about such trifling matters as outdoor smoking are those figures most likely to be prone to ressentiment, who harbour their own indignation about their general existence. These are the weak-willed subjects of ressentiment whose 'big idea' will transform things, even if it is never carried out by them, nor in the spaces they inhabit. Such directives are enforced by contract and general staff, such as the security services (ressentiment is part of the job description) who are grudgingly forced to do the dirty work for their superiors.

Ressentiment is conservatism. As Robert Sinnerbrink has noted, it is societal preservation, in particular, that, 'cultivates the reactive forces of consciousness and memory'[39]:

> (Individual) Responsibility as responsibility before the law, law as the law of justice, justice as the means of culture—all this disappears in the product of culture itself. The morality of customs, the spirit of the laws, produces the man emancipated from the law. This is

why Nietzsche speaks of a self-destruction of justice. Culture is man's species activity; but, since this activity is selective, it produces the individual as its final goal, where the species itself is suppressed.[40]

Control society

If, as Deleuze contended, the individual of the disciplinary system has been replaced by the 'dividual' of the control society, then within this contemporary paradigm, ressentiment has an even more virulent role to play. For example, wages paid to workers are subject to the constant variation of modulation as we are to all encompassing numerical parameters and as such, 'we no longer find ourselves dealing with the mass/individual pair. Individuals have become "dividuals," and masses, samples, data, markets, or "banks"'.[41] Symptomatic of a life spent in institutional organisations, the constant state of modulation reiterates the nihilistic impulse. It is the dominant model of the control society of advanced capitalism as 'it is more frequently the task of the individual to engage forms of competition and continuing education in order to attain a certain level of salary'.[42] The regulation of smoking, or any other activity for that matter, which is deemed to impact upon employment, reflects the overarching power of the institution in contemporary life, directives that continue to reinforce the basic inequalities that already exist in the work environment.

This returns us to the reactive forces of ressentiment produced by such institutional inequality. Of course, critics of smoking might contend that smokers are the ones who contribute to the inequality as they affect communal space. True enough, but when these directives become as encompassing as taking up a whole open campus, one wonders, as Chapman has, whether things have gone too far?

The opposition to smoking was not undertaken at the behest of the overworked academics, who have little to say on the matter. As Nietzsche contends, the 'strong-willed man' is not prone to dwell on such trifling matters, as he basically has better things to do. For it is precisely the 'dwelling upon' that exacerbates the ressentiment of the nihilist; the dwelling that hampers the affirmative 'yes' to life. As counter-intuitive as it may seem, smokers can actually be affirming the creative capacity of life, even if they are killing themselves in the process. Conversely, to speak of the 'unacceptable' is to enforce the reactive, and the excesses of anti-smoking policy are unacceptable in the sense that they present such reactive force, and reiterate a climate of dogmatism and antagonism. We hear a lot these days about the unwarranted intervention of the 'nanny state', and perhaps this might be considered a layperson's term for Nietzsche's 'herd mentality' that prevents active forces from creating and reactive forces from acting. Only affirmation will allow us to overcome nihilism and such affirmation can only come via the escape from history. 'To forgive and forget', instead of dwelling on posited values, enables us to replace them with new active processes of creation. When memory invades consciousness, our ability to 'forget' is lost. The 'ascent of memory into consciousness itself'[43] separates active force from what it can do. In everyday life, the reactive force of memory does serve a necessary function, as warning, as law (even if this is a history of respiratory ailments), which can, of course, help to ameliorate physiological condition. Not necessarily a bad thing, but it is this retraction into memory that can, of course, stop creativity too.

As the newly deputised take it upon themselves to enforce the law, it is usually at the expense of affirmation. One reacts with indignation and the reactive forces of ressentiment are thrust into consciousness. The cigarette break in the midst of creative thought is subject to remonstration, where one's conscious thoughts are subsequently given over to memory (and most likely calculated methods of torture toward the assailant in question). That we are 'constantly coerced into forms of "communication"',[44] is yet another pernicious development of the control society, as we find ourselves increasingly 'denied the privilege of having nothing to say, cultivating the particular kind of creative solitude that Deleuze values. It appears that we will increasingly lack a space for creative "resistance"'.[45] The communications process, driven by the reactive clichés of opinion, produces an ever more reactive society, negating individual autonomy and exacerbating the shift from the disciplinary to control society: 'control is short-term and of rapid rates of turnover, but also continuous and without limit, while discipline was of long duration, infinite and discontinuous'.[46]

Many smokers are well aware that the encroachment of their bodies by ever-encroaching forms of management is just another example of such continuous assessment. Furthermore, over-zealous measures do not assist, but merely justify smoking as a form of 'rebellion'. While undoubtedly a poignant example of cutting off one's nose to spite one's face, it may also be perceived as deliberately cutting off one's lung capacity as an essentially futile protest against a more pronounced social asphyxiation. A poor defence, to be sure, but the draconian restrictions placed on smokers will surely be extended to other 'problematic' sections of the 'community', as every personal idiosyncrasy is subject to clinicisation and restriction; 'the obesity epidemic' comes to mind here.

Resisting regulation

It is true that smoking is a problem, not only for the smoker, but for society as whole. It exacerbates illness, uses up important resources in the health system and it pollutes the environment (of course much the same could be said about any number of activities that we engage in daily). That said, I am not trying to defend smoking, but simply to say that as it is already banned in so many public spaces already, the public has generally been quarantined from its more egregious effects. In line with Chapman's concerns about the counter-productive effects of its more draconian manifestations, what is even more disconcerting is how eager some people seem to be about embracing a control society. The conditions that exacerbate regulation and surveillance have become so entrenched in everyday life that individual citizens are taking on the policing work. During work on this chapter, I was reminded of the 'don't dob/grass/snitch' ethos that governs so much of working-class life the world over. This is not to say that this is necessarily the correct approach, but no matter how unacceptable things might get, anything is preferable to delivering difference into the hands of reactive force. It is a philosophy that understands the will-to-power, of how to keep creativity outside the bounds of law. Yes, this can be problematic because 'active force is force that acts of its own accord. In doing so, it may impose forms upon lesser forces or otherwise appropriate or subordinate them to its own ends. Active force goes to the limit of what it can do, even to the point of its own destruction and transmutation into something else'.[47]

While a reluctance to snitch may lead to its own territorial destruction, better to affirm activity than to relinquish its creative capacity. Implicit in this idea of 'don't dob/grass/snitch' is an intuitive resistance to the more overwhelming sources of reactive power. In its own strange way it is an affirmation of active force, as 'active force affirms its own nature rather than seeking to oppose or limit that of the other'.[48] This is because there is often an intuitive understanding among the oppressed, that the common concept of political power is a reactive one. That calling upon the reactive, even if it may be immediately beneficial to your situation, has far worse consequences down the track. Empathy is a much better place to begin from when trying to summon active force.

Reaction is the easy option, as it reduces the capacity or power to live one's life actively, which is, of course, hardly a life lived at all. That is to say, only a fool believes that the law is on their side. We might only know reactive force, but there is no need to unnecessarily dwell upon it.

Notes

1. Marks, John, 'Control Society', in *The Deleuze Dictionary*, A. Parr (ed.), Edinburgh: Edinburgh University Press, 2005, p. 54.
2. Ibid.
3. Simon Chapman, 'Going Too Far? Exploring the Limits of Smoking Regulations', *William Mitchell Law Review*, 34(4), 2008, p. 1616.
4. Ibid., p. 1616.
5. David Lister, 'Smoke Rage Threatens Ireland's Ban'.
6. Detailed information on New South Wales, Australia smoking restrictions can be found here: http://www.health.nsw.gov.au/publichealth/health promotion/tobacco/faqs.asp.
7. Chapman's CV can be found on the 'Tobacco Control Supersite', http://tobacco.health.usyd.edu.au/simon-chapman-biography/.
8. Chapman, 'Going Too Far? Exploring the Limits of Smoking Regulations', p. 1619.
9. Ibid., p. 1609.
10. Ibid., p. 1611.
11. Macquarie University, 'Butt Out: University Campus to Go Smoke Free', *Macquarie University*, 23 November 2010, accessed 11 April 2011, http://mq.edu.au/newsroom/control.php?page=story&item=4299.
12. Derya Goren, 'Macquarie University Campus Ban on Cigarettes'. Goren mistakenly attributed Macquarie with 26 ha, when it should have been 126 ha.
13. Macquarie University, 'Butt Out: University Campus to Go Smoke Free'.
14. See Chapman, Thomson et al., 'Head to Head: Against Banning Smoking Outdoors', *BMJ*, 337 (a2804), p. 76.
15. Artwork can be viewed at http://www.heynick.com/posters/stay-in-your-homes.htm.
16. Macquarie University, 'Smoke Free Campus Policy'.
17. Gilles Deleuze, *Nietzsche and Philosophy*, Hugh Tomlinson (trans.), London: Athlone, 1983, p. 105.
18. Claire Colebrook, *Gilles Deleuze*, London: Routledge, 2002, p. 19.
19. Deleuze, *Nietzsche and Philosophy*, p. 169.
20. Daniel W. Smith, 'Critical, Clinical', p. 188.
21. Kenneth Surin, 'Force', p. 19.
22. Deleuze, *Nietzsche and Philosophy*, p. 40.
23. Ibid.
24. Ibid.
25. Ibid., p. 114.
26. Ibid.
27. Ibid., p. 41.
28. Ibid.

29. Sinnerbrink, Robert, 'Active Slaves and Reactive Masters? Deleuze's Anti-Dialectical Nietzsche', *Social Semiotics*, 7(2), 1997, p. 150.
30. Deleuze, *Nietzsche and Philosophy*, p. 64.
31. Sinnerbrink, 'Active Slaves and Reactive Masters? Deleuze's Anti-Dialectical Nietzsche', pp. 150–151.
32. Deleuze, *Nietzsche and Philosophy*, pp. 55–56.
33. Patton, Paul, *Deleuze and the Political*, London, New York: Routledge, 2000, p. 61.
34. Deleuze, *Nietzsche and Philosophy*, p. 68.
35. Sinnerbrink, 'Active Slaves and Reactive Masters? Deleuze's Anti-Dialectical Nietzsche', p. 154.
36. Ibid.
37. Deleuze, Gilles, 'Postscript on the Societies of Control', *October*, 59, Winter, 1992, p. 6.
38. Ibid.
39. Sinnerbrink, Robert, 'Active Slaves and Reactive Masters? Deleuze's Anti-Dialectical Nietzsche', p. 155.
40. Deleuze, *Nietzsche and Philosophy*, p. 137.
41. Deleuze, 'Postscript on the Societies of Control', 1992, p. 5.
42. Marks, 'Control Society'.
43. Deleuze, *Nietzsche and Philosophy*, p. 114.
44. Marks, 'Control Society'.
45. Ibid., p. 54.
46. Deleuze, 'Postscript on the Societies of Control', p. 6.
47. Patton, *Deleuze and the Political*, p. 61.
48. Ibid., p. 62.

References

Chapman, Simon, 'Going Too Far? Exploring the Limits of Smoking Regulations', *William Mitchell Law Review*, 34(4), 2008, pp. 1605–1620.
Chapman, Simon and Thomson, George et al., 'Head to Head: Against Banning Smoking Outdoors', *BMJ*, 337, 2008 (a2804), pp. 76–77.
Colebrook, Claire, *Gilles Deleuze*, London: Routledge, 2002.
Deleuze, Gilles, *Nietzsche and Philosophy*, Hugh Tomlinson (trans.), London: Athlone, 1983.
Deleuze, Gilles, 'Postscript on the Societies of Control', *October*, 59, Winter, 1992, pp. 3–7.
Goren, Derya, 'Macquarie University Campus Ban on Cigarettes', *The Daily Telegraph*, 25 November 2010, viewed on 11 December 2011, http://www.dailytelegraph.com.au/news/sydney-nsw/macquarie-university-campus-ban-on-cigarettes/story-e6freuzi-1225960441524.
Lister, David, 'Smoke Rage Threatens Ireland's Ban', *The Times Online*, 10 April 2004, viewed on 11 April 2011, http://www.timesonline.co.uk/tol/news/uk/article1058011.ece.
Macquarie University, 'Butt Out: University Campus to Go Smoke Free', *Macquarie University*, 23 November 2010, viewed on 11 April 2011, http://mq.edu.au/newsroom/control.php?page=story&item=4299.

Macquarie University, 'Smoke Free Campus Policy', *Macquarie University*, 2010, viewed on 9 December 2011, http://www.mq.edu.au/policy/docs/smoke_free/policy.html.

Marks, John, 'Control Society', in *The Deleuze Dictionary*, A. Parr (ed.), Edinburgh: Edinburgh University Press, 2005, pp. 53–55.

Patton, Paul, *Deleuze and the Political*, London, New York: Routledge, 2000.

Sinnerbrink, Robert, 'Active Slaves and Reactive Masters? Deleuze's Anti-Dialectical Nietzsche', *Social Semiotics*, 7(2), 1997, pp. 147–160.

Smith, Daniel W., 'Critical, Clinical', in *Gilles Deleuze: Key Concepts*, C. Stivale (ed.), Durhan: Acumen, 2005, pp. 182–193.

Surin, Kenneth, 'Force', in *Gilles Deleuze: Key Concepts*, C. Stivale (ed.), Durhan: Acumen, 2005, pp. 19–30.

Part II
Representing the Unacceptable

7
The Monstrous-Familial: Representations of the Unacceptable Family

John Potts

The focus of this chapter is the family. More precisely, I am concerned with the changing status and definition of family, including the accession to normative or acceptable status, within Western society, of a certain mode of family. This process has had, as a corollary, the construction of other types of family as unacceptable, undesirable, dangerous, even monstrous. Representations of these other families – outlawed, vilified, feared – are analysed in this chapter. There is no shortage of material in recent television, cinema and literature, because these other, unacceptable, families generate fascination as well as loathing within the judgement of acceptable society.

The term 'monstrous-familial' contains an allusion to the 1993 book by Barbara Creed, *The Monstrous-Feminine*. Drawing on the theory of the abject developed by Julia Kristeva in her book *Powers of Horror*, Creed analyses horror films as 'the work of abjection'.[1] Particular emphasis is given to the rendering of the maternal figure as the monstrous-feminine, in films ranging from *Psycho* to *Aliens*. Creed follows Kristeva in proposing that modern horror movies, like literature and art, have assumed the cathartic role once performed by religion: to 'purify the abject'. Horror functions to:

> bring about a confrontation with the abject (the corpse, bodily wastes, the monstrous-feminine) in order finally to eject the abject and redraw the boundaries between the human and non-human.[2]

This cathartic process is paradoxical, however, since 'abjection by its very nature is ambiguous; it both repels and attracts'.[3]

While the boundaries between the acceptable and the unacceptable may certainly be construed in the terms deployed by Kristeva and Creed, I take only limited inspiration from this approach. This is due to the largely ahistorical temper of the psychoanalytical study of cultural forms. Creed's cultural analysis, like the many other studies derived from Freud and Lacan, follows Freudian concepts as doctrine (even if, as in Creed's work, this involves a modification of Freudian theory). This doctrine posits a universal subject, with a universal unconscious, which acts out the same psychic scenario through history and across cultures. The doctrinaire application of Freudian principles to contemporary culture has resulted in the proliferation of Freudian clichés such as 'the return of the repressed'. This generalised approach reveals little of the historically contingent: that is, the way cultures evolve so that, in a particular time and place, cultural forms assume specific significance. Why have certain types of the family, at different times, been represented as socially unacceptable? I will consider changing representations of the family – acceptable and unacceptable – not only in horror, but in other genres and media forms as well. In order to understand this process, some historical context is required.

A brief history of the Western family

The word 'family' is derived from the Latin *familiare*, and classical sources provide insight into the status of the family group in the Roman world. This is true as well of Ancient Greece, although the Greeks emphasised not the family but the *oikos*, meaning household, including those who lived within it. The Greeks believed that the *polis* (city state) was an aggregation of *oikoi*: our words 'politics' and 'economy' (from the Greek for managing the household) stem from these Greek terms. The Greek family within the *oikos* was monogamous, comprising the conjugal family (husband, wife and children) as well as other dependent relatives and slaves. The *oikos* was run on strictly patriarchal lines, with separate quarters for men and women, while women were largely confined to the private world of the household.

Although the *oikos* was regarded as the basic economic unit, it was not esteemed within Greek culture. As Giorgio Agamben has observed, Ancient Greek thought made a distinction between *zoē* – simple or bare life – and *bios* – the public or good life. Aristotle confined simple or natural life to the 'home' or *oikos*, while the good life was the domain of the *polis*. The *oikos* was the site of 'merely reproductive life', with little political value.[4] There was nothing of the sentimental valuing of home and family found in modern Western culture; if family is mentioned by the Greek philosophers, it is at times in hostile terms. Plato proposed in the *Republic* that the family should be abolished for the ideal philosopher-rulers, because it was an impediment to their perfecting of moral judgement.[5] The Spartans imposed the authority of the state onto that of the family, removing male children from their families at the age of five. They lived until the age of 30 in a military mess, where they could devote themselves to military training and service to the state.[6] The Spartan instance was unique within the Greek world, but an elevation of the public life above that of the domestic household was true of all the Greek city-states. The life of the polis was public, male and communal, enacted in the agora and in male groupings; family life was the domestic zone of women and children, and was credited with little importance.

Roman civilisation exercised a similar upholding of the public or civic life over the domestic. Within the family, the authority of the father or *pater familias* was even more severe than in the Greek world; indeed the Greeks were shocked by the degree of power wielded by the father over his children, even when grown up: the *pater familias* reserved the right to sell his children as slaves, or even have them put to death.[7] Children effectively worked as servants within the family household: they were expected to wait on tables, but never to speak. They were raised by their mother or an elderly relative, with the help of slaves. Children were expected to observe *pietas* or dutiful behaviour to their parents, but they received little affection in return.

The medieval social order that developed after the fall of Rome depended largely on agriculture. Poverty was widespread, and bare subsistence on the land was the most that could be hoped for. The most common family form in Europe for many centuries was the extended family, defined as a three-generational family linked by a common economy and community of residence.[8] It was once assumed by historians that the extended family was the universal format in pre-industrial times, displaced by the nuclear family as industrialisation took hold. Recent historical research on the rural family has exposed this distinction as a simplification: throughout the middle ages, families came in a variety of types and sizes. High mortality rates and low life expectancy were significant factors: for one thing, this meant that grandparents did not always survive long enough to be part of the extended family household: as late as the end of the seventeenth century, the average life expectancy in England was 32.[9]

Despite this variety, however, the extended family was the most widespread form in pre-industrial times. The benefits of this structure for an agrarian society are readily apparent. In a peasant family which was of necessity self-sustaining, it was important that everybody in the family worked, including women and children; grandparents assisted with child rearing and domestic duties. Other extended family members – such as cousins – may have been part of the household, providing additional labour to work the land. Most households, then, comprised a selection of: grandparents, parents, children, servants and other kin.[10] The household was crowded, and privacy did not exist. Nor, according to French historian Philippe Ariès, did the ideas of childhood or family, as we understand them.

In his influential 1962 book *Centuries of Childhood*, Ariès argued that the medieval vision of a child was as a small adult, which was how they were depicted by artists. Once they reached the age of seven, children were sent out to work, often as apprentices, where they could work as domestic servants in the household of another family.[11] This common practice had two consequences: many households contained children who were not born of the parents; and many children were removed from their own families, preventing a consistent bond developing between parents and children. Ariès remarked that for many centuries, the family was a social, rather than a sentimental, reality.[12] His thesis was that 'the concept of the family was unknown in the Middle Ages [...] it originated in the fifteenth and sixteenth centuries [...] and reached its full expression in the seventeenth century'.[13]

One contributing factor to this process was the introduction of schooling, which progressively replaced apprenticeship from the fifteenth century. As children came to spend more time at home, the family changed its focus, to incorporate their presence; an 'increasingly sentimental relationship between parents and children' began to develop.[14] This change occurred first within wealthier families, including the emerging middle class; as late as the nineteenth century, the poor – that is, the majority – 'was still living like medieval families'.[15] But a significant shift, at least within the upper and middle classes, occurred when the family 'began to hold society at a distance, to push it back beyond a steadily extending zone of private life'.[16] This shift was first apparent in the Netherlands in the seventeenth century.

There were a number of factors which converged in the Netherlands in the seventeenth century. Holland was Protestant, embracing individualism and hard work, and, in its Calvinist inflection, cleanliness, order and thrift. Whereas the rest of Europe remained largely rural, the newly formed Dutch republic had no landless peasantry, and possessed a strong mercantile class. Most of the population lived in towns, where the middle class predominated: this was 'the first bourgeois state'.[17] People lived in households much smaller than the European norm: the average number per house in Dutch homes was 4 or 5, at a time when as many as 25 shared a household in Paris.[18] The Dutch had an advanced schooling system, and a limited use of domestic servants. These factors combined to produce a society where 'the family centred itself on the child and family life centred on the home, only in the Dutch home it occurred about a hundred years earlier than elsewhere'.[19]

Foreign visitors to Holland at the time expressed surprise at the degree of attention paid by the Dutch to their children, to their homes, and to domestic cleanliness[20]; surprising also was the authority exercised by the woman of the household. This new domestic zone was a feminised space, as reflected in the paintings of Vermeer. These works depict a novel interior mode: an ordered space, a still environment, 'a setting for private acts and personal moments' performed especially by women. The women in these portraits occupy the room completely, 'emphatically, contentedly at home'.[21] The Dutch housewife did her own domestic chores, including shopping, and supervised the managing of the household, especially the kitchen. This was the pattern which became very familiar, through advertising, in the twentieth-century nuclear family; it emerged first in the Netherlands in the seventeenth century, and was adopted in middle-class households throughout Europe a century later: 'Domesticity, privacy, comfort, the concept of the home and the family: these are, literally, principal elements of the Bourgeois Age.'[22]

The structure of houses changed in the eighteenth century to enhance the privacy and domestic intimacy savoured by the bourgeois family. The typical medieval household had beds throughout the house; now they were confined to discrete bedrooms, affording a new privacy. This interior zone of comfort and order was increasingly confined to parents and their children; servants, other kin and friends were excluded. As the middle class gained political power from the 1830s on, it imposed its ideal of the family. This ideal comprised the male breadwinner, wife and children cosily at home,[23] a newly sentimental and protective attitude to children lovingly depicted in painting and literature. In the early twentieth century, electricity and so-called 'labour-saving devices' entrenched the middle-class housewife as the household manager, especially in nations like the USA and Australia where few domestic servants were employed.

One final development took place in the early twentieth century to cement the strictly conjugal family as the norm in the USA and elsewhere in the western world. This concerned the status of the elderly, and was directly related to the rapid industrialisation and urbanisation in Western nations, particularly intense in the late nineteenth and early twentieth centuries. In the USA, the so-called 'scientific management' of the workforce produced studies correlating age with productivity, showing a decline for workers over 45. The result was the 'discovery of aging as a social problem',[24] the introduction of retirement, the problematising of old age – the word 'geriatrics' was coined in 1909[25] – and age discrimination. In social terms, unemployment and poverty became more common for the elderly, who were often separated from their families due to migration. If the aged could not be cared for by their extended family, their only refuge often was the 'poor-house', a Dickensian nightmare abode. The solution adopted by the state was the development of the old-age home, many of which were opened from the 1930s. If the elderly or infirm grandparents could now be consigned to institutionalised care with a reasonably good conscience, the stage was set for the flourishing of the two-generational nuclear family.

Whereas the rural extended family had been largely self-sufficient in terms of food production and basic needs, the nuclear family of the twentieth century operated within an industrialised consumer economy. The father retained patriarchal authority, but he was now a wage-slave hired on an individual basis: the factory or office, rather than the family, became the basis of social organisation.[26] Children, removed from the workforce by child labour legislation, became pure consumers. The mother, largely confined to the home, was the household manager, but deprived of the support previously provided within the extended family.

The term 'nuclear family' was coined in 1947, at the dawn of the nuclear age. Its 'golden era' was the 1950s, when it received theoretical support from American sociologists such as Talcott Parsons. Parsons argued that the 'isolated nuclear family' was 'the only type of family that does not conflict with the requirements of an industrial economy'.[27] He proposed that the nuclear family had two main functions: the socialisation of children; and 'tension management' of adults. In other respects, Parsons acknowledged the 'loss of function' of the modern family, since the family unit itself did not engage in economic production, while many of the family's traditional functions had been taken over by social structures.[28] Yet Parsons had no doubt of the superiority of the nuclear family model, which allowed the individual to pursue his or her interests 'free from the restraints imposed by customary or traditional group loyalties'.[29] Another advocate for the nuclear family, William Goode, celebrated in 1963 the worldwide changes in family life that allowed 'the emancipation of the individual from the authoritative control of the group', permitting 'the individual to escape from familial control'.[30]

It is important to note that while the nuclear family assumed normative status in the USA, Australia and many European nations by the 1950s, this was not the case in much of the world, where the extended family remains the norm. In Africa, for example, the traditional extended family is treasured, and the idea of sending grandparents to government-run homes for the elderly is considered a 'wicked' sign of ingratitude.[31] In China and Japan, likewise, until very recently older people were looked after by their own family members.[32] The 'generational contract' within three-generational families entails a reciprocity, whereby parents bring up children and in return are supported by their children in old age.[33] These reciprocal ties are much stronger in the extended family than in the nuclear. The jettisoning of this generational contract is sardonically depicted in an episode of *The Simpsons*, in which Homer recounts to his family how he persuaded his father to sell his house, transfer his wealth to Homer, and move in with the family. 'How long before you shipped him off to the Old Folks' Home?' asks daughter Lisa. 'About two weeks', Homer replies, to gleeful laughter from his nuclear family.[34]

Representing the acceptable family

There is ample representation of the acceptable – that is, nuclear – family in the twentieth century. The major generators of this imagery were advertising and American television. From the 1920s, advertising projected an image of the ideal nuclear family, united in its idyllic, insular domestic world – and united in consumption. Advertising targeted the housewife, constructed as the home manager and director of family consumption. She was often addressed directly in the ads, as the responsible provider, as the home-maker liberated from domestic drudgery by the newest labour-saving devices, and also as someone with a duty to maintain her physical attractiveness for her husband – with the aid of beauty and health consumer products.

A typical magazine advertisement of the 1950s, for the product Kellog's Pep depicts the husband returning home from work, telling his wife: 'Gosh, honey, you seem to thrive on cooking, cleaning and dusting – and I'm all tuckered out by closing time. What's the answer?' His wife, wearing an apron, holding a feather duster, while wearing lipstick and makeup, replies: 'Vitamins, darling! I always get my vitamins!'

The consumerist moral, spelled out at the top of the advertisement, is that 'the harder a wife works, the cuter she looks!'[35]

If the 1950s was the heyday of the nuclear family, this golden era was lovingly reflected in a number of popular American TV sitcoms, including *Father Knows Best* (1954–1960), which depicted the family from the parents' point of view, and *Leave it To Beaver* (1957–1963), which offered the child's perspective. These programmes showcased the nuclear family as an enduringly happy and hardy unit, able to overcome any problems or obstacles. Many sitcoms of this ilk maintained the advertising industry's idealised image of the modern family throughout the 1960s, as divorce became more prevalent, and the impact of the feminist movement revealed the intolerable burden often faced by women within the nuclear family. Sitcoms in the 1960s showed the nuclear family triumphing in all circumstances, including, in *Bewitched* (1964–1972), the incorporation of a witch, who repeatedly chooses to suppress her supernatural powers in the interest of conforming as a conventional housewife.

There were alternative families depicted in the 1960s TV comedies, but these were treated as adorable oddities, antiquated fish muddling through modernity's waters. *The Beverly Hillbillies* (1962–1971) featured a rural extended family, complete with a possum-eating granny, who are transplanted into the wealthiest part of modern Los Angeles. While their homespun honesty is respected, the hillbilly clan are the figures of affectionate fun: they are backward, rustic and recalcitrant in their outmoded ways. *The Addams Family* (1964–1966) similarly is out of place in the modern consumer world. They too are an old-fashioned extended family, incorporating a grandma, eccentric uncle and numerous other kin, as well as servants, within the household. The Addams Family is a relic of an aristocratic, pre-industrial world: Gomez the father does not work, but generates family wealth from shares; the children are not consumers; the family is oblivious to the charms of advertising and all aspects of the industrial consumer society. From the point-of-view of consumer modernity, they are a comical version of the unacceptable family, complete with comical monsters – the hand-creature Thing and hair-creature Cousin Itt – as kin within the old extended family.

American commercial television stubbornly clung to the idealised image of the nuclear family into the 1970s, even as internal tensions and family breakdown disrupted this image in messy reality. The producers of *The Brady Brunch* (1969–1974) originally wrote the character of Carol as a divorcee – but this acknowledgment of the real world was vetoed by the network. Single-parent families were invariably shown as the result of the unfortunate death of a spouse: single parents existed on TV only as widowed, temporarily. The sitcoms held out the promise, as in *The Brady Bunch*, of incomplete families being made whole again.

It was left to public television to provide a more realistic depiction of the modern family. The 1973, PBS series *An American Family* was celebrated at the time as a twelve-part exercise in TV verité, the forerunner of countless reality TV programmes. Its intimate portrayal of the Loud family – American middle class, nuclear – heightened the tensions and conflicts within the family, culminating in the family's breakup onscreen. The reality TV genre, which became a TV staple in the 1990s, often focused on the nuclear family, as in the 1992 Australian programme *Sylvania Waters*. Reality TV of this type collapses together the modes of documentary and soap opera, so that each episode follows a dramatic pattern leading to a cliff-hanger moment; strains and discord within the family are inevitably exacerbated.

Hollywood cinema of the 1980s was fascinated by the threat to the family from within, generally with the husband cast as the guilty party. Jack Nicholson's character in *The Shining* (Stanley Kubrick, 1980) at least has the excuse of being possessed by an ancient spirit as he terrorises his wife and son. In *Fatal Attraction* (Adrian Lyne, 1987), Michael Douglas's character endangers his family due to his infidelity. His affair unleashes his spurned mistress, transformed into an implacable monster, onto his family. *The Stepfather* (Joseph Ruben, 1987) offers an interesting twist to the menaced family, in that the danger emanates from a man who reveres the idea of family. The protagonist has so thoroughly absorbed the 1950s *Leave it to Beaver* ideal of the perfect family, that he is unable to tolerate any imperfection from family members. This psychopath finds single-mother suburban families, completing them – briefly – as the husband and father. When the reality inevitably falls short of the ideal, he murders the family and sets off for a new suburb and new family.

The violence in these 1980s films was also found in crime fiction, which from the 1960s increasingly focused on scarred individuals, the products of failed families or parental abuse. The guilty father is the subject of many crime novels, including the recent best-selling trilogy by Stieg Larsson, beginning with *The Girl with the Dragon Tattoo* (originally published in Sweden in 2005). This trilogy of novels, widely translated and adapted for cinema, constructs a stark moral universe in which the sins of the patriarchy are legion, in both private and public life. Patriarchal public figures are generally guilty of the sexual abuse of women alongside other heinous pursuits including anti-Semitism and the trafficking of prostitutes. Families are portrayed in this series as 'potentially dangerous insofar as they impose a closed world in which abuse can take place, or even be taught'.[36] The novels depict the efforts of the two heroes – one a crusading male journalist, the other a young female computer hacker – to disclose and thwart the sinister activities of powerful and clandestine hidden organisations, which are portrayed as 'an evil extension of the potentially perilous family that wields such power over us from birth'.[37]

A similarly adverse portrayal of the Western nuclear family was made in the film *Natural Born Killers* (Oliver Stone, 1994). This film, whose theme is violence and the representation of violence, contains a dark parody of the classic 1950s American family sitcom, entitled 'I Love Mallory'. In this travesty, the father is unemployed, abusive and violent. His crude behaviour, including sexual abuse of his own daughter and contemptuous disregard of his wife, is accompanied by comic sound effects and cued laughter from a studio audience. The discord between these sitcom conventions and the repulsive behaviour of the father reveals, in extreme form, the tensions within the nuclear family normally repressed in the cheery sitcom mode. The authority of the patriarchal figure is portrayed not as the centre of a benevolent family unit, but as the generator of incest, sexual abuse, female misery and ongoing violent behaviour.

In the twenty-first century, the notion of family in the West has shifted far from the 1950s model. Many parents co-habit but are not married; divorced parents share child custody; single-parenthood and step-parenthood are common; same-sex parenting is increasingly visible. Even commercial TV has relaxed some its taboos, depicting, in *Modern Family* (from 2009), same-sex parents and a step-parent family, alongside a conventional family. It should be noted, however, that all three of these modern families are variants of the nuclear family model, including the gay parent family. Alternative models of child-rearing practiced within the gay community, such as multiple parenting or mentoring, are not featured. Reality TV delights in detailing dysfunctional nuclear families, the more eccentric or irresponsible the better, as evident in the popularity of *The Osbournes* (2002–2005), featuring the drug-addled parenting of rock musician Ozzie Osbourne. Most of these families, however, survive – indeed relish – the attention of the cameras, unlike the Louds of the 1970s. *The Simpsons*, attacked by conservatives in the US for its unflattering depiction of the typical suburban family, likewise keeps the nuclear family intact. Wife and mother Marj has left her oafish husband and delinquent son on several occasions, but always returns as home-maker for her lovable misfit family.

Representing the unacceptable family

If the nuclear family was depicted in the popular culture of the twentieth century as the acceptable, desirable, modern Western family, how has the unacceptable family been represented? The unacceptable family has been portrayed in various guises, within different genres – but several common themes emerge. The first characteristic is that the unacceptable, dangerous family is generally some form of the extended family. Whereas the nuclear family attained normative status in White Anglo-Saxon Protestant (WASP) cultures, members of the extended family are often Catholic, emanating originally from old Europe, particularly the south of Europe where Catholic extended families still predominate. Whereas the nuclear family functions as a small unit of individualised members, the larger extended family is depicted as a network of reciprocal ties and obligations for family members. When this characteristic is portrayed in a critical light, the extended family is revealed as corrupt and corrupting. It is painted as a monstrous, unacceptable form of family organisation due to its crippling of individuals' freedom and potential.

The unacceptable nature of the extended family's bonds and obligations within a modern society are often dramatised in the figure of the immigrant, or offspring of immigrants, caught between the old culture and the new. An early example of this dramatic tension is found in the 1957 film The *Brothers Rico*, a late film noir directed by Phil Karlson. The protagonist of this film is Eddie Rico, an Italian-American who was once an accountant for the mob but is now a successful businessman in Florida. Eddie has an adoring WASP wife; they are about to complete their nuclear family by adopting a baby. On the very day they are due at the adoption agency to receive their baby, Eddie is contacted by his younger brother, who is still embroiled in the Mafia and is now fugitive from the mob. Eddie has turned his back on organised crime; with his glamorous wife and legitimate business, he is the picture of American modernity. He had previously mocked his Sicilian roots, its old country superstitions and peasant beliefs. But his Uncle Sid, a senior mob figure, appeals to Eddie to track down his two brothers, both of whom are in danger, having crossed the syndicate. Much to his wife's despair, Eddie is unable to resist the lure of the old family call. The extended family, mired in Mafia corruption, performs the role of the femme fatale in this film, luring Eddie away from his new family respectability and towards his doom.

The extended family members are portrayed as untrustworthy, repugnant individuals. Uncle Sid is the most sinister figure, manipulating

Eddie to locate his brothers so that they can be liquidated. Eddie's mother is shown to be complicit in the old world corruption and intrigue, despite her love for her sons. She is hysterical, Catholic – she has a shrine to Mary in her New York apartment – crippled (due to a World War II injury) but also crippling, her loyalty to Sid and the extended family proving a liability in Eddie's efforts to protect his brothers from the mob.

This is a film suffused with family, both new and old: hope and burden, prospect and trap. 'You can't buck the system', Eddie is told, as his brothers attempt to escape the clutches of their uncle. The younger brother wants to quit the mob to start a family with his young pregnant wife. Eddie's wife exhorts him to leave behind the 'filth and corruption and killing' represented by his old family. In a bloody denouement, Eddie's two brothers are killed, while Eddie only escapes by shooting his mob boss uncle in his mother's kitchen. He is free to start a new, non-corrupted, nuclear family, but only after violently severing all ties to his old, unacceptable extended family.

The best-known dramatisation of the Italian-American old world-new world conflict is found in *The Godfather* (1972) and *Godfather II* (1974), directed by Francis Ford Coppola. Here the extended Sicilian-American family is fused with the Mafia, a network of organised crime and violence. The family patriarch is also the Godfather, paternal figure exercising control over his community through fear and unquestioned authority. The Godfather's authority usurps that of the state, claiming the monopoly of violence exercised by the modern state. The citizens of the Italian-American community professing allegiance to the Godfather are like members of one huge extended family, complete with the reciprocal ties and duties binding the traditional extended family.

This relationship is apparent in the opening scene of *The Godfather*, when a member of the community asks Don Corleone for a favour on the day of his daughter's wedding. This Italian-American comes reluctantly to the Godfather for justice, as he had previously abided by the laws and values of the state. 'I believe in America', he tells the Godfather. 'I raised my daughter in American fashion.' When his daughter was savagely beaten, he 'went to the police, like a good American', only to feel betrayed by the courts when the perpetrators were given a suspended sentence. 'Then I said to my wife, for justice we must go to Don Corleone.' The Godfather's response is: 'Why did you go to the police? Why didn't you come to me first?' Initially indignant that this citizen had preferred the police and 'courts of law' for justice and protection, Don Corleone only grants the favour of vengeance when sufficient 'respect' is shown by his client, and when it is understood that this favour binds his subject to a reciprocal obligation, when he will be 'asked' in the future to perform a service for the Godfather.

The *Godfather* films exercised enormous appeal, much of it derived from the portrayal of this extended Sicilian-American family, operating as an exotic culture within the borders of American modernity. Family life is depicted as glamorous, exciting, passionate, coloured by Catholic rituals, full of internecine intrigue, and powered by a fierce loyalty to the family upheld by all its members. Yet ultimately this extended family is associated with violence, fear, corruption and death. Despite the great fascination the family exerts, it is portrayed as monstrous in its demands on individuals, most significantly on the figure of the Godfather.

The main arc of the two films concerns the fate of Michael Corleone, at first an outsider to the family business, then gradually drawn in to assume the role of Godfather. A flashback near the end of *Godfather II* shows a young Michael, mocked as a 'droopy thing' and 'Joe College' by his elder brother Sonny, the heir-apparent to run the family business. Sonny is enraged when Michael informs the family he has enlisted in the marines following the attack on Pearl Harbour. For Sonny and his father, enlisted men are 'saps' because they risk their lives for strangers. Michael counters that they 'risk their lives for their country', but a furious Sonny admonishes him: 'Your country ain't your blood.'

At this stage, Michael pledges loyalty to the state and to the nation above that of the family. His planned destiny lies outside the family business; when the family lawyer and adopted son tells him, 'Your father has plans for you', Michael retorts: 'I have my own plans for my future.' Michael's outsider status is shared by his girlfriend Kay, who first experiences the extended family allure at the wedding of the Don's daughter. Kay is a WASP who represents Michael's yearning for a life beyond his Sicilian-American family. As he is gradually drawn into the orbit of the family, assuming the Godfather position, Kay is increasingly revolted by the corruption and violence for which her husband is responsible. In a climactic scene, she condemns Michael and the extended family that has claimed him. She attacks the foundations of the family to which her husband demands complete allegiance, by revealing that she has had an abortion. In an emotional outburst, she likens their marriage to an abortion, 'something that's unholy, and evil'. Her revulsion is evident, as is Michael's fury, when she tells him: 'It was a son and I had it killed because this must all end.'

Kay is expelled from the family following her disclosure. It is Michael, however, who is revealed as the broken figure. The burden of his responsibility as head of the family, combined with the guilt associated with the violent acts he has authorised, has rendered him inhuman. He is a monstrous figure by the end, politically powerful yet profoundly alone.

The monstrous-familial

A monstrous version of the family appeared in several American horror films of the 1970s, at a time when the nuclear family had long been entrenched as the norm within industrial consumer society. The grotesque families portrayed in these films represent the monstrous Other of the acceptable family.

In *The Texas Chainsaw Massacre*, 1974, directed by Tobe Hooper, the massacre is conducted by a clan of cannibals presided over by the chainsaw-wielding Leatherface. Their decrepit house is located near the slaughter-house, where, we learn, family members had once worked. The furniture in the house is made from human bones, while they dine at family dinners on sausages of processed human meat. They are an extended family, as Grandpa is in residence. During the bizarre family dinner, at which the sole surviving member of a travelling group of young people is held captive, we are told that: 'Grandpa's the best killer there ever was. Did sixty in five minutes once.' Grandpa and the other family members, it seems, have been displaced from their profession as meat-workers by the advancing industrialisation of the industry.

Now the family survives by preying on strangers, who become their food. They are a grotesque parody of the traditional rural family: three-generational, self-sufficient, pre-industrial (except for the chainsaw). Leatherface and his clan represent a throwback to the old self-sustaining rustic family, rendered here irrationally violent, monstrous and terrifying. The dinner-party captive only survives because the family observes the ritual of allowing Grandpa to perform the kill, as he had once done in the slaughter-house. But the ancient grandparent is too feeble to perform the ritual slaying, allowing the terrified young woman to escape to a nearby road, to civilisation, and to modernity.

A similar throwback family is at the centre of *The Hills Have Eyes* (Wes Craven, 1977). This clan survives in the Nevada desert, led by the patriarch Papa Jupiter, who had been abandoned by his horrified father, disgusted by the 'monster child' that had grown into a 'devil man'. Jupiter raised a family in the desert with a prostitute: his three sons are malformed and more monstrous than their father. As they have grown up in a former nuclear testing site, the implication is that mutation has occurred, further warping a less than stellar genetic stock. Like the Texas Chainsaw family, this is a cannibal clan, hunting for any food, including human.

'Only animals live out there' is the warning issued to the middle-class American family intent on driving through this particular zone of the Nevada desert. In the tradition familiar to the horror genre, the victims ignore all advice to avoid the forbidden area, and soon become prey. Several family members are killed, and a baby is stolen, gleefully celebrated by the cannibals as 'thanksgiving dinner'. The baby is saved by the combined efforts of the family dog and Jupiter's daughter, who recoils from her family's cannibal activity, killing one of her brothers to free the baby.

The Hills Have Eyes suggests a parallel between the two families, as if the conventional middle-class family, strayed from its urban base, meets its dark reflection in the desert clan. This Other is deranged, violent and cannibalistic; it is also once again a travesty of the rural, poor, self-sustaining, pre-industrial family.

A similar parallel structures *The Lost Boys* (Joel Schumacher, 1987), in which a divorced single mother relocates her family of two sons to a part of California apparently teeming with vampires. Her elder son is taken in by a gang of delinquent vampires, and spends most of the film hovering between the two camps. The vampire clan is headed by Max, a patriarchal figure who seeks to unite the two families by converting the single mother to vampirism. This ambition is a dark parody of 1970s TV sitcoms: Max wants a 'bloodsucking Brady Bunch', as one of the characters remarks. The parallel between the acceptable and unacceptable families is relentlessly enforced, down to matching family dogs (one demonic). Ironically, the nuclear family is only saved by the actions of their grandfather, previously living alone in the area and wiser in the ways of monsters than his younger kin.

The polygamous family

Polygamy – or more technically polygyny, in which a man has multiple simultaneous wives – is a common practice in many parts of the world, including Africa and the Muslim world. In Islamic law, a man is permitted to have up to four wives; every Arab nation except Tunisia recognises the legitimacy of polygamous marriages.[38] Although the Old Testament contains several references to polygamy, the practice has been forbidden in Christian culture since it was condemned by St Augustine in the fifth century. Its presence in the West is mainly restricted to an outlaw existence within splinter groups of the Mormon church. Joseph

Smith claimed in 1831 that he received a revelation supporting 'plural marriage' for Mormon men. Followers of Smith practiced polygamy in Utah, despite opposition from the US Government, which declared the practice illegal in 1862. In 1890, the Mormon church was pressured by the state into renouncing plural marriage, resulting in 'Mormon fundamentalist' splinter groups leaving the church to continue practicing polygamy, as is still done today.

If the extended family has been represented as unacceptable from the perspective of the normative nuclear family, then the polygamous family is regarded in the West as highly unacceptable – hence its illegal status. It is not so much an extended as a multiple family. The several wives produce many children, presided over by the family patriarch (a pre-feminist gender dynamic it has in common with the traditional rural extended family). In other ways, however, the polygamous family shares characteristics of the nuclear family. A man with three wives and many children has a similar role to the husband/father of the nuclear family, except that the single wife is multiplied. This otherness yet familiarity of the modern polygamous family is explored in great detail in the HBO television series *Big Love* (2006–2011).

This series depicts the lifestyle of Bill Henrickson and his three wives in contemporary Utah. Due to the illegal status of polygamy, Bill publicly lives with his first wife Barbara, but the two 'sister wives' live in adjoining houses. Bill sleeps with a different wife every night, according to a roster system. *Big Love* plays with the fascination viewers may have with this unorthodox family structure and how it works (the answer, it is revealed in the first series, is with the assistance of Viagra).

This illegal family lifestyle is rendered more palatable in the series by the modernity of the household, which mirrors that of the conventional nuclear family. Bill is a very successful businessman, who can afford three houses for three wives; the wives and children consume the latest products and watch TV like members of any conventional family. Their suburban lifestyle is in contrast to the compound at Juniper Creek, where a cult-like Mormon fundamentalist group lives, in nineteenth-century puritanical dress, under the rule of a 'prophet'. The moral position adopted by the series casts the compound and its devious prophet as the unacceptable face of polygamy, while Bill's family is depicted more favourably. Bill – who shuns the reclusive and retrograde community in the compound – is, with the exception of polygamy, a model of American respectability: successful businessman, patriot, Republican (he runs successfully for the state Senate). The behaviour of the modern polygamous family, as represented in *Big Love*, is a strange combination of the familiar and unfamiliar, often shown to humorous effect. As an example, at one stage Bill is dating another woman with the prospect of making her Wife Number Four; he and the woman are in the front seat of his parked car, while two of the 'sister-wives' are in the back seat, contributing to the experience and to the prospect of gaining a new wife.

Bill's family ethos is unacceptable on many levels. An educated middle-class audience will find the sexist power dynamic offensive: Bill's wives are, for the most part, old-fashioned 'home-makers', whose chief duty is to produce and raise more children, the better to honour the family patriarch, and God. In a similar manner, the AMC series *Mad Men* casts a critical retrospective eye over the sexist behaviour of pre-feminist men, in the workforce and within the nuclear family, of the early 1960s: Don Draper's reprehensible attitude to women is revealed as the reason for the failure of his marriage.

Big Love recuperates the unacceptable family to the extent that the exotic is framed within parameters of the familiar. The familiar in this case includes the modern post-industrial consumer society, even the soap-opera nature of the domestic dramas occurring within the multiple family. This outlawed family system is represented not as monstrous or even as destructive (as the extended family is shown in *The Godfather*) but as an alien practice surviving in the domestic zone, the unfamiliar within the familiar, the unacceptable within the acceptable.

Conclusion

In this chapter I have concentrated on representations of the family from within a specific cultural sphere – Protestant, industrial, consumer society – which has enthroned the nuclear family as a chief social norm since the early twentieth century. From within this orbit, other modes of family, including the traditional extended family, have been represented as undesirable, unacceptable, even monstrous. Another cultural sphere, one in which the extended family were still the social norm, would have a different perspective, a different dividing-line between the acceptable and unacceptable. Such a perspective would regard the nuclear family as a 'parody' of the family, as it has been called,[39] for its callous jettisoning of the inter-generational contract, its emotionally cold assembling of atomised individuals, its intolerable strain on women, and its substitution of consumption for the support of extended family members. Many would find these characteristics of the nuclear family unacceptable, but the representations of the last century have told a different story.

Notes

1. Barbara Creed, *The Monstrous-Feminine: Film, Feminism, Psychoanalysis*, p. 10.
2. Ibid., p. 14.
3. Ibid.
4. Giorgio Agamben, *Homo Sacer: Sovereign Power and Bare Life*, p. 2.
5. I. M. Finley, *The Ancient Greeks*, p. 145.
6. John Boardman, *The Oxford History of the Classical World*, p. 7.
7. Ibid., p. 7.
8. Jan Turowski, 'Inadequacy of the Theory of the Nuclear Family: The Polish Experience', p. 23.
9. Diana Gittins, *The Family in Question: Changing Households and Familiar Ideologies* (Basingstoke: Macmillan, 1993), p. 8.
10. Ibid., p. 20.
11. Philippe Ariès, *Centuries of Childhood: A Social History of Family Life*, p. 365.
12. Ibid., p. 368.
13. Ibid., p. 353.
14. Ibid., p. 370.
15. Ibid., p. 404.
16. Ibid., p. 398.
17. Witold Rybczynski, *Home: A Short History of an Idea*, p. 54.
18. Ibid., p. 59.
19. Ibid., p. 60.
20. Ibid.
21. Ibid., p. 71.
22. John Lukacs, *The Bourgeois Interior*, cited in Rybczynski, *Home*, p. 51.
23. Gittins, *The Family in Question*, pp. 33–34.
24. Robert C. Atchley, & Amanda S. Barusch, *Social Forces & Aging: An Introduction to Social Gerontology*, p. 60.
25. Jill Lepore, 'Twilight: Growing Old and Even Older', p. 34.
26. Stuart Ewen, *Captains of Consciousness: Advertising and the Roots of the Consumer Society* (New York, NY: McGraw-Hill, 1976), p. 117.
27. David Cheal, *Family and the State of Theory*, p. 5.
28. Talcott Parsons, 'The American Family' in Michael Anderson (ed.) *Sociology of the Family: Selected Readings*.
29. C.C. Harris, 'The Changing Relation Between Family and Societal Form in Western Society' in Michael Anderson (ed.) *Sociology of the Family: Selected Readings*, p. 397.
30. Ibid.
31. Akpovire Oduaran, & Choja Oduaran, 'Grandparents and HIV and AIDS in Sub-Saharan Africa' in Misa Izhuhara (ed.) *Ageing and Intergenerational Relations: Family Reciprocity from a Global Perspective*, p. 103.
32. Ibid., p. 102.
33. Misa Izhuhara, 'Introduction' in *Ageing and Intergenerational Relations*, p. 5.
34. *The Simpsons*, 'Lisa's First Word', Episode 10 Season 4, Fox, 1992.
35. This advertisement is included in a section of 'Sexist Vintage Ads' on the website Sociological Images at http://thesocietypages.org/socimages/?s=cerealdm2711 (accessed 3 February 2012).
36. Tim Parks, 'The Moralist', p. 10.

37. Ibid., p. 12.
38. Philippe Fargues, 'The Arab World: the Family as Fortress', p. 346.
39. Ewen, *Captains of Consciousness: Advertising and the Roots of the Consumer Society*, p. 184.

References

Agamben, Giorgio, *Homo Sacer: Sovereign Power and Bare Life* (Stanford, CA: Stanford University Press, 1998).
Anderson, Michael (ed.) *Sociology of the Family: Selected Readings*, 2nd edition (Harmondsworth: Penguin, 1980).
Ariès, Philippe, *Centuries of Childhood: A Social History of Family Life*, trans. Robert Baldick (New York, NY: Alfred A. Knopf, 1962).
Atchley, Robert C. & Barusch, Amanda S., *Social Forces & Aging: An Introduction to Social Gerontology*, 10th edition (Belmont, CA: Wadsworth/Thomson Learning, 2004).
Boardman, John et al. (eds.) *The Oxford History of the Classical World* (Oxford: Oxford University Press, 1995).
Cheal, David, *Family and the State of Theory* (New York, NY: Harvester Wheatsheaf, 1991).
Creed, Barbara, *The Monstrous-Feminine: Film, Feminism, Psychoanalysis* (London: Routledge, 1993).
Ewen, Stuart, *Captains of Consciousness: Advertising and the Roots of the Consumer Society* (New York, NY: McGraw-Hill, 1976).
Fargues, Philippe, 'The Arab World: the Family as Fortress' in André Burguière et al. (eds.) *A History of the Family Vol. Two* (Cambridge, MA: Polity Press, 1996).
Finley, I. M., *The Ancient Greeks* (Harmondsworth: Penguin, 1963).
Gittins, Diana, *The Family in Question: Changing Households and Familiar Ideologies* (Basingstoke: Macmillan, 1993).
Izhuhara, Misa (ed.) *Ageing and Intergenerational Relations: Family Reciprocity from a Global Perspective* (Bristol: Policy Press, 2010).
Lenero-Otera, Luis (ed.) *Beyond the Nuclear Family Model: Cross-Cultural Perspectives* (London: Sage, 1977).
Lepore, Jill, 'Twilight: Growing Old and Even Older', *The New Yorker*, 14 March 2011, pp. 30–35.
Parks, Tim, 'The Moralist', *The New York Review of Books*, Vol. LVIII, No. 10, 9 June 2011, pp. 8–12.
Rybczynski, Witold, *Home: A Short History of an Idea* (London: Pocket Books, 2001).
Turowski, Jan, 'Inadequacy of the Theory of the Nuclear Family: The Polish Experience', in Lenero-Otera, Luis (ed.) *Beyond the Nuclear Family Model: Cross-Cultural Perspectives* (London: Sage, 1977).

8
Unacceptability and Prosaic Life in *Breaking Bad*

Elliott Logan

The American television drama series *Breaking Bad* is concerned with movements between states of the prosaic and acceptable, and the extraordinary and unacceptable. Set in contemporary Albuquerque, New Mexico, it tells the story of a formerly promising research scientist now cancer-ridden high school teacher, Walter White (Bryan Cranston). Faced with death and his family's financial ruin, Walt begins a criminal life manufacturing methamphetamine in the peripheral wilderness of the south-western desert, riven with cross-border conflict with Mexican cartels and US law enforcement. Modulating domestic, gangster and Western melodrama, the series structures oppositions between the prosaic or everyday and the extraordinary or spectacular; between the socially acceptable and the unacceptable.

Rita Felski described the everyday as 'the essential, taken-for-granted continuum of mundane activities that frames our forays into more esoteric or exotic worlds', providing 'the unavoidable basis for all other forms of human endeavour'.[1] The unacceptable and the acceptable might thus be understood as existing apart from each other; everyday, prosaic, acceptable worlds, and 'esoteric', 'exotic', unacceptable worlds forming frames of mutual separation.[2] A close examination of moments from the second season episode 'Over' shows how, moving between generically distinct spaces while blurring the lines that separate them, *Breaking Bad* unsettles conceptions of the unacceptable and the acceptable as being worlds apart.[3] In these moments, rather than unacceptable worlds and ways of life pushing in on their desired opposite, there is something unacceptable about or within the prosaic social world of contemporary bourgeois life that the series presents.

Frames of acceptability

Moving between worlds in *Breaking Bad* involves switching generic frames.[4] Switching generic frames, or lessening attention to one while focusing it upon another, *Breaking Bad* modulates its dramatic intensity. Marked shifts of generic frames and their possibilities may occur within episodes themselves, or individual episodes may be dominated more by the overtly heroic than the quietly prosaic, or vice versa. From the ultimate, heroic drama of the Western showdown, its characters must recover and resettle in the quiet, prosaic routines and performances of suburban life. The tension between these spaces is the subject of the melodramatic in Hollywood film as described by Deborah Thomas. For Thomas, such worlds are characterised by spatial dichotomy symbolising conflicts between social and other values. The world's social space – 'a domestic setting, a small town, a community, or some more general representation of civilisation' – is contrasted with an alternative space – 'the city's criminal underworld, a battlefield, the wilderness [...] where social values and expectations to some extent break down'.[5] These spatial boundaries do not define the limits of acceptability. The profitable harmony of the social space requires the repression or sublimation of individualist desires in favour of social interests. For Thomas, this repression in the domestic space gives rise to fantasies of 'augmentation' and fears of 'diminishment'. In the less constrained alternative space 'fantasies of violent self-assertion replace those which offer a mere appearance of domination – a front for the benefit of the outside world – within the marital and familial home'.[6] In Thomas's melodramatic world the prosaic, domestic space is not one of untroubled acceptability. It is a space of repression that gives rise to resentment and anxiety. Showing cracks in its veneer of domestic acceptability, the social space gives rise to fantasies of power and authority, qualities more able to be asserted in a more violent, less socially profitable, and more destructive alternative space elsewhere.

In Western and gangster films, this issue of acceptability and unacceptability is played out as violent drama between individuals set within or against a form of community. As Gilberto Perez put it, 'The reason the Western has the classic showdown between hero and villain take place on the main street of town is that the matter at stake is not a merely personal but a public, a social matter.'[7] Usually, the resolution of this conflict requires the repression of certain individual characteristics in favour of communal interests of peace, security, and profit. 'Usually what is seen as good,' wrote Perez, 'is what is seen to foster – and what is seen as bad is what it seen to threaten – the burgeoning social good'.[8] For the same reason, Robert Warshow claimed, the gangster striving for individual success and eminence is doomed. His doom is not because his means are unlawful, but because 'in the deeper layers of the modern consciousness, *all* means are unlawful, every attempt to succeed is an act of aggression [...] one is punished for success'.[9]

Robert B. Pippin suggested more exactly what the individual must sacrifice in favour of the communal interests Perez mentioned but did not describe:

> [I]f we believe writers like Albert Hirschman and many others, the central task in the founding of a modern political order was to find a way to denigrate, contain, and de-emphasize that chief pre-modern mark of distinction, *glory*, with all the militaristic and dangerous and violent dimensions of that task, in favour of a more scientific view of the primacy of the fear of death and the desire for peace.[10]

According to Pippin, the Western portrays this transition between social forms as deeply unsatisfactory and unstable:

> [T]he record of such an embourgeoisement is an incomplete and vexed one in the American experience, as the bourgeois virtues also seem to involve such a commitment to security, life, and peace that hypocrisy, self-deceit, and a prosaic form of life perhaps incapable of sustaining the required deep allegiance seem an inevitable consequence.[11]

Breaking Bad suggests that this dissatisfaction – the 'hypocrisy, self-deceit' and lack of 'deep allegiance' – still flow as undercurrents below the surface interactions of a 'prosaic form of life'. In its eruptions of hyperbolic, violent, passionate gesture, the series suggests that the troubling existence of these undercurrents can still be felt beneath – and will sometimes disrupt – the surface of everyday life.

Closely examining moments of the episode 'Over', the remainder of the chapter explores how through movements between worlds, and through varied repetitions of performance motifs across these movements, *Breaking Bad* articulates the split allegiance described by Pippin: between bourgeois acceptability and its deference to the social, and socially unacceptable assertions of individual eminence: the drive for glory.[12] Doing so, these moments trouble the conceptual separation of acceptable and unacceptable forms of life.

'Over'

The episode is notable for its sense of prosaic and domestic rhythms, rather than heroic and criminal exertions. The drama of Walt's narrative arc in the episode revolves around the hosting of a Sunday afternoon barbecue to celebrate his cancer remission, and his spirited involvement in home repairs during an extended leave of absence from his work as a teacher, and what is intended to be permanent leave from his work as a drug manufacturer. It is during the episode's barbecue sequence that the problem of Walt's relationship with his prosaic, domestic life explodes. Walt's everyday performance of timidity and deference is spectacularly shed, revealing his otherwise hidden, repressed desire to be recognised as holding authority and power, even if these qualities cannot be put to any positive social use.

The episode begins with a close-up of Walt's fist, its knuckles bruised and split. Walt sits in his bedroom considering his wounds received at the end of the previous episode upon receiving news of his cancer's remission. In the privacy of a bathroom, Walt responded to the life-giving information by pounding his fist into a wall-mounted hand dryer. The episode's opening moments thus invite consideration of Walt's ambivalent relationship to domestic life. With the unexpected retreat of Walt's cancer, the ultimate motivator to the achievement of something like a meaningful legacy – imminent death – has been stripped away. Its replacement is the promise of ongoing, prosaic life, with the limitations that accompany its attendant fear of mortality. Walt's dissatisfaction with this form of life in this domestic world – with the individual costs of its social demands, with its bland sublimations of personal creative energy and power – soon erupts at the barbecue held to celebrate the extension of just that life.

The barbecue sequence consists of two scenes. In the first, Walt's wife, Skyler (Anna Gunn), proposes a toast to recognise the struggle of Walt and his family with his illness, and the support given by their friends. She particularly recognises Elliott and Gretchen Schwartz, who are absent. The couple are Walt's former research colleagues, who are now wealthy, having obtained a patent related to the results of their research, from which Walt considers himself to have been excluded.[13] In the first season, Walt principally refuses their charitable offer to pay for his treatment but does not tell his family.[14] Thus, the phantom charity of wealthy strangers, rather than Walt's entrepreneurial skill and bravery in risk-taking, is recognised for keeping the family afloat. With these resentments riding high, Walt also makes a speech. Now taking swigs of beer, he explains that, when diagnosed with cancer, he asked himself 'Why me?' Now in remission, seemingly to live on, Walt tells his audience that he has asked himself the same, pitying question: 'Why me?' The apparent reassurance of continuing prosaic, everyday life provides no reassurance at all.

The second scene moves outside to the rear entertaining area where Walt, his teenage son Walter, Jr (R.J. Mitte), and his Drug Enforcement Administration (DEA) brother-in-law Hank (Dean Norris) drink tequila by the poolside. Walt, Jr is enraptured by Hank's stories of adventure; Walt is less engaged. On operations inside Mexico, Hank was involved in a deadly cartel bomb attack.[15] 'A little mercury switch, a 9-volt battery, three or four ounces of C4; that's how those cartel boys party,' is Hank's cavalier account of an incident that has left him with secret, post-traumatic stress that has shattered his previous confidence in his professional capacities and courage. Walt keeps himself at a reserved distance from Hank, who in his performative brashness asserts himself as an individual to form the scene's centre of gravity. Walt sits on the scene's periphery, apart from both his brother-in-law and his son, who in their mutual engagement in Hank's stories form a pair.

Hank unwittingly demonstrates his relative ignorance and intellectual clumsiness as he struggles to find the words to fully articulate the significance of his story of the cartel bombing. He verbally flails: 'What the hell's the word I'm looking for? Not a metaphor...not an analogy...it's a – Walt, what's the word I'm looking for?' His appeal to a higher intellectual authority is met only by Walt's drunken, contemptuous scoff. Moving on, Hank completes his story by denying the relevance or importance of the understanding he has failed to articulate. Hank further re-stabilises his place as the scene's centre of authority by gesturing to the tequila bottle with his hand and to Walt with his voice: 'Top me up there, will ya, buddy?'

It is under the implied, unquestioned thumb of Hank's self-assumed authority, supported by bravado rather than wisdom or ability, that Walt makes his reactive first move of the scene, albeit one that fails to transgress boundaries, or upset balances, of social acceptability. Filling Hank's shot glass and his own, Walt then tosses the contents of his son's cup into the garden bed, and pours a generous measure of spirit. An excited Walt, Jr looks to his father for further approval. Walt gives it in a truncated echo of Eastwood's famous dare. Eye cocked, leaning back, aloof, he finally breaks the tension: 'Go ahead.' Grinning, included in an exclusive club, Walt, Jr turns to his uncle with great enthusiasm. With his positive nod and encouraging grin Hank strengthens the sense of membership, stamps his own approval, and draws a new circle of authority, moving its bounds away from Walt. In contrast with Walt's distance, Hank leans in towards his nephew to join him in conspiracy. 'Better not let your mum see', he whispers. The three fire back their socially sanctioned shots. Walt, Jr's coughing and spluttering is met with roaring approval by Hank, who welcomes the young man into a masculine bond. 'I think I see a hair, maybe two!' The boy and his uncle are joined in shared jocularity and physical contact. In posture and expression, Walt maintains his resentful distance as Hank's boastful stories of excesses and achievements elsewhere progress.

Yet Hank's claims to individual eminence are surrendered the moment he notices Walt pouring the second shot of tequila into Walt Jr's cup. 'Kid's sixteen', he says, the register of his voice and posture now transformed. His bluster and laughter are replaced by the seriousness appropriate to defending a social boundary. Where he was loose, he is now tense. No longer unawares, he is now focused and ready. His body goes rigid as he grips his armrests. Dean Norris's performance signals Hank's choice to defend the boundaries of acceptability in this space. Walt also transforms his normal social performance. His face slips as if shedding a mask. In place of the apologetic and embarrassed manner that characterises his normal domestic facade is the face Walt wears in his other world, his world of driven criminal enterprise in which the community offers, in the words of Perez, 'no real fellowship but the fellowship of cash, no true sense of belonging but material belongings'.[16] Walt's eyes narrow and peer outwards, sunk in their sockets, accusing and threatening. Uncertain of where the boundaries of acceptability are now set, Walt, Jr again seeks unspoken advice from his uncle, the representative of social order. Walt's response is a demand for the recognition of his authority. Confronting his son with a scowl, and accusing his brother-in-law with a pointed finger while excluding him with an averted gaze, he shatters the atmosphere of mutuality between nephew and uncle by spitting at his son 'Waddya lookin' at *him* for?!'

Walt, Jr retreats into timid uncertainty as Walt reaches to refill his son's cup after the second swig. Escalation ensues. He is met with Hank's steely gaze and the bulwark of his hand. The two men stare across a raised hand versus a raised tequila bottle, a modern, bourgeois, domesticated echo of the Western showdown between gunslingers representing allegiance to the social good and its opposite. Hank's silent demand in response to Walt's attempts to pour his son a second drink – the gesture of dismissal and denial he makes with his face and hand – clashes extraordinarily with Walt's later violent, explosive, and publicly spectacular demand, made in full view of the assembled guests. Squaring off against Hank, Walt thunders, '*My* son! *My* bottle! *My* house!' Hank's is society's demand that Walt not do as he wants, that Walt defer his own desires to what is understood as the interest or at least the authority of the community; that he not let his son drink, or if he does, he allows only a taste, more a reminder of the acceptable limit than its transgression. By contrast, Walt's is a demand that he be recognised as independent from the authority of the community. The making of these demands, signalled through expressive performance, are choices as to how Walt and Hank will stake their positions in relation to the values of life in the social space. The defiant pouring of tequila over the barrier of Hank's hand enacts both choices through interrelated, decisive actions.

Following this third pour, Hank tries to restore the social balance. He physically imposes his authority by removing the bottle without permission of its owner, an imposition disguised by his resumption of safely nonchalant performance. He demonstrates his bond to the duty of enforcing social standards even when unbound from his badge and sidearm. Walt's next choice ultimately tips the scene's balance by publicly revealing the absence of his acceptable performance, and in this absence, revealing his everyday demeanour *as* performance. In the middle of the gathering, focusing its attention on his standoff with Hank, Walt demands recognition of his authority and power as an individual, as a man. '*My* son! *My* bottle! *My* house!' Yet in doing so, Walt destroys his home's congenial social atmosphere and attacks the familial bond between Walt, Jr and his uncle. It is significant that the face Walt wears when making this demand in the social space of his home is the same face he wears when asserting himself in the violent space of crime. Making such an assertion of individuality, such a demand for outright individual recognition and authority, Walt contaminates his acceptable, everyday social world with the unacceptable violence of the extraordinary and criminal.

The standoff between Walt and Hank is defused when Walt, Jr vomits in the pool. Rather than recognising the destruction wrought by staking his place away from the social – as Skyler and Hank do by moving to assist Walt, Jr – Walt sits in what seems to him to be splendid isolation, and finishes his drink in defiance of care for others. This is ultimately a hollow and pathetic demonstration of defiant unacceptability; the next morning Walt is sober, apologetic, and fully admits to the unacceptability of his actions. However, the episode refuses to give resolution to its conflict between individual, heroic desire and prosaic, social life. Instead, the remainder of Walt's narrative arc in 'Over' is centred on his inadequate efforts to sublimate into constructive home repairs his destructive passion for glory.

Unresolved bounds, unsettled places

The episode ends with a trip to the hardware store, where Walt recognises a fellow meth cook by the suspicious contents of his shopping trolley. Walt uses the occasion to offer generous advice and instruction to this competitor, who, confused by the generosity and made nervous by the exposure, flees. Walt moves on, and stands in line at the cashier with the other customers, each bearing their commitments to the domestic and its upkeep. Walt's brush with the criminal world in these surroundings seems to catalyse change. Stylistic choices invite its recognition. Each beep of another domestic item purchased is increasingly amplified, echoing in the space, as each sonic beep is matched with a visual cut that bring us closer and closer to Walt's face as it transforms once again. As by the poolside, Walt's face slackens and his eyes sharpen as a realisation is come to. Critic Donna Bowman wrote: 'His initial urge to school the slack-jawed druggie in proper acquisition technique gives way, as he stands in line with the other mundane suburbanites, to a different urge to educate.'[17] Walt drops his paint tins and exits, leaving unfinished his domestically oriented work. It is in the carpark that the nature of Walt's change following his encounter with another competitor becomes apparent.

Walt appears contained in himself as he walks towards his car. Almost as an afterthought he sees across the car park his competitor and the young man's older partner-in-crime; in appearance the two echo Walt and Jesse's partnership. Walt's face slips once again. He assumes the mask of the criminal as he strides to confront the two competing meth cooks. They notice Walt, who stands a few feet from them, half of his face shrouded in darkness, his eyes peering out from within the caverns carved by his cheekbones. The sense of roughly hewn pedagogical warmth that flowed from Walt to the younger meth cook in the hardware store is gone. There is only the stare of a man without compromise: the stare of the gangster, defending his deadly, destructive interests. Walt speaks in slow, measured tones: '*Stay out of my territory.*' In this moment, community and generosity of spirit do not co-exist with Walt's return to the criminal world, the challenges, exertions and rewards of which the prosaic rhythms of the domestic cannot seem to match.

Walt's life in the criminal world is not over; everyday, prosaic domestic life is not enough. In this final image of the episode, Walt once again drops his performance of social acceptability and reveals what it has both repressed and given rise to: a fantasy of, in Pippin's words, 'that chief pre-modern mark of distinction: *glory*'.[18] That across the series Walt repeatedly moves toward, away from, and returns to this form of life suggests the disturbing irresolution of his crisis; that it is represented in a serialised medium distinguished by its postponement of resolution strengthens this suggestion and this disturbance.

Never over

The aim of this chapter has been to explore how *Breaking Bad* unsettles assumptions about the acceptable or unacceptable characteristics of the series' generically framed worlds, situated in relation to the melodramatic tradition of Hollywood films as outlined by Deborah Thomas. *Breaking Bad* is striking for its juxtaposition of different worlds, in this instance the domestic and the criminal, that bring with them a raft of assumptions regarding their acceptability and unacceptability. The chapter's analysis has shown how, in moments of the episode 'Over', the series handles movements between these worlds and the forms of expression and action they allow. It does so in a way that disturbingly unsettles distinct relations in everyday, prosaic modern life between the acceptable and its ostensibly desired opposite. Rather than portraying the unacceptable as threateningly imposing itself from without the social world, *Breaking Bad* juxtaposes and mixes worlds and ways of being in them to suggest that the unacceptable is found within.

In 'Over', the disturbing undercurrents of dissatisfaction with the modern, prosaic form of life that characterises the series' social world disrupts the surface of that world through the transformation of serialised performance motifs. Attending to details of the barbecue sequence of 'Over', this chapter has illuminated ways in which acceptability and unacceptability thus exist in tenuous relation, governed by modes, choices, and details of performance in space. In its emptiness and falsehood, Hank's masculine brashness and bravado defuses the exertions and dangers of the alternative space, rendering them safe, to be performatively expressed in social space. When lines of social acceptability established or supported by Hank, as representative of social authority, are challenged, his false claims to being a maverick are immediately abandoned in favour of a seemingly less performative, more truthful presentation of his self more rigorously in line with the rules and interests of the social world. In contrast, Walter's everyday, acceptable performance of bland sublimation slips away into an extraordinary, unacceptably assertive performance of dangerous, glory-seeking passion that contaminates and disrupts social interests and authority.

At the episode's close, Walt again sheds his everyday performance to involve himself in the unacceptable world of the criminal. Rather than the clarity of a full stop, the moment offers the irresolution of a question mark. Set in a space that turns on the upkeep of bourgeois domesticity, Walt's final stare – flirting with direct address to the camera – offers the hint of a smile in the wake of a powerful assertion of self, suggesting that the profits of prosaic, modern life are not so easily balanced against their costs.

Notes

1. Felski, Rita, 'The Invention of Everyday Life,' *New Formations* 39 (1999–2000), p. 15.
2. Following James Walters and others, I refer to 'worlds' within fictional works figuratively, as more akin to social circles than to ontologically distinct or separate universes. See: Walters, James, *Alternative Worlds in Hollywood Cinema: Resonance Between Realms* (Bristol: Intellect, 2008), p. 10. See also: Perkins, V.F., 'Where is the World? The Horizon of Events in Movie Fiction', in John Gibbs and Douglas Pye (eds), *Style and Meaning: Studies in the Detailed Analysis of Film* (Manchester: Manchester University Press, 2005), pp. 16–41.
3. Gilligan, Vince, and Walley-Beckett, Moira, 'Over,' *Breaking Bad*, season 2, episode 10, directed by Phil Abraham, aired 3 September 2009 (Burbank, CA: Sony Pictures Television, 2010), DVD.
4. I take the idea of a generic frame from John Frow, for whom the 'regulative frame' or 'setting' of a text 'differentiates the genre of this text from other possible genres, alerts us to the way it works (its rhetorical function), and draws our attention towards some of its features and away from others', governing 'the different salience of their formal features, and of all the other dimensions of genre that are entailed in this shift of frame: a different structure of address, a different moral universe, and different truth-effects'. Frow, John, *Genre* (London: Routledge, 2005), pp. 9–10.
5. Thomas, Deborah, *Beyond Genre: Melodrama, Comedy, and Romance in Hollywood Films* (Moffat: Cameron & Hollis, 2000), p. 13.
6. Ibid.
7. Perez, Gilberto, *The Material Ghost: Films and Their Medium* (Baltimore, MD: Johns Hopkins University Press, 1998), p. 237.
8. Ibid., pp. 237–238.
9. Warshow, Robert, *The Immediate Experience: Movies, Comics, Theatre, and Other Aspects of Popular Culture, 1948* (Garden City: Doubleday, 1962), p. 133; original emphasis.
10. Pippin, Robert B., *Hollywood Westerns and American Myth: The Importance of Howard Hawks and John Ford for Political Philosophy* (New Haven, CT: Yale University Press, 2010), pp. 24–25; original emphasis. Pippin refers to Hirschman, Albert O., *The Passions and the Interests: Political Arguments*

for Capitalism Before Its Triumph (Princeton, NJ: Princeton University Press, 1977).
11. Pippin, *Hollywood Westerns and American Myth*, p. 25.
12. I take the idea of 'varied repetition' and 'performance motifs' from Sérgio Dias Branco. His doctoral thesis on these aesthetics of television fiction series develops the idea of such works being based on the varied repetition of sequenced units and motifs. Dias Branco, Sérgio, 'Strung Pieces: On the Aesthetics of Television Fiction Series', unpublished dissertation, University of Kent, 2010.
13. See Walt's confrontation with Gretchen in Gilligan, Vince, and Roberts, J., 'Peekaboo,' *Breaking Bad*, season 2, episode 6, directed by Peter Mendak, aired 6 August 2009 (Burbank, CA: Sony Pictures Television, 2010), DVD.
14. Gilligan, Vince, and Lin, Patty, 'Gray Matter,' *Breaking Bad*, season 1, episode 5, directed by Tricia Brock, aired 25 September 2008 (Burbank, CA: Sony Pictures Television, 2008), DVD.
15. Gilligan, Vince, and Shiban, John, 'Negro Y Azul,' *Breaking Bad*, season 2, episode 7, directed by Félix Enríiquez Alcalá, aired 19 April 2009 (Burbank CA: Sony Pictures Television, 2010), DVD.
16. Perez, Gilberto, *The Material Ghost*, p. 255.
17. Bowman, Donna, 'Over,' last modified 10 May 2009, accessed 16 January 2012, http://www.avclub.com/articles/over,27816/.
18. Pippin, *Hollywood Westerns and American Myth*, p. 25; original emphasis.

References

Bowman, Donna, 'Over,' last modified 10 May 2009, accessed 16 January 2012, http://www.avclub.com/articles/over,27816/.
Dias Branco, Sérgio, 'Strung Pieces: On the Aesthetics of Television Fiction Series,' Unpublished Dissertation, University of Kent, 2010.
Felski, Rita, 'The Invention of Everyday Life,' *New Formations* 39 (1999–2000): pp. 15–31.
Frow, John, *Genre* (London: Routledge, 2005).
Gilligan, Vince, and Lin, Patty, 'Gray Matter,' *Breaking Bad*, season 1, episode 5, directed by Tricia Brock, aired 25 September 2008 (Burbank, CA: Sony Pictures Television, 2008), DVD.
Gilligan, Vince, and Roberts, J., 'Peekaboo,' *Breaking Bad*, season 2, episode 6, directed by Peter Mendak, aired 6 August 2009 (Burbank, CA: Sony Pictures Television, 2010), DVD.
Gilligan, Vince, and Shiban, John, 'Negro Y Azul,' *Breaking Bad*, season 2, episode 7, directed by Félix Enríiquez Alcalá, aired 19 April 2009 (Burbank CA: Sony Pictures Television, 2010), DVD.
Gilligan, Vince, and Walley-Beckett, Moira, 'Over,' *Breaking Bad*, season 2, episode 10, directed by Phil Abraham, aired 3 September 2009 (Burbank, CA: Sony Pictures Television, 2010), DVD.
Hirschman, Albert O., *The Passions and the Interests: Political Arguments for Capitalism Before Its Triumph* (Princeton, NJ: Princeton University Press, 1977).
Perez, Gilberto, *The Material Ghost: Films and Their Medium* (Baltimore, MD: Johns Hopkins University Press, 1998).

Perkins, V. F., 'Where is the World? The Horizon of Events in Movie Fiction,' in John Gibbs and Douglas Pye (eds), *Style and Meaning: Studies in the Detailed Analysis of Film* (Manchester: Manchester University Press, 2005), pp. 16–41.

Pippin, Robert B., *Hollywood Westerns and American Myth: The Importance of Howard Hawks and John Ford for Political Philosophy* (New Haven, CT: Yale University Press, 2010).

Thomas, Deborah, *Beyond Genre: Melodrama, Comedy, and Romance in Hollywood Films* (Moffat: Cameron & Hollis, 2000).

Walters, James, *Alternative Worlds in Hollywood Cinema: Resonance between Realms* (Bristol: Intellect, 2008).

Warshow, Robert, *The Immediate Experience: Movies, Comics, Theatre, and Other Aspects of Popular Culture, 1948* (Garden City: Doubleday, 1962).

9
Sade's Constrained Libertinage: The Problem of Disgust

Naomi Stekelenburg

> *Voluptuaries of all ages and sexes – it is to you alone I offer this work. Nourish yourselves on its principles: they foster your passions; and these passions, with which cold and shabby moralists try to intimidate you, are simply the means used by nature to help human beings attain nature's goals.*
>
> –Sade, *Philosophy in the Boudoir*

Simone de Beauvoir says of Sade that 'the supreme value of his testimony lies in his ability to disturb us'.[1] Indeed, the work of Donatien Alphonse François, Marquis de Sade, is renowned for its associations with the 'unacceptable': with the *celebration* of excessive corporeal and moral repugnance. However, analysis of Sade using knowledge from the human sciences, particularly cognitive and affective neuroscience, reveals a hesitancy in Sade's transgressive impetus that is broadly unacknowledged by critics. Sade's determination to 'tell all' was tempered by the constraints imposed by social decision-making processes and evolutionary disgust, both of which work together to mediate the relationship between the author, characters and reader – a relationship highly significant in libertine fiction, due to its didactic imperative. Sade used textual strategies to encourage an alliance between narrator/educator and reader/student and to buffer the impact of the disgust evoked by his work. The result is a conflicted negotiation of social and moral transgression that, at times, concludes with conventionality and conformity.

In 1890, psychologist William James acknowledged the impact of impulse on decision making. James asserted that human impulses are complex, varied and often contradictory. Importantly, however, they *precede* reason. Once an impulse is initiated, the only phenomenon that will inhibit its generation is another impulse. Reason – as memory, associations and imagination – cannot inhibit impulse but merely serves to influence its course.[2] More recently, cognitive neuroscience has provided evidence to support James's ideas concerning the influence of precognitive emotional processes on decision making, especially in the social realm.[3] Social decision making is dissimilar from other forms of decision making, because it relies on assessment and predictions about human behaviour.[4] It moderates the navigation of relationships with others, as distinct from relationships with ideas or objects.

Literary output is subject to social decision-making processes in that it serves as an analogue of real-world interpersonal interactions and relationships.[5] When representations of human relationships transgress socially normative expectations, readers and writers are confronted by issues that prompt forms of social decision making such as, *How do I feel about that character/behaviour?*, *How would I respond in similar circumstances?* or *Is that behaviour fair/just and ethical?* Indeed, this is for Barthes the very source of pleasure in narrative, 'whenever the "literary" text (the Book) transmigrates into our life [...] in short, whenever a co-existence occurs'.[6] Of course, 'the Book' exists only due to the efforts of the human author. The human author is motivated by cognitions and affect, some of which are universal and predictable, even despite their manifestation as subjective experience. Therefore, such psychological phenomena have the capacity to illuminate how the text works to achieve meaning and value. To this extent, not only do literary worlds represent human social interaction, they exist within the social realm in and of themselves in that they are constructed by the joint participation of author and reader via the mediation of the text.

Booth[7] emphasised the significance of the psychic relationship between the author and reader. He described it as analogous to friendship: one of the most basic units of sociality. The nature of a friendship is defined by features such as the quantity and quality or kinds of experiences it offers, the level of reciprocity or dominion it invites or imposes, the degree of intimacy, the intensity of the engagement and the distance between the experiences of the friends. Importantly, Booth argued that these features can be used to determine the value of a literary work. The author, according to Booth, is far from dead, instead, he or she is an integral component of shaping the social decision making that is invoked by narrative.

This inherent feature of the literary experience is centralised in Sade's work because the imperative of the transmission of knowledge from author to reader completely underwrites the primary libertine didactic project, a project that aims to induct new members. The epigraph from *Philosophy in the Boudoir* serves as an example of this didactic impetus: 'Dialogues aimed at the education of young ladies. May every mother get her daughter to read this book.'[8] Sade's appeals to the co-option of the goodwill of the reader are explicit and necessary. Hénaff[9] noted this when he wrote: 'the whole apparatus of Sadean fiction functions precisely to turn the reader into an accomplice, one who thereby joins the Masters in their elite circle'. In *The 120 Days of Sodom*, this relational imperative is clear:

> [M]any of the extravagances you are about to see will doubtless displease you, yes, I am well aware of it, but there are amongst a few which will warm you to the point of costing you some fuck, and that, reader, is all we ask of you.[10]

In the same way that the pornographic is only valid if it produces a behavioural response in the reader/viewer, Sade's work maintains its stakehold in *libertinage* only to the extent that it prompts the reader to contemplate possibilities and to 'answer part of his secret stock of unanswered questions'.[11] Part of the means of achieving this is the exploration of ideas that are repugnant and alien, in order to discover the ones that provoke pleasure. In other words, the reader must become an accomplice in the Sadean universe, where boundaries are tested and limits of interpersonal relationships are exposed. As Delbène, the libertine nun from *Juliette* says: 'for a libertine intelligence, there is no more piercing pleasure than that of making proselytes'.[12] This process differs from pornography in that the pornographic presents only that which 'costs some fuck' even if the pleasure is as a result of displeasure or pain. The orgasm is a transitory physical phenomenon, whereas the induction into libertinage requires the exposition of the material body to trials and challenges that elicit ideological and moral transformation. If the language feeds the orgy in Sade,[13] then the orgy in its turn, feeds thought.

The tension that provides the force of Sade's libertine fiction is this need for society – for affiliation – between the reader and the author/narrator and between the characters, existing at once with the desire to radically disrupt inter-subjectivity through representations that are distinctly anti-social. This tension, as explained below, is augmented by the continuous presence of the threat (if not the actual evocation) of the disgust response, whose moral associations become significant when social transgression and social disunity exist. The orgy, which exists as a symbol for the extreme nature of libertinage sexuality and conversion, is by definition a social act. An orgy *requires* more than two people. However, the orgy is anti-affiliative and therefore anti-social. This is what Hénaff described as the 'constant alternation between suspicion and seduction'[14] experienced by the reader of Sade. The orgy seduces, but suspicion of it arises from the fact that it is fuelled by passion; never love. It results in death, rather than growth and is consumptive rather than generative; '[t]rue libertinage abhors progeniture'.[15] According to the 'Statutes of the Sodality of the Friends of Crime', the society of libertines in *Juliette*,[16] children borne of the orgy are to be raised in crèches in preparation for the consumption of them in seraglios. In the most tormenting of scenes, Juliette proves the extent of her libertinage by agreeing to sell her daughter, Marianne, to the aptly named Noirceuil, who thereupon throws her into the fire and roasts her alive with Juliette's assistance. Perhaps the provocation of this scene lies not in what Juliette does, but in her capacity to override the maternal feelings she has for her 'little dear'.[17]

The attempt by Sade to negate the maternal relationship has been written about at length.[18] To obliterate the mother is to attenuate sociality at its very foundation. Sade's attempt to negate maternal feelings is perhaps the surest indication of his desire to attenuate the relational foundations of the social. It is not surprising then that the titular character from *Justine*, who represents Sade's most developed and rounded character (if not the most frustratingly gullible) is also the one equipped to feel tenderness and affection, and this ultimately results in her suffering. Despite the claims by Sade that Justine suffers because of her virtue, Justine suffers more precisely because she experiences affiliation, even for her torturers. She says of Monsieur de Bressac, her captor and the man who attempts to co-opt Justine in the murder of his aunt:

> Whatever the foul treatment to which the Comte de Bressac had exposed me the first day I had met him, it had, all the same, been impossible to see him so frequently without feeling myself drawn toward him by an insuperable and instinctive tenderness.[19]

Justine recognises that such feelings are the source of severe punishment in the world of the libertine. This 'mistake', she acknowledges, is a 'folly, an extravagance [...] there has never been one equal to it'.[20]

Even the genitalia of the characters, which in pornography and erotic fiction are sources of desire, represent the need to protect characters from the physical and mental invasiveness of intimacy. Genitalia are militarised, making them mechanisms of defence rather than attraction. Part of the arsenal of the libertine is the monstrous penis. The cannibal Minski has a *'pike* (my emphasis) eighteen inches long by sixteen in circumference, surrounded by a crimson knob the size of a military helmet'. Minski's weapon is always vigilant: 'Aye, here it is', says Minski, 'behold its state, it is never in any other, even as I sleep at night, even as I walk in the day'.[21] Where Sade's men are fitted out with impossibly huge and unforgiving penises, libertine women have their own forms of grotesque defence. La Durand, one of Sade's most powerful female libertines, is vaginally impenetrable. Militarised genitalia do not titillate. By definition, titillation involves a sense of fixed attention resulting from attraction. The Sadean libertines work explicitly to repel each other and the reader, rather than attract them. To repel is unsociable and this constant negotiation of the unsociable within a medium whose impetus is necessarily *relational* represents a challenge for the writing of the obscene and unacceptable.

The nature of Sadean interpersonal practices at large means it is incumbent upon Sade to implement textual strategies to induce the reader's compliance. The result is that, while his libertine characters commit heinous crimes, they maintain a level of *personability*. This concept goes beyond the co-option of reader empathy or sympathy, the evocation of which is not particularly necessary and may even interrupt the assignment to the reader of genuinely libertine principles. Personability does, however, require a capacity to reassure the reader that, despite the chaos of the orgy, there will be limits, elements of control, both of which soothe the anxiety resulting from the proliferation of vice and anarchy. Of course, this does not mean that the libertines demonstrate kindness or compassion, or any other of the traits or behavioural tendencies ordinarily accredited with honour or ethics. However, they certainly exhibit moments of reasonableness and indeed, likability, despite their hideous and abhorrent behaviour. This is seen mainly in the interludes between orgies, when they declare their philosophical positions. For example, in *Justine*, Clément tortures Justine, but then settles in for a discussion with her. His language is avuncular: 'Let us lie down [...] perhaps you have suffered too much, my dear, even though not enough for me...'[22] During the philosophical discourse that ensues, Clément acknowledges the horror and disgust that Justine must be feeling in regard to the exposition of his philosophy. The acknowledgement is not necessary with respect to the relationship between the characters; Justine is Clément's victim and he demonstrates his ready capacity to treat her with cruelty. Instead, it demonstrates a sensibility on Sade's part that is not given due recognition by critics. Sade is not usually associated with sensitivity of any description; indeed, libertinage depends upon a general scorn for public opinion. But he employs a system of rhetorical devices that acknowledge the social dilemma within and produced by his writing. Empathy for the effects of his work on the reader is one such device.

In his negotiation of the social, Sade also instils a sense that the reader is not completely distinct (or as distinct as he or she, perhaps, would like to imagine themselves to be) from the other participants in the narrative. An example is this from *Juliette*: 'without a brain like mine, there is no conceiving such a thing, unless one has brains like yours, it is not to be comprehended'.[23] The materialism of the language, which is of course one of the stylistic markers of Sade's work generally, establishes the need for cognitive enlistment by those participating in the text. It evokes a sense of brains joined together and functioning to comprehend, echoing the joining together of bodies, which are functioning in order to orgasm, in the 'rosary'; the practice of the Bolognese nuns.[24] The acts of libertinage serve not to titillate, but they serve as prompts to contemplation. Often this takes the form of an aside: 'The reader will be pleased to take note that these comments proceeded from the most youthful member of the group.'[25] Here again is the companionable embrace that the Sadean narrator uses to coerce and seduce the reader. The use of the plural 'we' connotes inclusivity and alliance, as does the intimacy of the first person narration, which often manifests in the listing of details and attributes aimed at assisting the reader to comprehend the actions of the large numbers of characters. For example, in *The 120 Days of Sodom*, each of the main characters is profiled in detail and represented later, listed, as in encyclopedia form:

> so that should the reader, as he moves along, encounter what seems to him an unfamiliar figure, he will have merely to turn back to this index, and if this little aid to his memory suffice not, to the more thorough portraits presented earlier.[26]

This augments the sense that the text requires a scholarly approach, but it is an *affective* as well as cognitive thought experiment. 'Would I, or wouldn't I?' or perhaps more accurately, 'Could I or couldn't I?' are the foundational questions of the thought experiment. These questions are fundamentally social.

Disgust

The trope of social interactivity – and therefore the significance of social decision making in reading Sade's libertine novels – emphasises the importance of the affective response. In his 'somatic marker hypothesis', Damasio[27] suggested that the social realm operates differently from other realms of human cognitive output in that decisions made within it depend on emotional feedback. Negative emotions serve as deterrents against a set of behavioural choices. Positive-valanced emotions act as rewards and therefore motivate the performance of similar future decisions. Importantly, the impact of the emotions is pre-cognitive, meaning that it occurs prior to cognition, or understanding and awareness: consciousness. Damasio described this phenomenon as intuition, which he defined as 'the mysterious mechanism by which we arrive at a solution of a problem without reasoning toward it'.[28] The nature of Sade's thematic preoccupations: corporeal mutilation, infanticide, taboo and prohibited sexual practices, place the emotion of disgust at the centre of considerations about the affective component of Sade's fiction. Of course, as with any gut reaction, disgust may be overridden by cognition, and this is likely to be part of the processing that occurs in the appreciation of the disgust aesthetic. However, the impact of disgust cannot be discounted altogether in the consideration of how obscene literary works are created and read.

Damasio's ideas about social decision making provide a unique perspective on Sade's work. In the reading process, the most elemental of decisions is whether or not to continue reading; or, to reframe in more psychological terms, whether or not to continue the relationship with the author/characters in the narrative. The process of constructing texts from language is not liberated entirely from decision making simply by merit of the fact that it is predicated on creative and imaginative processes. In the same way that humans use emotional feedback in social interactions to decide what to say and how to behave, emotions such as disgust come to bear on the construction of literary worlds that seek to represent extreme forms of corporeally and morally subversive phenomena, as Sade's worlds do.

Sade's work is often discussed in terms of its capacity to defend 'impossibilities'[29] regarding extreme forms of human corporeal and moral behaviour. However, even in the defence of impossibilities, disgust necessitates the imposition of constraint and adjustment because of its capacity to cause unease. Sade manipulated and – at times, placated – disgust so that the outcome is, perhaps surprisingly, that his works can be read as confirming the established social order, or at the least, apologetically positioning themselves so that the anxiety evoked by transgression is cushioned. This being the case, the origins and functioning of disgust as it influences the powerful precognitive decisions, has much to contribute to the project of interpretation of Sade's work.

Disgust begins with the body: so too must any attempt to understand it.[30] Darwin noted that the experience of disgust is communicated facially by:

> the mouth being widely opened, as if to let an offensive morsel drop out; by spitting; by blowing out of the protruded lips; or by a sound as of clearing the throat.[31]

The physical markers of disgust demonstrate its associations with distaste and its origins in mediating avoidance of ingestion of harmful substances. Darwin prioritised the relationship between taste and disgust over the other sensory sources, but recent scholars have expanded Darwin's ideas by locating the genesis of the emotion to disease avoidance in general, with avoidance of oral ingestion of pathogens being just one of many ways the human seeks to maintain hygiene.[32] While the determination of what is a 'contaminant' is to some extent shaped and nuanced by culture, there are categories of phenomena that are universally disgusting.[33] Disgust can be induced by a variety of catalysts, but broad, universal categories of disgust have been established. These include: food that is culturally inappropriate or has been soiled in some way; body products such as faeces and mucous; sex that is culturally aberrant; slimy or dirty animals; body envelope violations, which occur as a result of body mutilation; death and cadavers; hygiene; and magical thinking, which manifests in the idea that any connection between a disgusting item and a neutral item makes the latter contaminated.[34] It is evident from these categories that the links between disgust and the unacceptable are founded on the limits and constraints on the ways bodies behave, interact and manage the substances emanating from them. This is highlighted when the associations between corporeal disgust and morality are examined.

At some point in the evolution of the human brain, disgust was co-opted by neural pathways serving to protect humans from moral contamination.[35] Disgust motivated hygiene of the body, but evolved into a guardian of purity of the 'soul'. There remains a robust association between bodily states identified with disgust and moral judgement.[36] Exposure to contaminated ideas, then, has the capacity to instigate hygiene response processes. The unacceptable is often viewed as a 'contagion' liable to infect an otherwise healthy organism. Indeed, the lexicon used to describe unacceptable cultural products reflects this. Obscene texts are 'filthy' or 'dirty' and their capacity to 'corrupt' is alluded to in the discourse on censorship. For example, in the legal case that established precedent for obscenity laws in Australia, the judge described obscenity in the following way:

> The test of obscenity is this, whether the tendency of the matter charged as obscenity is to deprave and corrupt those whose minds are open to such immoral influences and into whose hands a publication of this sort may fall.[37]

By extension, the imagination, which establishes mental associations between objects, experiences and people, can serve as a progenitor of disgust, and also of the concomitant hygiene behaviours motivated by the evocation of the emotion. In terms of the role disgust plays in the creation and interpretation of literary texts, it is significant to note that hygiene response behaviours can involve the seemingly contradictory impulses of avoidance and approach. The need to protect also commands concentration of attention onto the disgusting, imbuing it with the potential to captivate. Obscenity, often because of its representation of the body in transgression, balances precariously between these two precipices, and the negotiation of this is evident in Sade's fiction.

Disgust in Sade

The universal categories of disgust are of central importance in Sade's work. His libertine fiction challenged the boundaries of the body in eighteenth-century France, and it continues to challenge such boundaries in contemporary Western society. Sade did more than subvert the culturally conditioned behaviour of his historical epoch. Indeed, he was always less interested in the ways culture produces behaviour, than he was in interaction between human nature and the pejorative impact of irrational social practices on such nature:

> Our customs, manners, religious beliefs, codes, regulations – all these sordid local factors merit no consideration in this survey; the point is not to discover whether adultery is a crime in the eyes of the Laplander who permits it, or the Frenchman who hammers it, but

to make out whether humanity is wronged or Nature offended by this act.[38]

As such, to position his work as only a product of its time and not a response to and representation of human nature, reduces the capacity to acquire knowledge about it. The affective focus of Sade's fictional worlds is disgust and he worked to ensure that the gamut of disgusting acts was produced. He dedicated entire scenes to depicting transgressions involving the universal categories of disgust, sometimes all at once. In *Juliette*,[39] Clairwil and Juliette masturbate with the heart of one of their victims, Sbrigani and Minski gorge themselves on human flesh.[40] The virtuous Justine is witness to incest, murder and numerous acts of rape and brutality; too often to recount them all. The torturing of the disgust response, however, comes not so much from any singular act, *per se*, but from the excess of perversion. Excess of even that which causes initial pleasure can result in disgust. As noted by Miller, overindulgence in even those things that are pleasurable, such as food, drink and sex, produces feelings of sickness or unease due to surfeit.[41] The disgust aesthetic created by the excess, however, evokes a fascination that can be analysed in terms of the evolutionary origins of disgust.

Sade's libertinage is at once repulsive and compulsive – as well as excessive. The tension he evokes through the need to convert and calibrate the reader to libertinage is acknowledged in his negotiation of the powerful emotion of disgust which, as noted, has the potential to play a significant role in the social decisions represented and *required* by Sade's texts. The repulsion caused by the excessive behaviour of his characters is easy to identify and identify with. As in real life, however, the allure of the disgusting object is more difficult to comprehend. Evolutionary psychology provides some insight into this problem through its emphasis on the protective capacity of disgust. Jones and Fitness[42] identified individuals who are described as morally hyper-vigilant and whose tendency is toward both disgust sensitivity and to approaching repugnance in order to more skilfully avoid it in the future.

There is an aspect of this same moral hyper-vigilance when Sade is approached. His works compel because they offer a space for the imaginative examination of aspects of human behaviour and ways of being that are often not, or not *yet*, accessible in the real world. Sade portrayed images of disgust that make an important contribution to the exploration of the exchange of bodily products, death and sexual practices that exist at the boundaries of human experience. In this sense, Sade created imaginary worlds that allow for the exploration of phenomena that evoke a commentary on hygiene and contamination – phenomena very much in the central frame of human relationships and interactions with the external environment. As Miller said, 'To the extent that disgust defends us against pollution, it must be alert to the polluting; it has to know it and study it well.'[43]

Evolutionary literary critics[44] posit that the 'as if' experiences facilitated by the imagination activate feelings, emotions and thoughts that inform the individual's subjective experience of the world and the meaning they give to their lives. Indeed, as Frappier-Mazar points out, there is a metafictional component to Sade's work that allows for the acknowledgement of writing as a declaration of the imaginary[45] and, as pointed out above, the imagination in Sade facilitates understanding of the self and the world. Imagination is one of the foundational psychic mechanisms on which Sade's exploration of disgust is based. Juliette explains this to her proselyte, Madame Donis:

> summon up all those images and ideas you banished during the fasting period just elapsed, and indolently, languidly nonchalantly fall to performing that little pollution by which nobody so cunningly arouses herself or others as you do. Next, unpent your fancy, let it freely dwell upon aberrations of different sorts and of ascending magnitude: linger over the details of each [...][46]

Sade harnesses the human capacity for abstract, symbolic and imaginative thought in a way that is emotionally informative and in a way that facilitates knowledge about the social world in which humans exist. As Juliette tells us, understanding requires that 'one must allow one's imagination free play'.[47]

This reading of Sade's work, as a site for preparation and study of issues concerning contamination and hygiene, becomes even more compelling when the link between corporeal disgust and moral disgust is considered. This association is mirrored in Sade's work, bringing it in line with understandings from evolutionary affective psychology. On a macro level, Sadean orgies pre-empt explicit contemplation of socio-moral concerns. In this sense, the portrayal of excessive corporeal transgressions that create an aesthetic of disgust serves as an entry point, a source of lubrication, if you like, for dialogue between the characters about questions of morality. After the orgy, no topic is off limits and no idea is too 'dangerous' as it signifies a transgression that is finite.[48]

In *Philosophy in the Boudoir*, Saint-Ange conspires with her brother Chevalier to fill the young Eugénie's 'head with the principles of the most unbridled libertinage.'[49] Each lecture on being a libertine, we are informed by Saint-Ange, is to be followed by a demonstration. What she does not say, however, is that each orgiastic demonstration is also followed by another lecture, usually concerning the state of moral affairs of individuals and governments. After the first orgy, for instance, Dolmancé, one of the libertines given the task of 'educating' Eugénie, produces a monologue on the cultural construction of morality:

> There is no action, however bizarre you may picture it, that is truly criminal; or that can really be called virtuous. Everything depends on the customs and climates we live in.[50]

This routine of orgy into philosophical discourse reaches a climax when Eugénie loses her virginity and demands to be instructed to 'console me for the excesses I've plunged into'.[51] She says, 'I'd like to know whether a government truly needs a set of morals.'[52] A strange post-coital question, to say the least, but one that aligns with the constraint imposed by the emotion of disgust – the corporeal into the moral. At this point the pamphlet, entitled 'Frenchmen, Some More Effort If You Wish To Be Republicans', is read. Its first line, 'I am going to present you with some grand ideas',[53] captures the very purpose of the orgy: it is to mediate the transition from the material body to the abstract notions of right and wrong. Here, Sade employed a conventional approach in his manipulation of disgust. While, as Dolmancé commented, 'everything has been said',[54] the saying of everything takes place in order to enact the rich connection between corporeal disgust and moral disgust.

This is not the only way the Sadean vision is constrained by the mechanisms of disgust. While disgusting phenomena can captivate, the prospect of approaching them causes anxiety. Sade's libertine fiction is preoccupied with the need to control and manage the anxiety that comes with corporeal intimacy. Researchers interested in the emotion of disgust posit that human sexual behaviour is anomalous in terms of the disgust response as it necessitates the very thing that often initiates avoidance, contact with bodily fluids and pathogens.[55] The assumption here is speculative to the extent that there is little research in this area and, even if there were more, issues concerning sexual behaviour and disgusting phenomena would be difficult to unravel because of the difficulties generally in observation or self-report studies on such topics. However, even if it is accepted that at some point in sexual behaviour the disgust response must be subdued in order for sexual acts to occur, it must also be acknowledged that there is variation between individuals and instances where the subjugation of the response is more or less difficult. The most telling indications of Sade's concerns about hygiene, intimacy and anxiety come from the rules of the Friends of Crime. Ugly people, and those of lower social standing are permitted into the society, but never those who challenge the hygiene of the group. Article 34 states:

> Repulsive deformities or diseases will not be put up with. Someone so afflicted were he to present himself, would most surely be rejected. And were an already admitted member fall prey to such misfortunes, he would be asked to resign.[56]

Further, those who contract a venereal disease must sit out until given the clear by house physicians and surgeons. So fine is the detail concerning hygiene, that the Friends' rules outline toilet practices. Each toilet has an attendant who is equipped with:

> syringes, bidets, vessels in the English style, ordinary pots, high quality linens, cloths and swabs, perfumes and in general everything needed before and after the operation and while it is in its course.[57]

This detail is typical of Sade's insistence on saying everything. However, it is anomalous that such attention be given to assurances of cleanliness in a text that involves more than its fair share of scatological references, especially those referring to the pleasures of coprophagia and the celebration of base corporeality. Surely a society so libertine in its ideology and sexual practice has little need to make an explicit statement about the accoutrements necessary for toilet hygiene? The orgy necessarily involves the emission of bodily fluids and products, the eating of shit is a smelly enterprise – no matter how much perfume one uses – and if one is to use all body parts possible in the act of intercourse, what any libertine does after urinating or defecating is of little importance. This focus on cleaning the body is a concession made by one whose imagination leads to disgust. The details about sanitation calm and quell: instances of cleanliness despite the fraught sanitation of libertinage. Logically, of course, the effect of the attempts at hygiene is minimal. However, affect is intuitive, rather than logical, as James and Damasio reminded us. In this case, the need for hygiene even amid the corporeal chaos operates as an expression of intuitive affect to produce reassurance.

Juliette contemplates the connection between disgust and anxiety when she is imprisoned. She acknowledges that a life of vice leads to her having to 'put up with these familiar and tedious worries'.[58] She reconciles this by accepting the anxiety over the 'cowlike tranquility simple and stupid'[59] that she detests. Juliette's moment of contemplation represents a warning. Sade portrayals are not easy to take, but they are the ends that justify the means. His imaginary worlds allow for the exposure to events and characters that have the potential to cause disgust, but this is merely an opportunity to know and understand, which in turn facilitates the texts' didactic force. Sade was prepared to 'tell all' but not before providing the benefit of other warning devices. These exist as a means of controlling the anxiety produced by the moral and sexual transgressions Sade's characters are so intent on engaging with. However, the outcome of the devices is that, while they are necessary mechanisms to maintain equilibrium between the avoidance/approach response to the disgust aesthetic that is established, they also work to reinforce established socially and morally normative behaviour. In other words, even an author as reputedly transgressive and libertine as Sade was bound by the constraints imposed by disgust. In *Justine*, where, resigned to the horrible task of describing the misfortunes of Justine, the narrator begs the 'indulgence of my reader'.[60] This is a strategy to prepare the reader for what is to come, so that in the preparation there is a softening of the impact.

Setting also operates to attenuate the impact of disgust. Despite that Sade's libertines have fancies that have 'roved very far' and perhaps have gone 'beyond what one may imagine',[61] most of the orgies take place in settings that are cut off from the ordinary spaces of habitation. Sexual behaviour is hidden in bushes and boudoirs and remote castles, exactly the places you would expect to find it if the characters were sexually *constrained*. Discovery is, as Delbéne warns Juliette, the limit of debauchery.[62] This is not because of the fear of punishment by social institutions. Most of the libertines are so well connected that they are able to escape punitive measures of the law. It is a consequence of the need to reign in the anarchy so that it does not result in overwhelming disgust.

Barthes[63] wrote that the enclosure of the Sadean site allows for the system of the imagination necessary for the contemplation of libertine behaviour. But the system of the imagination must be yoked by mechanisms designed to temper the impact of its excess. For example, Shilling Castle in *The 120 Days of Sodom* is a 'remote and isolated retreat' that is surrounded by a mountain almost as high as Saint-Bernard, a crevice

1000 feet deep which is accessed by the party by a bridge that is destroyed, taking with it all access to the world on the other side, a 30-foot wall, another wall and then a moat. This shutting off from the rest of the world encapsulates and therefore controls the otherwise anarchic scenes that take place in the work. Of course, control is one of the reactions to feelings of anxiety and it manifests in forms other than setting. Sade was obsessive-compulsive in his focus on order, hierarchy and counting.[64] He used counting to soothe the anxiety associated with excessive corporeality. From *The 120 Days of Sodom*:

> In his youth, the Duc had been known to discharge as often as eighteen times a day, and that without appearing one jot more fatigued after the final than after the initial ejaculation. Seven or eight crises within the same interval still held no terrors for him, his half a century of years notwithstanding.[65]

So, while Sade abides:

> bloody corpses everywhere, infants torn from their mothers' arms, young women with their throats slit after the orgy, cups full of blood and wine, unimaginable tortures [...][66]

there is always a need to control through the assurance of numbers and order, as Delbéne demonstrates when she interrupts an orgy to ensure that all the participants are in their right places. Although ostensibly paradoxical, libertine passion is founded on a 'cool head'.[67] Delbéne seeks to re-establish order; order that confirms the status quo maintained by disgust. So while the orgy necessitates an invocation of the emotion of disgust in order to support the weight of its anarchy, it also requires mechanisms to ensure that the disgust is tempered; too potent, and it will overwhelm the text and produce irreconcilable anxiety.

By definition, the libertine seeks to completely evade constraints of sexuality and morality imposed by society. Regardless, constraints imposed by social decision-making processes facilitate and mediate the acquisition of apostolates. The didactic force of libertinage relies on the appointment of new members. To this extent, Sade was not entirely exempt from subjugation to social decision-making processes, which draw on feedback from powerful pre-cognitive emotions such as disgust. Sade may have successfully avoided constraints of social conventionality, but he could not evade constraints imposed by neuro-cognitive processes. In this sense, even while Sade worked to evade his humanity, it is exposed in his work. He used textual devices, such as the aside, the first-person narration, the closed-off settings and self-censorship, that permit the re-establishment of composure lost due to the excessive corporeality of his writing. This does not occur in the details of what he presented. It is without doubt that his work set out to challenge notions of vice and virtue. Sade's ostensible claim was to speak the unspeakable, but his anarchist impulse was, at times, interrupted or deterred completely by the pangs of unease caused by disgust. In this way, Sade presented us with a conventional view of the unacceptable.

Acknowledgements

I am grateful to Henry Martyn Lloyd, whose lively discussion and questioning sparked some of the ideas contained in this chapter.

Notes

1. De Beauvoir, 'Must We Burn Sade?', p. 64.
2. James, William, *The Principles of Psychology*, v.II, p. 1088.
3. Bechara, Damasio, Damasio, & Anderson, *Cognition*; Bechara, Damasio, Damasio, *Cerebral Cortex*; Le Doux, *The Emotional Brain*; Damasio, *Descarte's Error: Emotion, Reason and the Human Brain*.
4. Damasio, *Descarte's Error: Emotion, Reason and the Human Brain*.
5. Carroll, *Reading Human Nature*, p. 5; Carroll, Gottschall, Johnson & Kruger, *Reading Human Nature: Literary Darwinism in Theory and Practice*; Dissanayake, *Homo Aestheticus*, p. 212.
6. Barthes, *Sade, Fourier, Loyola*, p. 7.
7. Booth, *The Company We Keep: The Ethics of Fiction*, p. 180.
8. De Sade, *Philosophy in the Boudoir*.
9. Hénaff, *Sade: The Invention of the Libertine Body*, p. 65.
10. De Sade, *The 120 Days of Sodom & Other Writings*, p. 254.
11. De Sade, *The Misfortunes of Virtue & Other Early Tales*, p. 2.
12. De Sade, *Juliette*, p. 52.
13. Barthes, *Sade, Fourier, Loyola*, p. 32.
14. Hénaff, *Sade: The Invention of the Libertine Body*, p. 65.
15. De Sade, *Juliette*, p. 423.
16. Ibid.
17. Ibid., p. 1184.
18. Paglia, *Sexual Personae*; Gallop, 'The liberated woman'; Hénaff, *Sade: The Invention of the Libertine Body*, pp. 269–283; Carter, *The Sadeian Woman*, p. 121.
19. De Sade, *Justine or the Misfortunes of Virtue*, p. 511.
20. Ibid.
21. De Sade, *Juliette*, p. 582.
22. De Sade, *Justine or the Misfortunes of Virtue*, p. 121.
23. De Sade, *Juliette*, p. 311.

24. Ibid., p. 574.
25. Ibid., p. 23.
26. De Sade, *The 120 Days of Sodom*, p. 255.
27. Damasio, *Descarte's Error: Emotion, Reason and the Human Brain*.
28. Ibid., p. 188.
29. Barthes, *Sade, Fourier, Loyola*, p. 136.
30. The discussion that follows provides a background and context for analysis of evolutionary disgust in Sade's work. While it represents a degree of disjunction, hopefully it will become clear that the explanations given contribute to the analysis that follows.
31. Darwin, *The Expression of the Emotions in Man and Animals*, p. 256.
32. Curtis, *Proceedings of the Royal Society of London*; *Journal of Epidemiology and Community Health*.
33. Miller, *The Anatomy of Disgust*, p. 44.
34. Haidt, McCauley & Rozin, *Personality and Individual Differences*.
35. Rozin, Haidt & McCauley, *Handbook of Emotions*; Horberg, Oveis, Keltner & Cohen, *Journal of Personality*.
36. Wheatley & Haidt, *Psychological Science*; Schnall, Haidt, Clore & Jordan, *Personality and Social Psychology Bulletin*.
37. R. v. Hicklin, 1868, L.R. 3 Q.B. 360 at 371.
38. De Sade, *Juliette*, p. 63.
39. Ibid., pp. 544–545.
40. Ibid., p. 585.
41. Miller, *The Anatomy of Disgust*, p. 110.
42. Jones and Fitness, *Emotion*, pp. 613–627.
43. Miller, *The Anatomy of Disgust*, p. 111.
44. Carroll, Gottschall, Johnson, & Kruger, *Reading Human Nature: Literary Darwinism in Theory and Practice*; Swirski, *Of Literature and Knowledge*, see Chapter 4.
45. Frappier-Mazar, *Writing the Orgy*, p. 78.
46. De Sade, *Juliette*, p. 640.
47. Ibid., p. 163.
48. Baudrillard, http://www.egs.edu/faculty/jean-baudrillard/articles/between-difference-and-singularity/. Accessed 13 July 2011.
49. De Sade, *Philosophy in the Boudoir*, p. 7.
50. Ibid., p. 31.
51. Ibid., p. 103.
52. Ibid.
53. Ibid., p. 104.
54. Ibid., p. 173.
55. Oaten, Stevenson & Case, *Psych. Bulletin*, p. 308.
56. De Sade, *Juliette*, p. 424.
57. Ibid., p. 425.
58. Ibid., p. 201.
59. Ibid.
60. De Sade, *Justine*, p. 3.
61. De Sade, *Juliette*, p. 9.
62. Ibid., p. 80.
63. Barthes, *Sade, Fourier, Loyola*, p. 17.

64. Cryle, *SubStance*.
65. De Sade, *The 120 Days of Sodom*, p. 202.
66. Janin in Bataille, *Eroticism: Death and Sensuality*, p. 177.
67. De Sade, *Juliette*, p. 37.

References

Barthes, Roland, trans. Miller, R, *Sade, Fourier, Loyola*, Berkeley, CA: University of California Press, 1989.

Baudrillard, Jean, 'Between difference and singularity: an open discussion with Jean Baudrillard' The European Graduate School, accessed 13/07/11 http://www.egs.edu/faculty/jean-baudrillard/articles/between-difference-and-singularity/

Booth, Wayne, *The Company We Keep: The Ethics of Fiction*, Berkeley, CA: University of California Press, 1988.

Bechara, A, Damasio, AR, Damasio, H and Anderson, S, 'Insensitivity to future consequences following damage to human prefrontal cortex', *Cognition*, 1994, 50, 7–12.

Bechara, A, Damasio, H and Damasio, A, 'Emotion, decision-making and the orbito-frontal cortex', *Cerebral Cortex*, 2000, 10, 3, 295–307.

Carroll, Joseph, 'An Evolutionary Paradigm for Literary Study', in *Reading Human Nature: Literary Darwinism in Theory and Practice*, New York: Suny Press, pp. 3–54, 2011.

Carroll, Joseph, Gottschall, Jonathan, Johnson, John and Kruger, Daniel, 'Agonistic structure in Victorian Novels: Doing the Math', in Joseph Carroll (ed.) *Reading Human Nature: Literary Darwinism in Theory and Practice*, New York: Suny Press, pp. 151–176, 2011.

Carter, Angela, *The Sadeian Woman & the Ideology of Pornography*, New York: Pantheon, 1978.

Cryle, Peter, 'Les Cent vingt journées de Sodome', *SubStance*, 1991, 20, 1, 91–113.

Curtis, Valerie; Aunger, Robert and Rabie, Tamer, 'Evidence that disgust evolved to protect from the risk of disease', *Proceedings of the Royal Society of London*, 2004, 271, S131–133.

Curtis, Valerie, 'Dirt, disgust and disease: a natural history of hygiene', *Journal of Epidemiology and Community Health*, 2007, 61, 660–664.

Damasio, Antonio, *Descarte's Error: Emotion, Reason and the Human Brain*, New York: GP Putnam, 1994.

De Beauvoir, Simone, 'Must we burn Sade?', in A Wainhouse and R Seaver (eds) *Marquis de Sade: The 120 Days of Sodom and Other Writings*, New York: Grove Press, pp. 3–64, 1966.

De Sade, DAF, trans. Austryn Wainhouse, *The 120 Days of Sodom and Other Writings*, New York: Grove Press, 1966.

De Sade, DAF, trans. Austryn Wainhouse, *Juliette*, New York: Grove Press, 1968.

De Sade, DAF de, trans. Joachim Neugroschel, *Philosophy in the Boudoir*, New York: Penguin, 2006.

De Sade, DAF, trans. David Coward, *The Misfortunes of Virtue*, New York: Oxford University Press, 2008.

De Sade, DAF, *Justine*, London: Penguin (Perennial Forbidden Classics), 2009.

Dissanayake, Ellen, *Homo Aestheticus: Where Art Comes From and Why*, Washington, DC: University of Washington Press, 1995.
Frappier-Mazar, L, trans. Gillian C Gill, *Writing the Orgy*, Philadelphia, PA: University of Pennsylvania Press, 1996.
Gallop, Jane, 'The liberated woman', *Narrative*, 13, 2, 89–104.
Haidt, J, McCauley, C and Rozin, P, 'Individual differences in sensitivity to disgust: a scale sampling seven domains of disgust elicitors', *Personality and Individual Differences*, 1994, 16, 701–713.
Hénaff, Marcel, trans. Xavier Callahan, *Sade: The Invention of the Libertine Body*, Minneaoplis, MN: University of Minnesota Press, 1999.
Horberg, EJ, Oveis, C, Keltner, D and Cohen, A, 'Disgust and the moralisation of purity', *Journal of Personality*, 2009, 97, 963–976.
James, William, *The Principles of Psychology, v.II*, New York: Henry Holt, 1890.
Janin in Bataille, Georges, trans. Dalwood, Mary *Eroticism, Death and Sensuality*, San Francisco, CA: City Lights, 1986.
Jones, A and Fitness, J, 'Moral hypervigilance: the influence of disgust sensitivity in the moral domain', *Emotion*, 2008, 8, 613–627.
Le Doux, J, *The Emotional Brain*, London: Orion Books, 1998.
Oaten, Megan, Stevenson, Richard J and Case, Trevor, 'Disgust as a disease avoidance mechanism', *Psychological Bulletin*, 2009, 135, 303–321.
Paglia, Camille, *Sexual Personae: Art and Decadence from Nefertiti to Emily Dickinson*, London: Penguin, 1990.
Rozin, P, Haidt, J and McCauley, CR, 'Disgust', in M Lewis and J Haviland (eds) *Handbook of Emotions*, New York: Guilford Press, pp. 575–594, 1993.
Schnall, S, Haidt, J, Clore, GL and Jordan, AH, 'Disgust as embodied moral judgment', *Personality and Social Psychology Bulletin*, 2008, 34, 1096–1109.
Swirski, Peter, *Of Literature and Knowledge: Explorations in Narrative Thought Experiments, Evolution and Game Theory*, London: Routledge, 2007.
Wheatley, T and Haidt, J, 'Hypnotic disgust makes moral judgments more severe', *Psychological Science*, 2005, 16, 780–784.

10
Freedom of Expression has Limitations: Censorship of Performance in the USA

Timothy R. Wilson

Scheduled to appear in a 2010 episode of *Sesame Street*, Pop singer Katie Perry's duet with the lovable puppet, Elmo, was pulled by the programme's producers on the grounds that Perry's costume was too provocative for daytime television in the USA. With the video now widely available online from sites such as *YouTube*, people can determine for themselves the veracity of the censor's objections. The censorship of the Perry duet is yet another manifestation of the idiosyncrasies of US censors, and to understand the many incongruities that have framed our contemporary moral standards requires a broader examination and contextualisation of the US legal and constitutional frameworks. To this end, this chapter attempts to foreground some key events of the past and present landscape of censorship in the USA, to establish the over-zealous moral framework inherited by contemporary American audiences.

In developing the Constitution of the United States of America, the forefathers provided in the First Amendment for the rights of all Americans to engage in freedom of expression:

> Congress shall make no law respecting an establishment of religion, or prohibiting the free exercise thereof; or abridging the freedom of speech or of the press; or the right of the people peaceably to assemble, and to petition the Government for a redress of grievances. (December 15, 1791)[1]

While conventional wisdom dictates that the arts are immediately protected under the First Amendment rights of the Constitution of the United States of America, the arbitrary nature of interpretation continues to overshadow artistic freedom of expression in the USA. The contest over the interpretation of this freedom of artistic expression challenges both artist and audience. Some key artistic works make use of this inherent struggle.

The Cradle Will Rock

The Tim Robbins directed drama, *Cradle Will Rock* (1999) documents the production of the 1937 musical, *The Cradle Will Rock*, composed by Marc Blitzstein and sponsored by the Federal Theatre Project (FTP). One of the 'New Deal' economic programmes implemented by the Roosevelt government in the USA between 1933 and 1936, the FTP was under the jurisdiction of the Works Progress Administration (WPA), which sought to provide employment opportunities for theatre artists and technicians during the Great Depression. The FTP represented the first and only time that the USA founded a National Theatre in an effort to bring theatre/performance throughout the country.

As documented in Robbins's dramatisation, a troupe of passionate actors, including a young Orson Welles, risks everything to perform the infamous Blitzstein musical, whose leftist, Brecht-inspired critique of corporate greed and corruption was always likely to offend. Taking place within a generic 'Steel Town, USA', the play focuses on efforts to unionise workers so as to combat the evil capitalist 'Mr Mister', who controls the factories, the press, the church and the social organisations of the community. Given the fragility of the financial and social situation of the time, a musical that challenged the hegemonic order, and encouraged the notion of rising up against oppression – for the right of free expression, free work and free organisation – was a controversial subject to say the least. Due to its overt leftist sympathies, the musical's rehearsals were continually overshadowed by government accusations of the FTP's communist sympathies. What Robbins's film attempted to accentuate is how the committee hearings betray a complete ignorance of the history, purpose and intent of theatre as a necessary vehicle for critical thought, a quality of which the committee itself appeared to be in dire need.

The situation accelerated to the point where the US military was called in to block the entrance to the theatre on the eve of the performance so that its actors, stage technicians and musicians were refused entrance for rehearsal. Dismayed but determined, the actors took the show into an abandoned theatre, publicised via a parade through the New York streets. The new incarnation of the show came in the form of a scaled-down solo piano performance by its author and composer, Marc Blitzstein, who could perform because he was not part of the FTP or the musicians' union. The political censorship of the musical was juxtaposed with the destruction of a Nelson Rockefeller commissioned mural by Mexican Artist Diego Rivera, whose fate was sealed when the artist refused to remove an image of Lenin from the piece.

The Hays Code

With concern for the moral development of an unwitting American public, the introduction of the Hays Code not only governed what was fit to present in the cinema, but furthermore, reiterated the extraordinary power of the motion picture industry to shape moral rectitude. This set of censorship guidelines for the American film industry was established in 1930. To capture both the power and limitations entrusted to filmmakers, the following excerpts offer a glimpse into the language intended to guide the American film industry.

> **The Motion Picture Production Code of 1930 [The Hays Code] Excerpts:**
>
> If motion pictures present stories that will affect lives for the better, they can become the most powerful force for the improvement of mankind.
>
> Motion picture producers recognize the high trust and confidence which have been placed in them by the people of the world and which have made motion pictures a universal form of entertainment.
>
> They recognize their responsibility to the public because of this trust and because entertainment and art are important influences in the life of a nation.
>
> Hence, though regarding motion pictures primarily as entertainment *without any explicit purpose of teaching or propaganda,* they know that the motion picture within its own field of entertainment *may be directly responsible for spiritual or moral* progress, for *higher types of social life, and for much correct thinking.*[3] (Italicised segments offered for the purpose of emphasis.)

This Code proceeds for another twelve pages, warning of the potential evils of film, and provides commandments for things *Thou Shalt Not Include* in films, for example:

1. Crimes Against the Law
    a. The technique of murder must be presented in a way that will not inspire imitation.
    b. Methods of crime should not be explicitly presented.
    c. The use of firearms should be restricted to the essentials.
2. Sex
    a. The sanctity of the institution of marriage and the home shall be upheld.
    b. Adultery must not be explicitly treated, or justified, or presented attractively.
    c. Excessive and lustful kissing, lustful embraces, suggestive postures and gestures, are not to be shown.
    d. Sex perversion or any inference to it is forbidden.
    e. Miscegenation (sex relationships between the white and black races) is forbidden.
3. Vulgarity
4. Obscenity
    a. Obscenity in word, gesture, reference, song, joke, or by suggestion is forbidden.
5. Profanity
    a. Pointed profanity (this includes the word, God, Lord, Jesus Christ – unless used reverently – Hell, S.O.B., damn, Gawd) or every other profane or vulgar expression however used, is forbidden.
6. Costume
    a. Complete nudity is never permitted.
    b. Indecent or undue exposure is forbidden.
7. Dances
    a. Dances suggesting or representing sexual actions or indecent passions are forbidden.
8. Religion
    a. No film or episode may throw ridicule on any religious faith.

9. Locations
    a. The treatment of bedrooms must be governed by good taste and delicacy.
    b. Salacious, indecent, or obscene titles shall not be used.
10. Repellent Subjects
    a. Actual hangings or electrocutions as legal punishments for crime.
    b. Brutality and possible gruesomeness.
    c. Apparent cruelty to children or animals.
    d. The sale of women, or a woman selling her virtue.[2]

Despite the Code's detailed justification and clarification of its commandments, moral obligation was at the heart of its brief:

> The motion picture, because of its importance as entertainment and because of the trust placed in it by the peoples of the world, has special moral obligations.[3]

While the Code was discontinued in 1968, these guidelines live on through the Motion Picture Association of America film rating system, a situation that will be discussed later in this chapter.

The investigation of the Federal Theatre Project and the implementation of the Motion Picture Production Code provided evidence of an encroaching dogmatism that would further deter artistic freedom. Perhaps the apotheosis of this government campaign over morality came in the form of the House on Un-American Activities Committee (1947–1950). These events were presented in the Eric Bentley play, *Are You Now or Have You Ever Been* (1972), with dialogue taken directly from the transcripts of the committee proceedings. This method of scripting a play provides an early version of contemporary documentary theatre – presented not primarily as entertainment, but as an effort to effect social change. Through this series of hearings and transcripts, one is aware of the sheer terror awaiting those who affirmed allegiance to the Communist Party.

Producers, directors, actors and artists were brought before the committee to justify affiliations with communism, whether real or imagined, if only to avoid being blacklisted from employment completely. Questionable phrasing simply aided the witch-hunt: 'Are you now, or have you ever been, a member of the Communist Party or the Screen Writers Guild?' While the fear of communism infected the USA at that time, this interrogation of artists and their influence on social or political values would have ongoing consequences into the future.

Federal Communications Commission

Yet another landmark in the regulation and maintenance of contemporary community standards of decency was the Federal Communications Commission (FCC) regulation of television and radio broadcasting. While the regulation did not explicitly state the words to be avoided, the absence on the airwaves of the swear words – shit, piss, fuck, cunt, cocksucker, motherfucker, tits (words still considered offensive by the FCC although current regulation allows a statement that uses them to stand, albeit to bleep-censor the actual word) – was lampooned by the comedian George Carlin in 1972, in his monologue, *Seven Words You Can Never Say on Television*.[4] Carlin himself would eventually fall foul of FCC censors after a broadcast of this routine on radio station WBAI-FM received complaints.[5]

Despite the ensuing court case over the broadcast monologue, there was one at least one small victory for artistic freedom. The United States Supreme Court established the 'safe-harbour' provision that grants broadcasters the right to broadcast indecent (but not obscene) material between the hours of 10 pm and 6 am (even if the FCC remains somewhat capricious in regulating its enforcement). For example, the 'After Oscar Special' of *Jimmy Kimmel Live* preceding the 80th Annual Academy Awards (2008), featured a video entitled *I'm Fucking Matt Damon*, where Damon utters, 'Hey Sarah, he's got bigger tits', which was aired without incident. In contrast to the subdued response to the Kimmel programme is the Madonna 'fuck' incident of the *Late Show with David Letterman* (2011). According to the FCC 'count' the F-word was used by Madonna thirteen times in conjunction with many other offending words – all of which were bleeped for air, even though this segment appeared after the officially sanctioned 10 pm–6 am safe harbour indicated in the 1972 George Carlin case by the FCC. Questioned on the controversy surrounding her appearance, and the censorship it attracted, Madonna argued against the moral ambivalence of the FCC: 'You can show a person getting blown up, and you can't say fuck? It's such hypocrisy. The fact that everyone counted how many fucks I said – how small minded is that?'[6]

Feuds over public funding

US artists and arts organisations can apply to the taxpayer-funded National Endowment for the Arts (NEA), for financial support for projects and performances. The grant requests are read by appointed peer artists who determine the strength of the project and the value to the arts community. In 1990, Congress amended the statute governing the National Endowment for the Arts to require that the NEA Chairperson consider 'general standards of respect and decency for the diverse beliefs and values of the American public'[7] when awarding art grants.

The 'NEA four', Karen Finley, Tim Miller, Holly Hughes and John Fleck, are performance artists whose provocative work pushes the boundaries of contemporary art. While they work independently of each other, they share a collective passion for creating new works of performance, and they enjoy an international reputation. Yet their reputation preceded them, and in an astonishing sequence of events in the late 1990s, these four individual performance artists had their funding support from the National Endowment for the Arts withdrawn as a result of the NEA's 'decency clause'. They took their case before the Supreme Court in protest. While their right to maintain government funding was previously upheld by the California courts, subsequent challenges brought about primarily by Republican Senator Jesse Helms (North Carolina) pushed the issue to the national courts. The concept of 'decency standards' adds some imprecise considerations to an already subjective process. The outcome of this legal challenge was that all four of these individual artists received compensation surpassing their grant amounts in 1993 when courts ruled in support of the four artists.[8]

The NEA Four's legal battles were foreshadowed by the controversial award of $15,000 given by the NEA-funded Southeast Center for Contemporary Arts to visual artist Andres Serrano, for his work *Piss Christ* (1987). The apparent blasphemy is readily apparent in the title of the work, and understandably confronts the sacred nature of artistic images of Christ throughout the ages. Without the title, one is simply confronted with a photo of a transparent soft blending of shades of yellow-orange-red-pink around a beautifully lit crucifix. When coupled with its provocative title, the work takes on a dramatic new dimension, and has invariably set off a series of protests wherever the picture is shown.

Such is the taboo on Christian iconography in the art world, that Cosimo Cavallaro's life-size and anatomically correct, suspended 'chocolate Jesus' sculpture entitled, *My Sweet Lord* (2007) was cancelled before it even opened at the Roger Smith Hotel's, Lab Gallery.[9] With its opening scheduled to coincide with Holy Week, 2007, the public outcry resulted in the cancellation of the exhibition.[10] In fact, most of the work's actual notoriety was generated through images circulated on the internet, without which the exhibition would have likely proceeded without incident. The outcry was amplified by the Catholic League for Religious and Civil Rights, who forced the president of the hotel in which the gallery resided to finally cancel the exhibition. Matt Semler, the Lab Gallery's artistic director, resigned in protest, stating that the action to cancel was at the instigation of those who had not even seen the show.[11]

Perhaps some of the struggles encountered by the aforementioned artists are best addressed by American-based, Mexican performance artist, Guillermo Gomez-Pena, who, in a 2006 article in *The Drama Review*, confronted 20 years of US censorship of his performance troupe, La Pocha Nostra. He states that during his tours of the USA he has come across innumerable situations in which the content of his 'politically direct', 'racially sensitive' and 'sexually explicit' material had to be adapted and translated for specific performance sites. The underfunding of the arts, paired with an institutionalised neo-conservatism and the imposed culture of panic, has created an incendiary environment for the production of critical culture and resulted in a growing unemployed class: the 'radical' experimental artist. He recites a letter from his agent, Nola Mariano, where he was told that 'Besides the ideological censorship exercised during the Bush administration, I believe that we have entered a new era of psychological censorship [...] Unable to quickly identify the opposition, we find ourselves shadowboxing with our conscience and censoring ourselves.'[12] Those artists like Guillermo Gomez-Pena who continue to push the boundaries of conventional artistic expression are taking direct action, instead of waiting to be censored. Gomez-Pena, for example, has drafted a letter to be sent prior to his performance:

Dear Curator, Producer, Arts Presenter,

Think twice before inviting this performance to your institution.
His new work might be overtly political and too sexually explicit
for these times. He might, challenge – even offend – your audience.
If you insist on inviting him, make sure that your board members

approve, and that the local community is prepared. We don't want to ruffle the feathers of our donors or the media. Remember this is post-9/11 America, the Bush era, and these are extremely delicate times.

Sincerely,
The Artist
USA, 2005[13]

The Motion Picture Association of America

Perhaps some of the more elusive forms of censorship are perpetrated by the Motion Picture Association of America (MPAA). As exposed in the compelling documentary by Kirby Dick, *This Film Is Not Yet Rated* (2006), the MPAA Ratings Board uses a panel of 'average American citizens', whose identity is not disclosed, to view films prior to release to provide a guideline for potential audiences. In the American system, the following letters provide an indication of the nature of language and images which may provide concern for the viewer:

> G General Audiences [...] nothing that would offend parents for viewing by children.
> PG Parental Guidance Suggested [...] may concern some material parents might not like for their young children.
> PG13 Parents STRONGLY Cautioned [...] some material may be inappropriate for pre-teenagers.
> R Restricted [...] Contains some adult material. Parents are urged to learn more about the film before taking their young children with them. [Note: under 17 not admitted without parent or guardian.]
> NC17 No one under 17 admitted [...] Patently adult material. Children are not admitted.[14]

On the surface, this could serve as a valuable guide for parents, if they choose to be involved in their child's entertainment choices. It would hold additional value if one were to believe that the MPAA was an open, transparent and honest system of review. In Dick's film, we learn otherwise; he hires a private detective to gather information about the raters, the process of review and the potential for a filmmaker to successfully market and distribute a film. In the process, Dick uncovers some troubling information on the process of qualifying and quantifying objectionable material. The arbitrary nature of MPAA review means that, for example, the term 'fuck' can be used as a noun, but not as a verb, or that 'shit' is acceptable as exclamation, but not as bodily function.[15]

'Acceptable' bodies

Dick's investigation also encounters the politics of the 'acceptable' body. In the film, *Boys Don't Cry (1999)*, which originally received an NC-17 rating, the director was told that Lana – a young woman who identifies as a male – had an orgasm deemed 'too long'. The rating system did not appear to extend the same concern to the film, *Coming Home (1978)*, in which Jane Fonda is the recipient of an extremely protracted orgasm, courtesy of the disabled Vietnam vet, Luke Martin, played by Jon Voight. We learn that sex is permissible when the shot focuses on the upper bodies, but once the camera maintains full body-shot, perhaps exposing pelvises in action, censorship beckons. Pubic hair still remains a taboo, although that also remains an ambivalent category, as nudity is seemingly more permissible among women than men.

The penis has been covertly introduced into contemporary cinema, albeit not in a state of sexual excitement but only as flaccid appendage. In the original *Sex in the City* (2008) feature film, the camera offered a side glimpse of Giles Marini's chiselled body in an outdoor shower with his manhood fully exposed. This scene was casual with the only intention left to the responsibility of the viewer. In *Forgetting Sarah Marshall* (2008), actor Jason Segal, with his somewhat soft body, presented full frontal nudity with a sense of vulnerability. The most recent controversial concern for a film rating depicting male nudity was in the 2011 film *Shame*, starring Michael Fassbender. Appropriate to the character being played, a sex-addict, Fassbender appeared completely nude in several scenes. What is unique about this film is that it received the rating NC-17, which usually places limitations on film promotion and the potential acknowledgements during the awards season. Yet *Shame* has broken barriers of acceptability and has earned recognition both for the film and its lead actor; among a plethora of film awards, Fassbender won Best Actor in a Leading Role at the Golden Globes (although he was conspicuously absent from the Oscars).

It would appear that such accolades are still the bastion of the heterosexual world. As recounted in Dick's film, 'straight' sex earns an NC-17 rating; sex involving same-sex couples earns an R rating. One can simply compare two films released in the same year of 1999: *But*

I'm a Cheerleader and *American Pie*. In the former example, teenagers are sent to a sexual rehabilitation camp in order to 'change' their sexual persuasion from gay or lesbian to 'straight'. In one scene, we find one of the 'gay' girls alone in her room, masturbating, albeit fully clothed. It received an R rating. In the coming-of-age comparison film, *American Pie*, the straight male can, with buttocks exposed, fuck a pie on the kitchen table, and merely get off with a PG-13. An MPAA rating that can access wider audiences means a lot in terms of distribution and advertising revenue. Films rated R and NC-17 find it hard to compete for the same mass-market attention.

This most accessible artistic medium enters American homes daily. With a broad range of programming for network, cable and independent broadcast venues, the standards of acceptability continue to evolve, but the editing for content, image and language is quite persistent. The control of television standards by the Federal Communications Commission (FCC) seems driven by an arbitrary set of values, and notable for their stasis. While the FCC standards haven't changed, the lifestyles of its viewers have. Although the 10 pm to 6 am slot enjoys its 'safe harbor' provision, the lifestyle of the American teenager has changed. Twenty-four hour access to any form of entertainment, images or language which interests them is not uncommon. Perhaps the FCC is upholding a set of values no longer in step with contemporary social mores. The sitcom *Modern Family*, for example, features three different kinds of families: traditional, gay and inter-generational, and the programme continues to capture the attention of the American audience as well as garner awards for writing and acting.[16] The teen-focused drama of *Glee* is similarly provocative in its presentation of issue-oriented situations of concern to its demographic.

Some of the measures taken by the FCC incite more curiosity that they probably should. The use of 'the black bar of censorship', sometimes evident as 'a pixilated oval' intended to cover buttocks or breasts, are a common feature of reality television, viewer submitted videos, as well as some cable presentation of films. This is one of the most imaginative and distracting forms of censorship in American television. One would believe that according to television censors, Americans cannot handle the image of the human buttocks or breasts, even while such apparently unacceptable images are perfectly acceptable in other countries.

A bizarre demonstration of the American proclivity for the use of pixilation is apparent in the 1994 film, *Threesome*. We witness a scene in which three college roommates (two men and one woman) are at a lake in a remote wooded area, when the woman decides to enjoy some 'skinny dipping'. One of the two males eagerly drops his clothes and dives in, while the other more reluctant male finally gives in and runs in after his friends. This charming and somewhat innocent scene becomes farce, as the American television audience is greeted with three pixilated ovals covering three sets of buttocks and one set of breasts. One is led to believe that this editorial choice was, once again, political in nature as this film was being played on Logo – Gay & Lesbian Network (owned by MTV, owned by Viacom).

Yet on the same network – in approximately the same late-night-time slot, there is a weekly broadcast of an episodic show entitled, *Nip/Tuck* that has a somewhat more heterosexual pedigree, and less censorship. In the Season 3 episode, *Fraternity Prank* (2005), two freshmen pledging the fraternity have their faces super-glued to another male's buttocks, all of which is quite permissible for the audience to see. In Season 4, Episode 3 the well-sculpted Mario Lopez plays a guest plastic surgeon and is seen to be taking part in a communal shower with his co-worker, played by Julian McMahon. Both men are completely nude from the back and freely comment on each other's physical development. Presented under the guise of 'surgeons curious about how much work the other has had on his body', the scene also escapes the pixilated ovals. As further reflection on this somewhat biased representation, one could also cite the apparent lack of scrutiny given to network broadcasts of *NYPD Blue* (1993–2005), a hard-hitting and highly regarded drama, which often contained nudity. The series continues to air uninterrupted without any attempt at censorship, and no pixilated ovals or black bars are in sight.

Given the vagaries of FCC regulation, there have been attempts at competing rating systems. Home Box Office (HBO), a cable broadcast service, has promoted its own system of ratings advice:

TVY	Appropriate for all children
TV7	Directed to older children
TVG	For General Audiences
TVPG	Parental guidance suggested
TV14	Parental guidance strongly suggested
TVM	Mature Audiences only[17]

Although this is not dissimilar to the system generated by the MPAA, where HBO goes into further detail is in the following list, which is provided as indication of content advisories and is appropriately shown both in the printed programme guide as well as onscreen at the beginning of the broadcast.

AC	Adult Content
AL	Adult Language
GL	Graphic Language
MV	Mild Violence
V	Violence
GV	Graphic Violence
BN	Brief Nudity
N	Nudity
SC	Strong sexual content
RP	Rape[18]

This manner of working provides a transparency that is lacking from that of the FCC. While this might, for some, represent a little too much information, for others it is just enough to allow freedom of choice. Nevertheless, the feature film is at least presented as it was intended.

Reflecting the vast changes in morality since the inception of FCC regulation, the Supreme Court of the USA is currently reviewing the policing of curse words and nudity on broadcast television in the 24-hour cable era. The Supreme Court was also troubled by the many inconsistent standards that allowed certain words and displays in some contexts but not in others. At issue in this current debate is a 1978 decision that upheld the FCC's authority to regulate radio and television content primarily at least in the hours when children are likely to be watching or listening (before 10 pm). The networks indicate that the FCC's current policy is too hard to follow and penalises the use of particular words in some instances but not in others. The interpretation of the First Amendment to the Constitution of the United States continues.

In the process of making an informed choice, there seems to be no explanation and much inconsistency in the practice of censorship. In all areas – performance, film, and television – the rules remain unclear. It is a capricious process and the artist is left juggling personal artistic integrity with the potential for work being altered by someone else or for the work not being seen.

Censorship of school programs

The backlash from parents and administrators during recent attempts for high school theatre programmes to present the acclaimed work,

Rent, resulted in the performance being cancelled in communities in California, Virginia and Texas. *Rent*, loosely based on Puccini's opera, *La Boheme*, and running on Broadway for more than 12 years, centres on a group of artists, straight and gay, living in the East Village in New York City. Some of the protagonists occupy marginal positions in the community, some are HIV-positive; some are drug addicts; some are in recovery. Rowlett High School, a Texas community near Dallas, cancelled a production of *Rent*, after protests from some of the parents in the community. Although the show was announced in advance of the school year, and rehearsals were ongoing, it was not until the eve of the show's opening that the controversy erupted. Attending to the mounting pressure, the school's theatre director, Brandon Tijerina, made a decision to cancel:

> In light of everything that has happened, I need to think of my students first and foremost. They are dealing with pressures they don't need at their age. The best thing for my students is for me to cancel the show, not because of the controversy, but because I honestly truly care for my students.[19]

There was at least a happy ending to this unnecessary saga; in the aftermath of the decision, Tijerina eventually garnered community support and a local radio station covered the cost of the music and secured an alternate venue outside of the school district jurisdiction at Southern Methodist University in Dallas.[20]

Less fortunate was the fate of the play *Corpus Christi*, by Terrance McNally (1998). A reimagining of the story of Jesus Christ (referred to as Joshua because his mother's husband, Joseph, thinks the name Jesus 'sounds like a Mexican'), the play dramatises a story of Jesus and the Apostles as gay men living in modern-day Texas. A condensed version of the play, featured as part of a student directing class at St Edward's University in Austin, Texas was performed in 2001, without incident. However, as a class project in 2010, John Jordan Otte, of Tarleton State University in Stephenville, Texas, was stopped from performing the play. The small liberal arts public college in Texas became the centre of a political maelstrom, to the extent that the Lieutenant Governor of Texas, David Dewhurst, was drawn into the debate. Dewhurst was to comment: 'Every citizen is entitled to the freedom of speech, but no one should have the right to use government funds or institutions to portray acts that are morally reprehensible to the majority of Americans.'[21] Although it had the grudging support of the university president, the play succumbed to pressure from the governor's office and the performance was cancelled.

The arts in the USA form a vibrant and essential dynamic which offer reflection as well as opportunities to continue to explore and understand diverse ways of being. If there is a solution to the current practice of censorship – whether identified as such or subsumed under the rubric of provisional guidelines – the American public can only become responsible consumers through a consistent set of values. From the evidence presented from recent censorship controversies, this is still sadly not the case.

Notes

1. http://www.firstamendmentcenter.org (accessed 16 April 2012).
2. http://www.artsreformation.com (accessed 16 April 2102).
3. Ibid.
4. James Sullivan, *7 Dirty Words: The Life and Crime of George Carlin*, Da Capo Press, Cambridge, MA, 2010.
5. Ibid.
6. Stransky, Tanner, 'Madonna Shocks Letterman', *Entertainment Weekly*, Issue #1148, 1 April 2011. Accessed 13 April 2012.
7. California State University Long Beach, 'Finley v. National Endowment for the Arts (Excerpts) 1992'.
8. Robert Ayers, 'Karen Finley, Tim Miller, Holly Hughes, and John Fleck – the "NEA Four" – at New York University, 15 April 2004', *franklinfurnace.org* (accessed 15 April 2012).
9. Associated Press, 'Display of "Chocolate Jesus" Sculpture Cancelled', Foxnews.com. 30 March 2007 (accessed 11 April 2012).
10. Ibid.
11. Ibid.
12. Guillermo Gómez-Peña, 'Disclaimer', *The Drama Review* 50(1), 2006, p. 151.
13. Ibid., p. 150.
14. http://www.MPAA.org, 'What Each Rating Means' (accessed 14 April 2012).
15. Kirby Dick, *This Film is Not Yet Rated*, Red Letter Entertainment/Independent Film Channel, 2006.
16. Joe Jackson, Joe, 'Emmy Awards 2011: "Modern Family" Wins Big, "Mad Men" Takes Top Prize', *Time.com*, 19 September 2011 (accessed 13 April 2012).
17. http://www.HBO.com (accessed 11 April 2012).
18. Ibid.
19. Holly Yan, 'Director Cancels Production of "Rent" at Rowlett High', *Dallas Morning News*, 12 December 2008.
20. http://www.Dallasvoice.com, 'RHS theater students set "Rent" revue', 23 January 2009 (accessed 13 April 2012).
21. Reeve Hamilton, 'Play Cancelled at Tarleton State University', *TexasTribune.org*; 20 March 2010 (accessed 11 April 2012).

References

ArtsReformation.com, 'The Motion Picture Production Code of 1930 (Hays Code)', *artsReformation.com*, accessed on 11 April 2012, http://www.artsreformation.com/a001/hays-code.html

Associated Press, 'Display of "Chocolate Jesus" Sculpture Cancelled', Foxnews.com. 30 March 2007, accessed on 11 April 2012, http://www.foxnews.com/story/0,2933,262602,00.html

Ayers, Robert, 'Karen Finley, Tim Miller, Holly Hughes, and John Fleck, The "NEA Four"', New York University, April 15, 2004', *franklinfurnace.org*, accessed on 15 April 2012, http://www.franklinfurnace.org/research/essays/nea4/ayers.html

BBC.co.uk, 'Chocolate Jesus Exhibit Cancelled', *news.bbc.co.uk*. 31 March 2007, accessed on 11 April 2012, http://news.bbc.co.uk/2/hi/6513155.stm

California State University Long Beach, 'Finley v. National Endowment for the Arts (Excerpts) 1992'. *Csulb.edu*, accessed on 11 April 2012, http://www.csulb.edu/~jvancamp/doc4.html

Dallasvoice.com, 'RHS theater students set "Rent" revue', *Dallasvoice.com*, 23 January 2009, accessed on 13 April 2012, http://www.dallasvoice.com/local-briefs-january-23-2009-1018665.html

Dick, Kirby, *This Film is Not Yet Rated*, Red Letter Entertainment/Independent Film Channel, 2006.

FirstAmendmentCenter.org, 'About the First Amendment', FirstAmendmentCenter.org, accessed on 11 April 2012, http://www.firstamendmentcenter.org

Gómez-Peña, Guillermo, 'Disclaimer', *The Drama Review* 50(1), 2006, pp. 149–158.

Hamilton, Reeve, 'Play Cancelled at Tarleton State University', *TexasTribune.org*; 20 March 2010, accessed on 11 April 2012, http://www.texastribune.org/texas-education/higher-education/play-canceled-at-tarleton-state-university/

HBO.com, accessed on 11 April 2012, http://www.hbo.com

Jackson, Joe, 'Emmy Awards 2011: "Modern Family" Wins Big, "Mad Men" Takes Top Prize', *Time.com*, 19 September 2011, accessed on 13 April 2012, http://newsfeed.time.com/2011/09/19/emmy-awards-2011-modern-family-wins-big-mad-men-takes-top-prize/

MPAA.org, 'What Each Rating Means', *MPAA.org*. Accessed on 14 April 2012, http://www.mpaa.org/ratings/what-each-rating-means

Stransky, Tanner, 'Madonna Shocks Letterman', *Entertainment Weekly*, Issue #1148, 1 April 2011, accessed on 13 April 2012, http://www.ew.com/ew/article/0,,20476158,00.html

Sullivan, James, *7 Dirty Words: The Life and Crime of George Carlin*, DaCapo Press, Cambridge, MA, 2010.

Yan, Holly, 'Director Cancels Production of "Rent" at Rowlett High', *Dallas Morning News*, 12 December 2008, http://www.dallasnews.com/sharedcontent/dws/news/localnews/stories/121108dnmetrent.388b0b1.html, archive copy at *WFAA.org*, accessed on 14 April 2012, http://www.wfaa.com/news/local/64496887.html

11
Why Saying 'No' to Life Is Unacceptable

Claire Colebrook

Just what counts as acceptable or unacceptable is obviously a cultural, social and historical variable. That being so, it might still be possible to make claims regarding broader structures of unacceptability, and certain motifs that, within epochs, dominate cultural production. We can perhaps begin by asking – today – just what might count as unacceptable *in general*. That is to say, one can imagine all forms of socially refused content, ranging from prohibited actions and lifestyles to censored content. But on what grounds or by what logic is the border between the acceptable and unacceptable drawn?

The problem can be given some generality and purchase today if we ask what the rationale for accepting or refusing something might be, and – further – what forms the limit of acceptability today. I would suggest that despite dispute over what counts as acceptable, the governing rationale for dispute is the concept of *life*: one either argues for an intrinsic 'right to life' or one asserts one's rights to choose on the basis of the autonomy of one's life. One either argues against gay marriage, single parenting or other alternative lifestyles on the grounds that it threatens 'our way of life' (including the family, reproduction, maintaining humanity as it is), *or* one insists on the right to determine one's life. Cultural production also reinforces this unquestioned affirmation of life: from lifestyle channels, to reality television's display of life, to celebrity culture, to legal and medical dramas and the increasingly close-angled camera work displaying the minutiae of life: all external criteria give way to the value of *life itself*.

At first glance it appears that the Enlightenment project of removing all forms of transcendent justification – church, state, privilege and prejudice – has been achieved, and now there is nothing other than life. And yet, such a frenzied surge in an unquestioning insistence on the value of life is accompanied both by an inability to confront the imminent demise of life (whether that be by way of accelerated extinction due to climate change, or disaster scenarios resulting from terrorism, nuclear warfare, viral pandemic or bio-weapons and resource depletion – or, the inevitable panic that would follow on from and exacerbate the appearance of any of these threats). In addition to the shrill insistence on the primacy of life, and alongside the deluge of information regarding increasing and exponentially accelerating threats to life, there has been a strange incapacity to ask the question of life. That is to say: now that life appears to be in danger of disappearance, diminution or mutation beyond recognition, living humans indulge both in greater and greater insistence on the sanctity of life, *and* seem incapable of directly confronting the intensifying threats that menace the present.

The hinge of the acceptable is life, both because acceptability is negotiated on the basis of life, and because any *question* of life is evidently unacceptable. This inadmissibility is most clearly the case precisely when the question of life seems to have been posed. That is, when cultural production turns directly (as it does occasionally) to the problem of life, it is precisely at that point that the question of life refuses to be asked. The question of what we accept and do not accept, what we can consider or question and what remains beyond question, is probably always a query of some interest. But the question of the value of life should gain in interest (if not urgency) for us now, and for three reasons. First, the question or problem of life is now an actual question that is everywhere being asked (and yet also deferred in the very mode of the question's formation). We are no longer simply confronted with the 'meaning' of life, or the enigma of existence, for it is quite possible, probable or increasingly certain that we will begin to witness the beginning of the end of life (mass extinctions, resource depletion threatening human order, climate change that is moving at a pace beyond predictions of exponential acceleration, and even the strange mutation of the human brain via digital technologies and visual culture that may spell the 'end' of cognitive man).

Yet, oddly enough, despite the urgency of this problem, the question of life has – more than ever – been articulated in terms of *meaning*, with a flurry of supposedly deeply philosophical accounts of the unavoidable horizon of meaning when approaching what appears as life.[1] Further, and despite recent academic and philosophical insistence upon life's meaning, there has been a surge of cultural production focusing on life's termination – ranging from disaster fiction and cinema to survival guides for end-of-the-world scenarios. In addition to a flourishing genre of post-apocalyptic cinema and literature, there have also been documentaries and non-fictional thought experiments about the world without humans, the aftermath that would follow catastrophes, and other human-witnessed post-human scenarios. In sum, the problem of the continuation of life *ought* to be at the forefront of reflective inquiry (and is indeed played out in a series of fictional and semi-fictional scenarios) but the problem is (in that very process of being played out) displaced. It is as though cultural production, at least in its dominant mode, is indulging in Freud's grandson's *Fort-Da* game: we play and replay the disappearance and reappearance of life, and do this to anticipate and master an event that concerns our (in this case, very real and possible) non-existence.

Third and finally, even in its barely articulated, suggested, but not fully posed mode, the form of the question of life has altered in the twenty-first century. Until recently, if the problem of life were posed it took the form of theodicy, or justification: of how 'we' can explain life's utter cruelty and seeming disregard for human suffering. It is this question that is played out in Job, in Greek tragedy, in Milton's *Paradise Lost* and even perhaps in modern novels, such as William Godwin's *Caleb Williams*, where inscrutable injustice is now politicised (and can be attributed to corrupt and therefore remediable institutions). These modern novelistic explorations of life's cruelty are tales of fortitude, and of the nobility and dignity of withstanding the force of existence. The endpoint of this tradition might be Kafka or Beckett, in which the individual confronts a life that is tragically void of all sense and (for that individual at least) hope. It is perhaps thoroughly modern to shift from a tragic acceptance of the brute contingency of life to some sense that the struggle itself is one of personal meaning. (This was why Nietzsche so admired the ancient Greeks, for having the capacity to experience the violence and festive cruelty of life's force, without moralising.[2]) Today, and for some time, the tragic mode has become less acceptable *as tragic* and some form of resolution or compensation usually closes narrative form. The forces of good triumph in the end, or suffering itself is given meaning: Hollywood cinema rarely allows itself a conclusion void of redemption, while tales of suffering – from *Born on the Fourth of July* (1989) to *The Pursuit of Happyness* (2006) and *127 Hours* (2010) are morality plays of individual triumph rather than an exploration of cosmic indifference. Even so, and despite a refusal to confront the limits of life just when the historical actuality of life's end is becoming apparent, though not witnessed, it is possible to note a shift of genre away from human-to-human adversity to, at least initially, something like a war between humans and the cosmos (and this despite all the deep ecology proclamations of our oneness with life).

A new mode of the question of life has come to dominate cultural production: not 'Why are humans subjected to the brutal force of existence?' but 'Given human brutality and life-destructiveness, by what right will humans continue to survive?' It is no longer life that needs to be justified, but the human species' malevolent relation to life. Nietzsche had already charted the ways in which 'man' as a moral animal had been effected from an inability to accept the violence of the forces of life. Whereas Ancient Greek tragedy was initially akin to a theatre of cruelty, not yet indulging in justification, the positing of a 'higher world' that would justify life created man as a slavish animal.[3] When that higher world was turned inward, it was not God who enslaved man, but 'humanity': we are now always already guilty, chastened and humiliated by an ideal of our own making, and fall into nihilistic despair if the once imagined higher world seems no longer real. We simply cannot live existence without granting it some sort of meaning. Yet today it is not nihilistic despair in the face of non-meaning that seems to be the concern. On the contrary, not only is meaning now the seemingly unquestionable horizon of human existence – ranging from 'philosophical' studies to the Oprah Winfrey Network and projects of individual self-development: cultural production reaches its points of tragic despair by questioning the rampant violence of humans in relation to life rather than life's lack of concern for humans. It is not humanity that is cruelly placed in an inhuman world, so much as an inhuman humanity that has become unjustifiable in an anthropomorphised world.

The post-apocalyptic

The opening of the twenty-first century is marked by a supposedly new genre (or the efflorescence of an old genre) of the post-apocalyptic. However this term is used, one way we can make sense of the *post*-apocalyptic is to note that scenes of near-destruction of the human milieu are followed by an exploration of what will survive or remain, or what ought to survive or remain, after the absence of humanity as we now know it. The post-apocalyptic is best read as a question posed: just as the human species starts to approach the real possibility of its actual non-existence (whether through climate change, viral pandemic, terrorist use of nuclear or bio-weapons, wars on the terror aiming to avert the latter, resource depletion, panic, or any conjunction of the foregoing), there is a barely perceived and half-articulated problem of how and whether humans ought to survive. What is it about humanity that one would want to accept? Further – as the very use of the word 'post-*apocalyptic*' indicates – the genres and modes in which this problem is posed preclude the problem from being posed. There is a constitutive inability to confront the very content that 'we' are nevertheless constantly replaying.

According to Freud, art is primarily a rendering acceptable of otherwise indulgently unacceptable private content.[4] Jokes, similarly, allow otherwise unacceptable content to circulate, allowing what can be thought but not *really* said to find some outlet (thus explaining, for Freud, the body's explosion in laughter). Beyond Freud, and in a line that runs at least from Adorno to Jameson, there is a commitment to the idea of narrative and form as processes that render the intolerable tolerable. Despite its debt to Marx, this strand of what I would refer to as existential or Hegelian Marxism problematises a Marxist concept of 'the political' that has tended to dominate whatever is left today of ideology critique. According to this basic Marxist imperative of politicising or denaturalising whatever appears as simple, inevitable, universal or irrevocable, one ought to historicise the present, and account for the genesis of the social and political world on the basis of 'man's' transformation of that world. What appears as intolerable should be regarded as an outcome of the division of labour and the conditions of production. Nothing should simply appear as transcendent, inhuman and inscrutable.

For Adorno, working against theodicy, there is an imperative to maintain an irresolvable negativity or disjunction between the sense we make of the world and a 'world itself' that can only be given as other than the human.[5] The shudder of existence, or the brute otherness of life that simply cannot be lived, is tempered in general by the projective processes that form the world. What appears today in the form of 'the aesthetic' enables us to have some sense of a historical trajectory in which the radically alien and contingent force of life has passed through a process of animism, or a mythologising reduction of the world, through enlightenment (or the reduction of the world to so much calculable and 'disenchanted' matter) through to modernism.[6] Modernism, for Adorno, is counter-bourgeois and counter-kitsch, an experience of form in its deadness, in its incommensurability with life. Without endorsing Adorno's high modernist resistance to the easily consumed and already circulating forms that render the world always already amenable, it is nevertheless worthwhile to pursue this crucial insight: art can be seen as having a *humanising* function, a rendering of the world into some form of manageable order. In quite different ways, Paul de Man, also indebted to Hegel in some respects, and also less ready to see language's ordering of the world as a process of meaning or familiarity, sought to draw attention – however impossibly – to language and form as radically *inhuman*.[7] For both Adorno and De Man, the text or art operates as a disjunction, negation or instance of 'deadness' or 'afterlife.' It is the lure of 'the aesthetic' to imagine that art is somehow an expression of 'life'.

If art in general is a formalising process that grants the raw violence of life some moralising structure, then certain modes of narrative would seem to intensify what Fredric Jameson (writing after Adorno) has summarised as the ideological transformation of existential horror into social symbolisation. Science fiction, for example, codes otherness into the delimited and opposed figure of the alien or invader.[8] (Spy fiction has its different narrative modes of discerning or reading just who or what counts as a threatening other, or just where the limits and readability of self and other lie). In so doing, narrative passes into a temporal project – an overcoming of adversity – what could not be confronted as such: our subjection to life.

The novelistic imagination tends to personalise, or even render familial, the symbolising order that had once – in epic or tragic modes – required a confrontation with forces that required more than 'life management'. If one examines cultural production today, the manifest content that seems at first to confront radically threatening forces is ultimately returned to the genres of family drama and romance, as though even the end of human existence could be Oedipalised. That is, there is an efflorescence of disaster and post-apocalyptic narrative, but always with a narrative resolution that restores a basic human binary (such as the romance ending that allows humanity to triumph in *The Adjustment Bureau* (2011) or the victory of New Age humanoids over corporate and military greed in *Avatar* (2009)). Even a story as bleak as Cormac McCarthy's *The Road* (especially in its cinematic adaptation of 2009), devolves around a father–son relation: the man and boy wander a landscape while struggling for survival against remaining humans; the journey concludes with a sense of the possible renewal of the family-maternal bond as the son is taken in by a potential new family.

In blockbuster entertainment, the 2008 film *Traitor* figured the 'war on terror' and the conflict between fundamental Islam and US security and espionage as ultimately a problem of fraternal misunderstanding: the warring individuals find common cause in the discovery of their underlying humanity. It is as though terrorism and militarism could be overcome if only we could return, once again, to face-to-face encounters. One might add to this continual anthropogenicism any number of disaster epics that are organised into human–human agonistics: it is never the earth, the climate, contingency or catastrophe as such that is presented as the intruding force of destruction; rather, it is some identifiable face that allows the sheer violence of adversity to be translated into a resolvable and symbolised other.

Occasionally, however, within narrative trajectories there have been moments when the *question* of life reaches articulation. If life – or the idea of a body that goes through time, manages an external world, and then arrives at its own end – has always been figured through some narrative imaginary that renders stark contingency into a mastered and acceptable *sense*,[9] then the question of life seems to destroy narrative. I want to cite two pre-contemporary examples before looking at the different ways in which the question of life's acceptability has changed its structure in the twenty-first century.

Narrative life

In Milton's *Paradise Lost*, a self-proclaimed theodicy or justification of the apparent intolerability of life, Adam asks God why he (Adam) was made so unfairly and impossibly free. If we accept that man deserves to be expelled from paradise because he chose to transgress the order of Eden, it does not follow that man deserved to be given this task in the first place. Adam's lament cries out against the burden of human freedom, or man's capacity to act against life. Why did God make him thus?

> Did I request thee, Maker, from my Clay
> To mould me Man, did I sollicite thee
> From darkness to promote me, or here place
> In this delicious Garden? as my Will
> Concurd not to my being, it were but right
> And equal to reduce me to my dust,
> Desirous to resigne, and render back
> All I receav'd, unable to performe
> Thy terms too hard, by which I was to hold
> The good I sought not. To the loss of that,
> Sufficient penaltie, why hast thou added
> The sense of endless woes? inexplicable
> Thy Justice seems; yet to say truth, too late,

> I thus contest; then should have been refusd
> Those terms whatever, when they were propos'd[10]:

God responds by unfolding a vision of history: Adam will witness increasing violence and destruction, but will eventually see man benefit from grace and forgiveness. If, after all this evil, God will still sacrifice his son, allowing man to receive a law that is now internalised and accepted from a condition of forgiven fallenness, then life once more make sense. Human life, for all its apparent perversity, is ultimately a higher good, all the better for having turned away from, and then re-found, itself. One might say that all narratives are theodicies, or ways in which the seemingly senseless destruction of existence is given redemptive form. The unacceptable is rendered acceptable, not just in the sense of what is socially frowned upon being presented as more palatable, but in a more radical sense in which something like *the social* is formed. Narrative creates the lure of a world in common, an order of sense and humanity, in which otherness is personalised and rendered familial and familiar.

This has specific purchase today: it is almost as though the more unimaginable the possible forces of destruction appear to be, the more local our narrative imagination becomes. In addition, though, to the process of narrative as social symbolisation – in which order as such is constituted – the problems, intolerable conflicts or disjunctions to which narrative responds are varied. One can imagine the ways in which race, sex, social disintegration, internecine conflicts, historical transitions and so forth, all need to be worked through by narrative.[11] What is suggested by Adorno's approach, and in Jameson's concept of ideology, is that these 'political' figures are ideological precisely because they give a binary and humanised form to existential conflict:

> The fantasy level of a text would then be something like the primal motor force which gives any cultural artifact its resonance, but which must always find itself diverted to other, ideological functions, and reinvested by what we have called the political unconscious.[12]

On the one hand, then, there is an ordering or meaning-producing function of narrative, a function that answers what might be referred to in general as the problem of existence. On the other hand, there are historically specific ways in which the modes of this question or conflict are formed; the ways in which life presents itself as intolerable are expressed in figurations that vary according to just what the horrific other of humanity is deemed to be.

In *Paradise Lost*, and theodicy generally, the problem is the burden of human freedom in relation to a God and life that *must be* conducive to harmony. In Mary Shelley's *Frankenstein*, the similarly formed question is now directed to man (Victor Frankenstein) by his monstrous progeny. Here the question is not so much human freedom as humanity's creation of a world in which its offspring are then abandoned. What duty do we owe to the future? If Victor Frankenstein plays God, he does so not only in his creation of a living being who is at once a mirror of his own being and yet deemed by him to be lesser, but also in his tyrannical laying down of terms the monster cannot accept. Allegorically, Shelley can be seen to be posing Milton's question again, somewhat blasphemously: what sort of God creates a being and then leaves it wandering in a world of despair? Or, as the monster accuses Victor: 'You, my creator, abhor me; what hope can I gather from your fellow creatures, who owe me nothing? They spurn and hate me? The desert mountains and dreary glaciers are my refuge.'[13]

The creature's plea to his maker is also an allegorical questioning of humanity's relation to production: how can we leave a populace of the future so miserably orphaned? In Shelley's case, this is sharpened by the fact that the monstrous being of the future promises to be less rapacious than man (even though he is refused by his creator):

> My food is not that of man; I do not destroy the lamb and the kid to glut my appetite; acorns and berries afford me sufficient nourishment. My companion will be of the same nature as myself, and will be content with the same fare. We shall make our bed of dried leaves; the sun shall shine on us as on man, and will ripen our food. The picture I present to you is peaceful and human, and you must feel that you could deny it only in the wantonness of power and cruelty.[14]

Shelley's novel is a play of mirrors (directly rewriting *Paradise Lost*), in which 'man's' plea against existence is at once given a political-allegorical form (so that the monster appears to be a disenfranchised other who could, in theory, be redeemed and included), at the same time as the monster's creator and pseudo-God also feels the utter horror of what it has meant to be a free, creative and world-transforming being. The maliciously and thoughtlessly reproductive Victor poses the same question to himself: how can one go on living when existence is intolerable, when one's free actions yield such monstrous outcomes: 'Cursed, cursed creator! Why did I live? Why, in that instant, did I not extinguish the spark of existence which you had so wantonly bestowed?'[15]

Shelley's formulation aimed to give some political purchase to the existential question, suggesting that it is Victor's theological imaginary that prompts him first to play God and then to hold on to proper notions of man and morality in the face of the monster's rather ecological and reasonable request. Even so, Shelley – like Milton – began by posing the question of the intolerable terms of life *for man*. If Milton sought resolution in grace, a 'paradise within' and a future when the world shall be 'all in all', Shelley suggested a more radical response: the truly human future does not close itself off to the non-carnivorous generations who will live in the glaciers and deserts. Something like the properly human functions as Shelley's political answer to the question of life. Like Marx, Adorno and Jameson after her, Shelley suggested that the existential shudder of existence should properly be understood not as a relation between man and world, but among men.

To varying degrees all these writers – from Milton and Shelley, to Marx, Adorno and Jameson – recognised that it is ideological and hasty to present adversity as a simple problem in the form of an isolated and humanised other, but it is also insufficient to abandon thinking and fall into an existential despair with regard to the brute violence of existence. Criticism, in this tradition, has as its task to hold on to the notion that damaged life might be redeemed, while avoiding the easy fantasy solution that would lie in attributing evil to some binary other. To this end, Shelley undertook a genealogy of the self: she described the genesis of Victor's monster, who first encounters the sensations of life and then becomes humanised by overhearing a reading of Milton's *Paradise Lost* (and then Volney's *Ruins of Empire*). After this basic training in humanity the monster is, however, spurned by those he encounters, primarily because of his visible difference from the humans with whom he feels such kinship. Shelley's politicisation of what seemed for Milton to be a problem of human freedom (or the relation between life and law) is – if we accept Jameson's definition of ideology – a counter-ideological gesture. What appears as the pure horror of life, or what for the moralising Victor can only be the menacing threat of beings who are radically other, was seen ultimately by Shelley to be a problem of critical enlightenment. What appears as existentially unacceptable should be transformed through social and political revolution. If recognition were granted to the potential hordes of the future one would be faced not with violence but sympathy and pity. *Political* solutions are therefore akin to the formalising procedures of art: what appears as intractable, unacceptable, intolerable or horrifically other can be given resolution by transforming torment as such into an anthropogenic problem. If Jameson argued that ideology is the way in which politically unacceptable structures are given imaginary resolution, and that the social symbolism of narrative completes a redistribution that should properly be revolutionary, then this is because of his post-Marxist commitment to transforming seemingly natural, universal or intractable problems into human-to-human struggles.

Minus the political

An entire genre of what has come to be known as post-apocalyptic film and literature currently and repeatedly, with ever increasing verve, plays out a fantasy of human near-disappearance and redemption. It does so precisely when our energies ought to be focused on what humans have done to the planet and how they might desist from so doing. In response to this deluge of cultural production, we would need to adjust the Marxist approach to politics and humanisation. Marxist critique aims to humanise and historicise, the two gestures being the same: what appears to be simply and universally intolerable needs to be recognised as having a history, where history is a history of labour and human relations. When those human relations are naturalised or 'frozen' – when the family or the male–female couple appears as the fantasy frame through which all horrors can ultimately be resolved – then it is the figure of bourgeois man that needs to be criticised and historicised. But what if the problem today were not that of a justice among humans? What if social political revolution among human beings were still to leave the relation between the human species and life in the same place? A new mode of critique that would *not* be political would be required. Indeed, it is the *political* gesture, or the understanding of conflicts as ultimately intra-human, that needs to be questioned. One needs a hypo-Marxism or counter-Marxism whereby the very condition of Marxism – man as a labouring animal who furthers his own life – needs to be recognised as the limit of thinking. For what 'we' cannot accept is the obvious counter to this assumption: man is not an animal who furthers his own survival.

For Milton and Shelley, the problem was that of the violence of life for an ill-equipped human. Whereas Milton responded theologically – arguing that God's grace and the unfolding of human history will justify the seemingly unjustifiable torments of life – Shelley adopted a more modern and political approach: humanity is capable of living well, living in a humane manner, if only social and political structures were conducive to sympathy and recognition (if we came into existence like Frankenstein's monster – through sensations and reading, rather than through doctrines of piety). Shelley diagnosed human despair and regarded its genesis as human, but for that very reason also resolvable. And this is in accord with the tradition that I have already cited whereby Adorno regarded the violence of existence to be something humanity finds intolerable and will thereby either mythically project onto an animated other, or 'rationally' subject to its own order. Critique or dialectics recognises that the sense or acceptability we have projected onto the world is at once *not* the world's own and yet – politically – demands to be brought into being.

Things have changed. The overwhelming question that presses itself upon us – requiring incessant repression and working through – is not the question of how we humans were placed in a world in which the task was too hard, the conditions too bleak or the burden of freedom too confronting. The question is not one of how we humans can justify life, but how we can possibly justify ourselves given our malevolent relation to life.

The current vogue for what is misleadingly called post-apocalyptic fiction seems to indicate that we are now feeling (if not thinking) a new relation between the human species and time. More accurately, we are experiencing humanity *as a species*, not just a humanity that emerged from the depths of time but a 'man' as a specified mode of organism that will one day have had its time. Just as post-Darwinian nineteenth-century literature had a sense of deep time – feeling some alarming presage of a time before humans – and adjusted its plot structures accordingly, literary and cinematic form is struggling with forms of expression that might capture a new mode of inhuman time. We rehearse over and over again our near annihilation, playing a cosmic version of the *Fort-Da* game, in which we replay our disappearance (semi-traumatically) and then stage our return and redemption.[16] *This* problem now focuses not on creation – why was man created given the hard terms of his existence? – but on extinction: what reasons might we fathom for wanting our survival? (Here it is not a question of justifying the life that man must face, but of justifying the man who has done so much to de-face life). Humanity has been violent, all too violent; it is not the horror of existence that tortures humanity but a humanity that can do nothing other than destroy itself and its milieu, and all – perversely – for the sake of its own myopic, short-circuited and self-regarding future.

Living extinction

In 2008, *The Day the Earth Stood Still* featured a deadpan alien (played appropriately by Keanu Reeves) who informed humanity that its violence and destructive modes of consumption no longer entitled it to life on earth. The narrative of the film proved this judgement and diagnosis to be peremptory: Keanu is given the chance to see the benevolent side of humanity through the eyes of a young boy, and the annihilation of the human species is delayed. A common motif in science fiction narratives of alien invasion, the judgement of humanity as life-denying and life-unworthy is neither refuted nor answered, but simply set aside as the plot hurtles toward redemption. Humanity is split in two: the worthless, violent, historical and life-denying humans perceived by the judging aliens, and the proper humanity that is disclosed by the morality tale of the narrative.

In *The Adjustment Bureau* of 2011, human freedom – that which makes us human and therefore supposedly worthy – is judged to be the cause of sufficient destruction to the point where its existence can no longer be permitted. This adaptation of a Philip K. Dick story features a team of intervening agents whose task is to allow humanity to run its proper and seemingly free course while making minor corrections if events appear to stray from their appropriate end. The heart of the film concerns a love story that is at odds with the prescribed order of events. Despite a series of more and more complex adjustments, and in the face of all adversity, the lovers – even with one of them knowing about the 'adjustments' – remain committed to their love. They stand firm, despite the warnings of the catastrophes that follow. The tale is heroic and Promethean, but not tragic; for in the end it is this miniscule and possibly disastrous granting of human love and freedom that wins the day. One of the adjusters had already explained to the male lead (Matt Damon) that human freedom, when given free reign, has led to the dark ages and (among other things) World War I and II (including the Holocaust). Even so, narrative sympathy is with the love and freedom that asserts itself against such bureaucratic calculation, and this is in accord with a common motif of science fiction's postulates of the end of man. There is something pernicious, evil or *apolitical* in simply denying the right to existence of humanity; such diagnoses appear as unacceptably ruthless, as having no feeling for the love and passion that makes us human. This is so much the case that dystopian visions of the world need be no different from the present other than presenting the absence of human passion, even if that absence creates a world of peace and happiness. The classical statement of this malaise is *Brave New World* (Huxley, 1932), but the reasoning is the same in *The Adjustment Bureau*; there is something insidious about a world that might be managed, for our benefit, or in which it had been decided that we ought to be guided away from our freedom to be violent.

As I have already suggested, the once common question of theodicy that challenged the goodness of life and man's tragic subjection to a violence beyond that of his own comprehension, has been reversed into a problem of human destructiveness towards an otherwise neutral, if not benevolent, milieu. In the 2007 Oliver Hirschbiegel film *The Invasion*, the central character played by Nicole Kidman faces a world in which a virus is released when a space shuttle crashes to earth. The virus causes its hosts to become inhumanly robotic, void of all passion. Despite the absence of war and violence that would ensue, the narrative has a typical redemptive trajectory that sees the virus vanquished with the world returned to its human order. (Or disorder: the film concludes with newspaper headlines of war and other returns of violence.) Why, we might ask, do *Brave New World* scenarios of passionless peace seem so objectionable, and why – precisely when we do indeed face a future of possible human non-existence (and sooner rather than later) – is present discourse focused on *how we might survive*, rather than whether we ought to survive?

Or, if we accept the parochial desire to survive, why can we not hear all the voices that accuse us of an existential worthlessness? The present seems to be split between two myopias of the future: the first is evidenced by climate change policy's discourse of managerialism. We speak of adaptation, mitigation, sustainability, cap and trade and even – despite cataclysmic game-changers – of recovery and renewal. Given the stark facts, how could 'our' survival possibly be adjusted in terms of using slightly less, or at a slower rate, or with one part of the globe trading its destructive emissions with another? Even beyond the crises of climate change, other disaster scenarios – ranging from terrorism and viral pandemic to panic and systemic collapse – seem to require something that is a difference in kind, not degree. It could not be a question of either adjusting our desires and expectations to a diminished future, or finding *other* resources of energy and maintenance. For the problem lies not in the substance of energy – of what, if you like, we accept as our milieu – but the mode of acceptance as such. As long as there is something like *life* that presents itself as that which must be sustained, or – worse – as that by which we value sustainability (such that the good is what allows life to continue as it is), we have failed to ask the question that is being repeatedly articulated and yet never addressed.

I want to conclude by looking at the new dominant mode of reaction-formation questions. These are questions that at first glance appear to face forward to the future but are ultimately ways in which the reality of the future is covered over. In short, one may say that it is precisely at the point in humanity's history when the question of the acceptability of the species ought to be asked that this very question mutates into a defence mechanism. By asking *how* we will survive into the future, by anticipating an end unless we adapt, we repress the question of whether the survival of what has come to be known as life is something we should continue to admit as the only acceptable option.

The violence of the question

Before looking at the culturally dominant modes of the question, I want to consider a philosophical example, for it brings the flagrant self-delusion of humanity into sharp focus. For quite some time, the philosopher Peter Singer has posed a rather uncomfortable thought experiment: I am wearing a pair of designer shoes and I pass by a child drowning in water that is deep enough to kill the child but insufficiently deep to pose any risk to me. I decide not to save the child because doing so would damage my shoes.[17] (In an earlier version, Singer simply set saving the child against allowing our clothes to become muddy.[18]) Singer suggested that few, if any, of us would accept this decision. We would save the child. And yet, he goes on to argue, we continually choose small and not highly significant or necessary material pleasures over the minor and barely noticeable material sacrifices it would require to save the lives of distant others. If we faced up to the real situation of our choices – which Singer suggested we ought to do by extending the range of our consideration beyond the immediate sympathies of those who are present to us – then we would conclude that we ought to give up a not too significant portion of our material wealth for the sake of benefiting an other in a way that is far more life-preserving than the minor life-enhancement of a pair of designer shoes.

In response to this provocation, Richard W. Miller[19] started to assess the degree to which sympathy and sacrifice for others diminish what is integral to the self. He argued that it might make sense, in terms of a person's self-definition and the duty they owe to themselves, to act more kindly to those closer at hand (including one's children and one's self). Singer's case was already thoroughly (but perhaps disturbingly) reasonable. He was not asking us to sacrifice all inequalities or benefits for the sake of saving other lives, just those that would not diminish our own pleasures and happiness significantly. Singer accepted a limitation of sympathy and an apparently non-negotiable selfishness, such that his argument – for all its audacity as a thought experiment – was really quite compatible with a world in which some people just do have more than others. The critical responses to Singer's principles of sympathy and charity disclose the degree to which human selfishness or self-maintenance is not only the accepted principle of living well, but lies at the heart of moral philosophy. Morality is deemed to be a question of doing what is required in order to *be the being that I am*.[20] There is, it seems, a sense in which either acting without principle *or* giving up too much of one's wealth would threaten the very being that I am. What is scandalous, I would suggest, is not that humans have placed their own survival as more valuable than other lives, but that at the heart of moral philosophy is an assumption that nothing is more valuable or definitive of value than human life's capacity to maintain itself. We ground value on life, either the sustainability of life, or our capacity to give our lives form and definition, or – to really face up to the circularity – we value life because it is life that makes value possible.

Life is, properly considered (which is to say, always considered in terms of what defines humanity), selection: we say that something is living if it maintains or strives to maintain itself through time. The dispersed, the haphazard, the inert, the contingent, the diffuse and the unformed – these are not living. They are therefore not only not *valuable* but also (significantly) not valuing. We value what values: we defend animal life because it too makes its way in the world, possesses a degree of choosing this rather than that, and is therefore on its way to something like meaning or sense. We seem to think not only that the prima facie value of life lies in its modes of flourishing, but that something like destruction and annihilation are *other than life and therefore unacceptable.*

This brings us back to the new mode of the existential question: how can humanity be at once the figure of that which renders life self-evidently valuable (because humanity is that animal that values) and yet be the being that has – through valuing itself – annihilated not only others of its own kind, but precipitated the end of all modes of life, valuing and otherwise? How is it that humanity defines itself as that being that inevitably chooses life, and yet has done so by saving only its own life? Why is it that the increasingly shrill affirmation of life – not just human life, but life as a living that furthers and values itself – occurs precisely at the moment in the history of life when it is at its most destructive and at its most evident end?

In series three, episode nine, of *True Blood* (2010), the villainous anti-hero Russell Edington appears suddenly on live National News to tear out and chew the spine from the broadcasting newsreader. Edington announces an end to vampire–human reconciliation – the seeming motif of *True Blood*'s ongoing elegy to the desirability of human passion – and declares that a vile, destructive, violent and planet-destroying humanity must give way to another more worthy species. The question is not so much answered as deflected. The narrative trajectory of *True Blood*, its romantic propulsion, lies in the desirability of being human: while the villainous vampires embrace their immortality, the heroic central figure seeks the love that is only possible with human finitude. Despite this, of course, the vogue for vampire fiction and the fanzine embrace of Edington as the twenty-first century's 'mad, bad and dangerous to know' type suggests that the manifest yearning for being human covers over a deeper flirtation with a sense of the end of man. If humanity has always asked questions about its predicament, it has – as I have suggested – begun to consider the violence of its being in relation to the very figure of life that has rendered the human exemplary of life as such.

Now, when the actual end of man approaches, when it seems necessary to ask what mode of the human – if any at all – should live on, the discourse of life can apparently only consider questions of degree rather than questions of kind. We ask *how* we might survive, adapt, mitigate or even trade our way into the future; we do not ask whether there is a future *for us*, and we cannot ask this because the 'we' of the question is at once that which has defined life *and* that which is essentially hurtling towards its own extinction. What disturbs us today is not theodicy, or how human life can live with the violence of its milieu, but anthropodicy, or how human life can avoid asking how it might justify itself.

Finally

How has the common figure of the self-evident value of human life *as life itself* given way to an increasing sense of species guilt and preliminary mourning? Why, just as humanity begins to have some sense of its end, are policies of survival, adaptation, mitigation and climate change, accompanied by a wide sense and figuration of the unacceptable nature of human life? Nothing defines the concept of reaction formation better than the present: everywhere there is evidence of the nonviable and unacceptable modus of human life, and yet the one notion that is unacceptable – incapable of being heard – is that human life has no value. This is not to say that – being without value – what has come to be known as humanity ought to extinguish itself, but rather to say that what is left of the human needs to confront the absence of value. For it is value and the holding on to that which saves itself, preserves itself, values itself and maintains itself that has precluded confrontation with the question that we are at once screaming out and yet also not hearing.

One way to pose the question of the unacceptable is to consider what we, as a species, might affirm as our own or reject as inhuman. This is a standard and complex border, played out in the thought experiments of monstrosity and the supposedly post-apocalyptic. If we imagine a future where certain aspects of humanity take over, then we may adjust ourselves accordingly. Dystopias are warnings, or cautionary tales in which a tendency of the present may be averted. (This is perhaps why many post-apocalyptic dystopias have considered unacceptable solutions to the problem of energy (ranging from the cannibalism of *Soylent Green* (1973) and Kenneth Cook's *Play Little Victims* (1978) to the faux humans bred for maintaining the rest of us in *Brave New World* and *Moon* (2009).) Such dystopias would, presumably, act as salutary cautions against us following the course of our current actions to the nightmarish conclusions that would follow. If we imagine another species – vampires – who are defined by a certain inhumanity that has manifested itself in the human species, then the battle for humanity *as life* becomes a figural war against the future. That is: we imagine what it might be for the inhumanity within ourselves – a rapacity, ruthlessness and consuming rage – to become a species in its own right (figured as the dystopian man of the future). Rather than deal with humanity's war on itself, we have narrativised and figured the horror of humanity into some distant other. We imagine that it is *in the future* that man becomes cannibalistic, void of empathy, ruthlessly calculative, and so dependent on technology that he ceases to think; in this exercise of the imagination we preclude considering all the ways in which this 'other' dystopian 'man' has already (and has always already) arrived.

We are against the future in two senses: humanity's end presents itself to us, and rather than ask the question this poses we instead imagine external threats to the species that are then warded off in a clear species-species agonistics. (One would not want to read too much, or perhaps anything at all, into the current vogue for vampire fiction, except perhaps to note that, like late eighteenth-century gothic, it occurs alongside the frenzied affirmation of the life of man against various forms of threatening transcendence.) We also war against the future by presenting the world of the present – a world of species self-annihilation and global rapacity – as a future dystopia, or as a possibility that may occur unless humanity saves itself. What we do not ask, and herein would lie a possible acceptance of the future, is not whether man ought to survive, but why this question is so unacceptable as to be constantly displaced and disfigured.

Notes

1. John Cottingham, *On the Meaning of Life*; Terry Eagleton, *The Meaning of Life*; Susan Wolf, *Meaning in Life and Why It Matters*.
2. Friedrich Nietzsche, *The Birth of Tragedy*.
3. Friedrich Nietzsche, *On the Genealogy of Morality*.
4. Sigmund Freud, 'Creative Writers and Day-Dreaming', pp. 141–154.
5. Theodor Adorno, *Negative Dialectics*, p. 361.
6. Theodor Adorno and Max Horkheimer, *Dialectic of Enlightenment: Philosophical Fragments*.
7. Tom Cohen, Claire Colebrook and J. Hillis Miller, *Theory and the Disappearing Future: On De Man, On Benjamin*.
8. Fredric Jameson, *The Political Unconscious: Narrative as a Socially Symbolic Act*, p. 141.
9. Peter Brooks, *Reading for the Plot: Design and Intention in Narrative*.
10. John Milton, *Paradise Lost* 10: 742–757.
11. Jameson, *Political Unconscious*, p. 214.
12. Ibid., p. 129.
13. Mary Wollstonecraft Shelley, *Frankenstein*, p. 184.
14. Ibid., pp. 128–129.
15. Ibid., p. 121.
16. Sigmund Freud, *Beyond the Pleasure Principle*, Trans. James Strachey. New York: Norton, 1961.
17. Peter Singer, *The Life You Can Save*.
18. Peter Singer, 'Famine, Affluence and Morality', pp. 29–243.
19. Richard Miller, *Globalizing Justice: The Ethics of Poverty and Power*.
20. Wolf, op cit.

References

Adorno, Theodor, *Negative Dialectics*, Trans. E.B. Ashton. London: Routledge, 1973.
Adorno, Theodor and Max Horkheimer, *Dialectic of Enlightenment: Philosophical Fragments*, Trans. Edmund Jephcott. Stanford: Stanford University Press, 2002.
Brooks, Peter, *Reading for the Plot: Design and Intention in Narrative*. New York: A.A. Knopf, 1984.
Cohen, Tom, Claire Colebrook, Claire and Miller, J. Hillis, *Theory and the Disappearing Future: On De Man, On Benjamin*. London: Routledge, 2011.
Cottingham, John, *On the Meaning of Life*. London: Routledge, 2003.
Eagleton, Terry, *The Meaning of Life*. Oxford: Oxford University Press, 2007.
Freud, Sigmund, 'Creative Writers and Day-Dreaming', *The Standard Edition of the Complete Psychological Works of Sigmund Freud, Volume IX* (1906–1908): *Jensen's 'Gradiva' and Other Works*, Trans. James Strachey. London: Hogarth Press, 1908.
Freud, Sigmund, *Beyond the Pleasure Principle*, Trans. James Strachey. New York: Norton, 1961.

Jameson, Fredric, *The Political Unconscious: Narrative as a Socially Symbolic Act*. Ithaca, NY: Cornell University Press, 1981.

Miller, Richard, *Globalizing Justice: The Ethics of Poverty and Power*. Oxford: Oxford University Press, 2010.

Nietzsche, Friedrich, *The Birth of Tragedy*, Trans. Douglas Smith. Oxford: Oxford University Press, 2000.

Nietzsche, Friedrich, *On the Genealogy of Morality*, Ed. Keith Ansell-Pearson and Trans. Carol Diethe. Cambridge: Cambridge University Press, 2007.

Shelley, Mary Wollstonecraft, *Frankenstein*, Ed. Johanna M. Smith. London: Palgrave Macmillan, 2000.

Singer, Peter, 'Famine, Affluence and Morality', *Philosophy and Public Affairs*. 1972. 1.1: 229–243.

Singer, Peter, *The Life You Can Save*. New York: Random House, 2009.

Wolf, Susan, *Meaning in Life and Why It Matters*. Princeton, NJ: Princeton University Press, 2010.

Index

127 Hours, 205

abortion, 82, 94, 98, 149
abstinence, 110–11
abuse, 15, 48–9, 51, 53, 59, 66–7, 69, 72, 74, 77–9, 103–6, 110, 112–15, 117, 145–6
activism, 7, 10
addiction, 103–8, 111
Adjustment Bureau, The, 208
adoption, 5, 14, 83, 85–8, 90–3, 99, 112, 147
Adorno, Theodor, 10, 207–8, 210, 212, 214, 221
adultery, 176, 190
aesthetics, 24, 26, 28, 33, 37, 43–4, 166
Afghanistan, 107
Africa, 143, 151, 154
Agamben, Giorgio, 11, 19, 36, 43, 138, 154–5
ageing, 66, 154–5
AIDS, 67, 114, 154
Albury, Kath, 78–9
alcohol, 9, 117
amendment, 4, 187, 199, 202
America, 1, 14, 17, 85, 104, 148, 187–8, 191, 195
American Cancer Society, 122
American Pie, 197
amphetamines, 113
Amsterdam, 15, 105–6, 108–9, 114, 116–17
anarchy, 172, 181–2
Anderson, Michael, 155
anthropogenicism, 209
Anti-Oedipus, 26
anxiety, 14, 48–9, 51, 53, 57, 67, 68–9, 74, 157, 172, 175, 179–82
Apostles, 200
Arellano, Silvia, 100–1
Ariès, Philippe, 140, 154–5

aristocracy, 3, 70–1
Aristotle, 138
art, 5, 10, 12–13, 27, 44, 70, 79, 124, 137, 186, 189, 193, 207–8, 212
arthouse cinema, 43
artists, 17, 77, 105, 140, 188, 191–4, 200
arts, 76, 78, 187, 193–4, 200–2
asexuality, 58
Asia, 108–9, 124
Assange, Julian, 19
Atchley, Robert C., 155
audiences, 16, 17, 26, 45, 71, 86, 92, 146, 153, 160, 187–8, 194–5, 197–8
Aunger, Robert, 185
Australia, 1, 4–5, 14, 32–3, 69, 74, 76–9, 121, 123, 132, 141, 143, 176
authoritarianism, 91, 95, 105
authority, 2–3, 6, 8, 23, 35, 59, 64, 71, 73–4, 111, 122–3, 139, 141–2, 146, 148, 157, 159–62, 164–5, 199
Avatar, 208
Ayers, Robert, 202

Bachmann, Christian, 116–17
bans (prohibition), 6, 15, 29, 42, 119–23
Barbaro, Michael, 19
Barthes, Roland, 185
Barusch, Amanda S., 155
Bataille, Georges, 186
Baudrillard, Jean, 185
BBC (British Broadcasting Corporation), 202
beatniks, 14, 106, 113
Beckett, Samuel, 205
belief, 73, 147, 176, 193
Belleville (Paris), 108
Bentley, Eric, 191
Bergeron, Henri, 111
Bertolucci, Bernardo, 38, 40, 43

Big Love, 16, 152–4
binaries, 34, 41, 53
Bin Laden, Osama, 37
bisexuality, 6, 64
blasphemy, 30, 193
bleeping (censorship), 17, 192
Blok, Gemma, 117
Boardman, John, 155
body, the, 1–2, 64, 120, 126, 130, 173, 175, 196
Bogad. L., 66
Bondebjerg, Ib, 44
Booth, Wayne, 185
Borg, Gérard, 116–17
Born on the Fourth of July, 205
Botello, Blanca, 99–100
Bowman, Donna, 166
Boys Don't Cry, 196
Breaking Bad, 16, 156–8, 164–6
Brecht, Bertolt, 188
Britain, 3, 33, 47, 64, 66, 103
Brito, Alejandro, 99–100
Brooks, Peter, 221
brutality, 18, 177, 191, 206
Burroughs, William, 106
Butler, Judith, 62–3

Cabrera, Rafael, 99–100
Cahiers du Cinema, 37–8, 118
Calcutta, 107
Caleb Williams, 205
California, 47, 69, 98, 151, 185, 193, 200–2
Calvinism, 140
campaigns, 5, 28, 90–1, 114, 122,124, 191
Canada, 4, 67, 89, 96
Canberra, 79
cancer, 65, 110, 120, 122, 156, 159–60
cannabis, 103, 106, 112–13
Cannes, 13, 24–8, 30, 33, 41–2
cannibalism, 16, 150–1, 172, 220
capitalism, 10, 36, 39, 42–4, 106, 129, 166, 188
Carroll, Joseph, 185
Carter, Angela, 185
Case, Trevor, 186
Castañeda, Jorge, 100

Catholic Church, 6, 14, 51, 81, 84, 86, 89–90, 92–5, 147–9, 194
censorship, 1–5, 8, 9, 13, 17–18, 23, 65, 78, 95, 176, 183, 187, 189, 192, 194–9, 201, 203
chaosmos, 12
Chapman, Simon, 133
chauvinism, 81
Cheal, David, 155
childhood, 1, 5, 14, 48, 57–8, 63–6, 68–73, 77–9, 140, 154–5
children, 3–5, 14, 46, 49, 51–2, 57–8, 60–1, 63–4, 66, 68–79, 90, 108, 124, 138–44, 152–3, 171, 191, 195, 198–9, 217
China, 4, 109, 112, 143
Chocolate Jesus, 194, 201–2
Christianity, 2–3, 5, 15, 28, 76, 92, 110, 112, 115–17, 151, 193
cinema, 18–20, 37–8, 100, 102, 137, 145, 165, 167, 189, 196, 204–5
citizenship, 6, 65
civilisation, 8–11, 15, 18, 20, 98, 103–7, 112–13, 116, 139, 150, 157
classification, 1, 5, 69
cleanliness, 17, 140, 180
Clegg, Stewart, 44
clinicisation, 131
cocaine, 103
coercion, 24, 34–5
coffee, 111–12
cognition, 168–9, 173–4, 182, 183, 185, 204
Cohen, Peter, 117
Cohen, Tom, 221
Comber, C., 62, 65
comedy, 144, 165, 167, 192
Coming Home, 196
communism, 4, 27, 188,191–2
Conformist, The, 37, 38
conformity, 15, 38–40, 112, 144, 168
conscience, 8, 125, 142, 194
conservatism, 6, 9, 14, 32, 46, 48, 68, 74, 80–1, 83–4, 86, 92–3, 95, 98, 104, 111, 116, 128,146, 194
consumerism, 5, 46, 106
control society, 119–20, 129–34
Cooper, Robert, 44

Coppel, Anne, 116–18
Coppola, Francis Ford, 148
coprophagia, 180
corporations, 4, 30, 69, 78–9, 120, 128, 188, 208
corporeality, 16–17, 64, 66, 119, 168, 174–5, 178–80, 182–3
Corpus Christi, 200
cosmopolitanism, 81, 114
Cottingham, John, 221
counterculture, 103, 105–6, 108, 111, 113
Courtwright, David, 117–18
crack, 103
Cradle Will Rock, The, 188
Crawford, Kate, 79
Creativity, 1, 130–1
Creed, Barbara, 155
crime and criminality, 1, 5, 10, 28, 31–2, 51, 64, 66, 105, 110–11, 114, 116, 145, 147–8, 156–7, 159, 161–5, 171, 172, 176, 179, 180, 190–1, 201–2
criminology, 64, 66–7, 117
Crisis of the Modern World, The, 107
cruelty, 173, 191, 205–6, 211
crusading, 5, 9, 111, 122,146
Cruz González, René, 99–100
Cryle, Peter, 185
Cuenca, Alberto, 99, 101
culture, 1, 6–7, 10, 12–13, 18, 20, 26, 29, 32–3, 37–8, 40–1, 60, 65–6, 69, 72, 75, 77–9, 97–8, 110, 112–13, 127–9, 138–9, 147, 149, 151, 165, 167, 175–6, 194, 203–4
Curtis, Valerie, 185
cyberphobia, 66
cyberspace, 66

Damasio, Antonio, 185
Damned, The, 38
Darwin, Charles, 175, 184
Darwinism, 183–5, 214
Day the Earth Stood Still, The, 214
DEA, 160
Dean, Mitchell, 44
De Beauvoir, Simone, 185
decriminalisation, 98, 111–12
degeneracy, 37, 40–1, 115

Dehesa, Rafael de la, 99, 101
De Kort, Maartje, 117–18
De Las Heras, María, 99, 101
Deleuze, Gilles, 11–13, 15, 19, 26–7, 42, 44, 119–20, 125–30, 132–4
Delhi, 107
democracy, 4, 42, 82, 91–2, 95, 98, 106, 116
Democratic Party (US), 4, 10, 32–4, 80, 82, 84, 95, 98
demonisation, 66, 114
Denmark, 42
depression, 188
De Sade, 16, 168, 183–5
Descartes, 113, 117–18, 183–5
desire, 9, 13, 23–7, 30, 33, 35, 38–41, 49, 51, 53, 55, 57–61, 65–6, 69, 104, 108, 158–9, 162, 170–1, 216
detoxification, 110
deviancy, 15, 46–7, 56, 64, 66, 111–12, 116
dialectic, 126–7,133, 214, 221
Dias Branco, Sérgio, 166
Díaz, Gloria, 99, 101
Dick, Kirby, 202
Dickson, Albert, 19
didacticism, 17, 127, 168–70, 181–2
difference, 1–2, 54–5, 61, 64, 126–8, 131, 185, 212, 216
diplomacy, 43, 113, 117
directives, 119–20, 122, 125, 127–9
discipline, 30, 57, 77, 120, 129–30
discourse, 1, 14, 34, 41, 43–4, 54, 58, 63, 65, 91, 95, 104, 115–16, 172, 176, 179, 216, 219
discrimination, 4, 6, 61, 89, 91, 93–4, 97–8, 142
disgust, 10, 13, 16–17, 45, 168, 170, 172, 174–86
Dissanayake, Ellen, 186
divorce, 144, 146, 151
documentary, 145, 191, 195, 205
dogmatism, 12, 129, 191
Downfall, 26
drinking and drunkenness (alcohol), 39, 55, 56, 121, 160
drugs and drug use, 1, 14–15, 55, 104, 106–8, 111, 113–18, 146, 159–60, 163, 200

drug trafficking, 108–10, 145
Dutch, the, 15, 105–6, 110–12, 114–15, 117, 140–1
dystopia, 71, 215, 220

Eagleton, Terry, 221
earth, 18, 209, 214–16
ecology, 206, 212
education, 45, 48, 50, 58, 64–7, 77, 129, 170, 202
egalitarianism, 89, 98
Ehrenberg, Alain, 111, 117–18
elitism, 89, 94, 105, 170
Ellis, V., 63–4
Elmo (*Sesame Street*), 187
El Universal (Mexican Newspaper), 99, 101
emancipation, 128, 143
emotion, 16, 60, 99, 104, 149, 153, 169, 174–7, 178, 179, 182–6
empathy, 131, 172–3, 220
empire, 2, 212
England and English people, 25, 55–7, 60, 69, 106, 108, 116, 139, 180
enlightenment, 33, 40, 83, 98, 113, 203, 207, 212, 221
Ennew, J., 63–4
EPA, 123
epidemiology, 184–5
equality, 85, 87–8, 98
eroticism, 8, 10, 24, 29, 36, 37–41, 48, 55, 58–60, 65, 66, 69, 72, 76, 78–9, 171, 185–6
Escoffier-Lambotte, Jacques, 113
ethics, 24, 33, 41,172, 183, 185, 221–2
ethnography, 46, 65
eugenics, 27, 37
Europa/Zentropa, 27–8
Europe and Europeans, 1, 3, 26, 29, 38, 65, 71, 75, 98, 104, 106, 107, 112, 116, 118, 139–41, 143, 147, 185
euthanasia, 82
Ewen, Stuart, 155
excrement, 10, 175
existence, 15, 25, 36, 105, 112, 128, 151, 158, 169, 204–8, 210–16, 218

experimentation, 11, 82, 110, 112, 173, 186, 194, 205, 217, 220
extinction, 204, 214, 219

Facebook, 92, 100, 102
falsehood, 31, 86, 111, 164
family, the, 1, 4–5, 15–16, 24, 27–8, 33, 42, 53, 59, 61, 70–1, 73–4, 77, 79, 86, 94, 137–56, 157, 159, 162, 197, 201–3, 208, 210, 213
famine, 221–2
fantasy, 56–7, 61, 63, 164, 210, 212–13
fanzines, 219
Fargues, Philippe, 155
fascism, 13, 24–6, 28–30, 32–3, 36–42, 43–4, 91, 114
fashion, 2, 5, 28–30, 33–4, 38, 60, 69, 76, 78–9, 121, 148
Fassbender, Rainer Werner, 196
fatherhood, 9, 27–8, 43, 74, 76, 139, 142–6, 149–50, 152, 160, 208
Faulkner, Joanne, 73, 78–9
FCC, 192, 197–9
fear, 9, 36, 52, 66, 68, 72, 75, 148–9, 158–9, 181, 192
Felski, Rita, 165–6
female(s), 37–8, 48–9, 51, 55–7, 59–60, 65–7, 146, 172, 213
femininity, 38, 40, 56–7, 63, 76, 88, 137, 141, 154–5
feminism, 4–5, 53, 63–5, 100, 144, 152–5
femme, 28, 36, 38–40, 147
fetish, 29–30, 36, 39–40
fiction, 16–18, 145, 165–8, 170–1, 174, 176, 179, 183, 185, 204, 208, 214–15, 219–20
film, 5, 10, 13, 16–17, 23–30, 33, 37–40, 42–4, 60, 114, 137, 145, 146–8, 149–50, 151, 154–5, 157, 164–5, 167, 188–91, 195–9, 201–2, 208, 213, 215–16
Filth, 10, 16, 109, 148, 176
Fine, M., 63, 65
Finley, I. M., 155
First Amendment, 4, 187, 199, 202
Fitness, J, 186
Fonda, Jane, 196

food, 10, 31, 142, 150–1, 175, 177, 211
Foucault, Michel, 11, 19, 24, 26, 30–2, 34, 37–8, 42–4, 52, 54, 61–3, 65, 77, 79, 119
Fox News, 201–2
France, 3, 14–15, 28–9, 37, 103–6, 108, 110, 113–15, 117, 176
François, Donatien Alphonse (Marquis de Sade), 16, 168, 183–5
Frankenstein, 211, 213, 221–2
Frankenstein, 212
Frankfurt, 10, 39
Frappier-Mazar, L, 186
freedom, 4, 6, 17, 34, 95, 104, 147, 187–8, 191–2, 199–200, 209, 211–12, 214–15
French, 6, 15, 28–9, 83, 105–6, 108–11, 113, 115–17, 140, 176, 179
Freud, Sigmund, 7–10, 18–19, 28, 57, 70,138, 205, 207, 221
Frow, John, 165–6
fucking, 170, 192, 196–7
fundamentalism, 152

Gaddafi, Muammar, 37
Gallop, Jane, 186
gangsters, 16, 156–8, 163
Gare de Lyon, Paris, 109
Gay, 6, 14, 18–20, 64, 66, 80–1, 83, 85–90, 92, 94, 96–7, 99–102, 146, 197–8, 200, 203
gaze, 52, 68, 72–3, 78, 161
gender, 1, 4, 53–4, 56, 60–1, 64–6, 71, 74–6, 87, 152
genealogy, 212, 221–2
Geneva, 116
genitalia, 171–2
genre, 16, 25, 59, 138, 145, 147, 151, 165–7, 205–8, 213
Germany and Germans, 24, 26–9, 33, 37, 113
Gilligan, Vince, 165–6
Ginsberg, Allen, 106
GIRE, 100–1
Girls, 46, 51, 56, 59–60, 64–6, 75–9, 93, 145, 197
Gittins, Diana, 155

globalisation, 36, 51, 103, 123, 154–5, 220–2
God, 115, 153, 190, 206, 209–13
Godfather, The, 16, 148
Godwin, William, 205
Gómez-Peña, Guillermo, 202
Gómez Quintero, 100–1
Gottschall, Jonathan, 185
government, 3–4, 7, 17, 23, 32, 42, 44, 64, 74, 82–5, 90–1, 93, 95, 97, 109, 143, 152, 179, 187–8, 191, 193, 200
governmentality, 31–2, 34, 41, 44
Grass, 106, 131
Greece, 11, 32, 138–9, 154–5, 205–6
Green, Al, 37
grotesques, 150, 172
Guattari, Félix, 12–13, 19, 26–7, 42, 44
Guénon, René, 107
guilt, 8, 18, 39, 150, 219

habit, 15, 117–18, 120–1, 146
Hague International Opium Convention, The, 113
Haight-Ashbury, 106
Hall, Stuart, 61, 65
hallucinogens, 103, 105, 113
harm, 15, 69, 74–5, 109–12, 116–17, 123
Hartley, John, 79
Hartmann, J.P.E., 27
Harvard, 65, 101, 117–18
HBO, 152, 198, 201–2
health, 48, 50, 66, 77, 103–4, 109–10, 115–17, 119–20, 122–3, 131–2, 143, 184–5
Hegel, 207–8
Hegemony, 3, 45–6, 53, 64, 188
Hénaff, Marcel, 186
Henson, Bill, 68–9
Heresy, 1, 3
heroin, 103, 108–9, 112, 114
heterosexuality, 6, 8, 45–7, 53, 57, 59, 64, 66, 196, 198
Higonnet, Anne, 79
Hills Have Eyes, The, 150
Hindess, Barry, 44

Index

Hippies, 105–7, 108, 113–14, 116, 118
Hispanics, 98
Hitler, Adolf, 26
HIV, 154, 200
Hjort, Mette, 44
Hobbes, 36, 43–4
Holland, 104–6, 108, 114–15, 140–1
Hollywood, 5, 16, 145, 157, 164–7, 205
Holocaust, 26, 28, 32, 39–40, 215
homology, 115
homophobia, 40, 46–7, 67, 91–2, 97
homosexuality, 6, 36, 39–40, 48, 53, 67, 80, 82, 85, 88, 91–3, 95, 97, 99–102, 115
horror, 13, 16, 19, 58, 65, 137–8, 150–1, 172, 208, 211–12, 214, 220
Huffington Post, 43
humanism, 25, 28, 30, 32, 41
Huxley, Aldous, 215
Hygiene, 175–6, 178, 180, 185
Hypocrisy, 43, 158, 192
Hysteria, 9, 148

I'm a Cheerleader, 197
iconography, 33, 38, 40, 193
identity, 3, 6, 10, 14, 26, 29–30, 46–7, 53–5, 57–9, 61, 64, 66, 73–4, 79–81, 96, 107, 195
ideology, 11, 39, 45, 65–6, 127, 154–5, 170, 180, 185, 194, 207, 208, 210, 212–13
imaginary, 13, 45, 54, 57–61, 177, 181, 209, 212–13
immigration, 6, 28, 108–9, 112, 114, 147
immorality, 6, 90, 92,
imperialism, 36, 105
India, 106–7
indigenous cultures, 74, 97
individualism, 6, 33, 37, 41, 53, 57, 92, 107, 116, 119, 121–2, 127–9, 140, 145, 147, 149, 153, 157, 162, 177, 179, 208
indulgence, 181, 205–7

industrialisation, 3, 28, 139, 142, 150
inequality, 36, 74, 92, 120, 129, 217
infanticide, 174
infantilisation, 124
infants, 182
innocence, 14, 37, 58, 60, 65–6, 68, 70–3, 78–9, 198
Inquisition, The, 3
institutions, 1, 6, 11, 21, 31, 45, 47–8, 51–2, 58, 66, 68, 74, 80, 82–3, 86, 87, 89, 91–2, 103, 109, 112, 119–20, 123, 125, 127–9, 135, 142, 156, 168, 181, 187, 190, 194, 200, 203, 205
Internet, 4, 7, 63, 65, 75, 92, 194
intolerability, 11–12, 28, 144, 153, 207, 209, 210–14
intolerance, 80, 89, 91–2, 98, 99
Invasion, The, 216
Iran, 4, 107
Ireland, 121, 132–3
Islam, 208
Islamic, 6, 29, 151
Israel, 25
Italy, 33, 38, 147–8
Izhuhara, Misa, 155

Jail (Gaol), 60, 64
James, William, 183, 186
Jameson, Fredric, 222
Japan, 94, 143
Jenkins, Henry, 79
Jesus Christ, 190, 193, 200
Jews, 24, 26–8, 30, 33
Jiménez, Eugenia, 101
Johnson, John, 185
journalism, 25, 64–5, 94, 107, 146
Juárez, Benito, 89
judgement, 137, 139, 175, 215
junkies, 105, 107–9, 114–15, 117

Kafka, Franz, 205
Kershaw, Ian, 26, 42, 44
Kidman, Nicole, 216
Kimmel, Jimmy, 192
Kincaid, James 48, 62–3, 65, 69, 72, 78–9

kitsch, 27, 40, 207
knowledge, 11, 31, 39, 58, 61, 71–5, 168–9, 177–8, 184, 186
Kristeva, Julia, 9–10, 19, 62, 65, 137–8
Kruger, Daniel, 185
Kubrick, Stanley, 145

labour, 23, 77, 112, 114, 140–3, 207, 213
Lacan, Jacques, 9, 19, 138
La Nauze, Andrea, 79
Lancelot, Michel, 116, 118
language, 9, 17, 24, 30, 41, 43, 56–7, 97–8, 110, 170, 172–4, 189, 195, 197, 199, 208
Latour, Bruno, 34, 43–4
law, 1–2, 4, 6–10, 13–15, 23, 28–9, 32, 40, 65, 81–7, 89–90, 93–4, 110–12, 122, 128, 130–3, 148, 151, 156, 160–1, 181, 187, 190, 210, 212
law enforcement, 15, 112, 122, 156, 160, 192
Leary, Timothy 106
left, the, 82, 188
legalisation, 6–7, 14,18–19, 82–5, 88, 90, 92–3, 95, 98
legislation, 4, 6–7, 82–91, 94–5, 111, 121, 142
Lenero-Otera, Luis, 155
Lepore, Jill, 155
lesbian, 6, 56, 64, 83,101, 197–8
Letterman, David, 192, 201–2
Levine, Judith, 79
liberalism, 4–5, 10, 32–6, 40–1, 48, 82, 88–9, 94–5, 98, 114, 116, 200
libertarianism, 4, 116
libertines, 17, 168–72, 174, 176, 179–83, 186
liberty, 72
libido, 8–9, 33, 40
liminality, 72, 78
Lin, Patty, 166
literature, 5, 13, 37, 43, 76, 78, 137, 141, 184, 186, 205, 213–14
Logo (US Television Network), 198
Lolita, 60
London, 20, 42, 44, 63–7, 78–9, 106, 117, 132–4, 155, 165–6, 184–6, 221–2

López, Lorena, 83–5, 99–102
love, 16, 28–9, 38, 46, 66, 75, 146, 148, 152–3, 171, 215, 219
LSD, 64, 103, 105–6, 108, 118
lust, 59–60, 64
Luxembourg, 116, 118

Macquarie University, 119, 122–4, 132–4
Mad Men, 153, 201–2
madness, 11, 31
Madonna, 192, 201–2
mafia, 105, 147–8
mainstream, 1, 4, 6–7, 16, 47, 103
males, 6, 8, 40, 46, 49, 51, 53, 55, 57, 59–60, 66–7, 74, 88, 93, 115, 138, 139, 141, 146, 149, 152–3, 161, 172, 196–8, 200–2, 212, 213, 215
Mandala group, 105, 118
Mapplethorpe, Robert, 63
Marcuse, Herbert, 10, 19–20, 112, 117–18
marketing, 5, 69, 75–6, 128
Marr, David, 79
marriage, 1, 6–8, 14, 18–20, 40, 59–60, 76, 80–3, 85–99, 149, 151, 152–3, 190, 203
Marx and Marxism, 9–10, 39, 83, 207, 212–13
masculinity, 48–9, 53–4, 63–4, 161, 164
masochism, 24, 29–30, 36, 38
masturbation, 30, 52, 177, 197
Materialism, 173
McCarthy, Cormac, 208
Mckee, Irwin Robert, 100–1
McMahon, Julian, 198
McNally, Terrance, 200
McRobbie, Angela, 62, 66
medicines, 65, 103
Melancholia, 25
Melbourne, 79
melodrama, 16, 156–7, 164–5, 167
memory, 38–9, 43–4, 71, 128, 130, 169, 173
Merino, José, 100–1
Methadone, 109–10
methamphetamine, 156, 163
methodism, 200

Mexico, 14, 80–91, 93–102, 156, 160, 189, 194, 200
Militarism, 29, 139, 158, 172, 188, 208
Miller, Peter, 44
Miller, Richard, 222
Milton, 205
Mino, Fernando, 99, 101
minorities, 4, 6, 75, 91, 93, 97–8
miscegenation, 190
misogyny, 25, 27, 88
modernism, 207
modernity, 63, 80–1, 90, 95–6, 98, 99, 101, 107, 127, 144, 147, 149–50, 152
modulation, 16, 120, 129
monogamy, 8, 138
monstrous, the, 15–16, 66, 115, 137, 144, 147, 149–51, 153–5, 172, 211, 220
moral panics, 1, 9, 45–7, 58, 64, 67
morals and Morality, 1–6, 9, 15–17, 28, 36, 39, 41, 45–7, 55, 58–9, 61, 64–7, 90, 92–3, 95, 98, 103, 110–11, 113, 116, 125, 127–8, 139, 144–5, 152, 154–5, 165, 168, 170, 174–5, 177–9, 181–2, 186–7, 189, 191–2, 199–200, 205–6, 208, 212, 215, 218, 221–2
Moreno, Eva Díaz, 100–1
Mormons, 151–2
morphine, 103
mortality, 73, 139, 159
Mosso, Rubén, 100–1
mothers and mothering, 27, 55, 57, 59, 74, 76, 139, 142, 145–6, 148, 151, 170–1, 182, 200
Motion Picture Association of America (MPAA), 195–8, 201–2
MTV, 75, 198
Mumbai, 107
Murphie, Andrew, 7
Muslims, 6, 37, 43, 151
mutilation, 8, 174–5
mysticism, 106–7
myth, 9, 35, 64, 78–9, 165–7, 207, 214

narcissism, 39
narcotics, 110
Nassif, Alberto Aziz, 100–1
Nazism, 13, 24–9, 30, 32–3, 37–8, 42
NEA Four, The, 193, 201–2
Nefertiti, 186
Netherlands, 14, 103, 106, 109, 115, 140–1
Neuroscience, 168–9
New Zealand, 67
NGOs, 92
Nietzsche, Friedrich, 125–30, 132–4, 205–6, 221–2
Night Porter, The, 38
Nihilism, 94, 125, 127, 129–30, 206
Nip/Tuck, 198
Nixon, Richard, 104, 113
normalisation, 30, 53, 111
normality, 35, 48–9, 53–5, 92, 123–4, 161
normativity, 16, 46–7, 53–4, 57, 59, 137, 143, 147, 152, 169, 181
Now or Have You Ever Been, 191
nudity, 17, 27, 68, 190, 196, 198–9

Oaten, Megan, 186
Obama, Barack, 37, 43
obesity, 131
obscenity, 5, 30, 172, 174, 176, 190
occident, 116–17
oedipalisation, 208
offensiveness, 28, 30, 153, 175, 192
ontology, 52, 58, 127, 165
opium, 104, 112–13
Opium Regie, 112
order, 7, 9–10, 12, 15, 17, 36, 43–4, 46, 51, 54, 65, 69, 84, 90, 96, 99, 112, 129, 137–41, 158, 161, 170, 173, 175, 177, 179, 182, 188, 197, 204, 208–10, 214–16, 218
orgasm, 170, 173, 196
orgy, 170–2, 178–80, 182, 184, 186
orientalism, 105–8
Osborne, Roger, 20
Osbournes, The, 146

paedophilia, 1, 5, 13, 49, 51–4, 60, 63–5, 69, 73, 78–9
Paglia, Camille, 186
pain, 25, 113, 170
Pakistan, 107
pandemics, 104, 204, 206, 216
Pantoja, Sara, 99, 101
Paradise Lost, 205
parents and parenting, 27, 42, 52, 72, 74–7, 103, 107–8, 139–41, 143–6, 195, 199–200, 203
Paris, 13, 15, 28–9, 39, 42, 106–9, 116–18, 141
Parks, Tim, 155
parrhesia, 32–3, 41
Partido de la Revolución Democrática (PRD), 82–8, 90–1, 99–100
Partido Revolucionario Institucional (PRI), 82–4, 87, 95
Pasolini, Pier Paolo, 38
passion, 69, 104, 112, 115, 149, 158, 163, 165, 166, 168, 171, 182, 188, 190, 193, 215–16, 219
pathology, 35–6, 39–40, 55, 59, 115
patriarchy, 16, 56, 138, 142, 145–6, 148, 150–3
Patton, Paul, 133–4
Paz, Octavio, 96, 100–1
PBS, 145
pedagogy, 49, 59, 63, 66, 128, 163
Perez, Gilberto, 165–7
Peril, Lynn, 79
permissiveness, 5
Perry, Katy, 187
Peyrefitte, Alain, 116, 118
phallus, 57
phantasm, 52, 54, 61
Philosophy in the Boudoir, 170
Piss Christ, 193
Plato, 139
pleasure, 8, 13, 23–4, 26, 29–30, 33, 37, 40–1, 59, 169–70, 177, 221
poetics, 66
police and policing, 4, 6, 13, 15, 23, 28, 56, 64–5, 69, 73, 109–12, 121, 125, 131, 148, 199
politics, 1, 7, 10, 12–14, 19, 24, 26–8, 30–7, 39–41, 43–6, 48, 51, 64, 66, 75, 77–8, 81–90, 93–5, 98–9, 101–2, 104, 110, 112, 116, 126, 131, 133–4, 138, 141, 158, 165–7, 189, 192, 194, 196, 198, 200, 207, 210, 212–13, 221–2
polygamy, 16, 93, 151–2
pontius, 84
pornography, 1, 5, 30, 37, 43, 45, 50, 63, 68, 74, 78, 170–1, 185
poverty, 12, 72, 77, 139, 142, 221–2
power, 1, 4, 6, 10–11, 13, 15, 18–19, 23–4, 26, 32, 34–44, 47, 57, 66, 81, 89, 95, 122, 126–9, 131–2, 139, 141, 146, 153–5, 157, 159, 162, 189, 211, 221–2
Power, Michael, 44
prisons, 11, 19, 31, 104, 110–11
privacy, 140–1, 159
profanity, 190
Prometheus, 215
prostitution, 77, 109, 145, 150
protestantism, 3, 112, 140, 147, 153
psychedelics, 105–6, 108
psychiatry, 11, 104, 115
psychoanalysis, 7, 9–10, 26, 37, 57, 138, 154–5
psychology, 9, 16–17, 90, 168–9, 174, 177–8, 183–4, 186, 194, 221
psychopathology, 8, 27, 145
psychotherapy, 33, 38
Puccini, 200
puritanism, 37, 96, 152
Pursuit of Happyness, The, 205

Queer, 63, 67

Rabie, Tamer, 185
race and racism, 1, 4, 26–7, 32, 46–7, 65, 71, 114, 194, 210
Rajchman, John, 77, 79
rape, 46, 177
ratings, 195, 198, 202
Ravetto, Kriss, 44
reactive, 125–34, 160
Reagan, Ronald, 113
reason, 35, 53, 108, 113, 124, 126, 153, 157–8, 168–9, 183–5, 214
Reeves, Keanu, 18, 214–15

Reforma, 100–1
regulation, 2–4, 8–9, 13–14, 46, 65–6, 112, 119–20, 123–5, 127, 129, 131, 192, 198–9
religion, 1, 2, 3–7, 10, 18–19, 23, 36, 40, 61, 71, 80, 89–91, 93, 99, 107, 112, 115–16, 137, 176, 187, 190, 194
Renn, Heinz, 116, 118
Rent, 200–2
representation, 1, 3, 5, 10, 12, 13, 15–17, 24, 30, 38, 41, 42, 47, 49, 55–6, 58, 60–1, 63–5, 67, 69–71, 78, 97, 114–16, 137–8, 143, 146, 153, 157, 169–70, 176–7, 198
repression, 2, 3, 7–10, 13, 15, 19–20, 23, 58, 95, 109–10, 112, 157, 214
Republican Party (US), 152, 193
repulsion, 59, 90, 177
resistance, 11, 29, 39, 66, 70, 87, 119, 130–1, 207
ressentiment, 125, 127–30
restriction, 8–9, 61, 87, 117, 120, 127, 130–2
Revista, 102
RHS, 201–2
risk, 31–3, 41, 47, 50–1, 63, 67, 69, 72, 74–5, 77–8, 87, 116, 123, 149, 159, 185, 188, 217
ritual, 43–4, 149–50
Rivera, Diego, 189
Rivera, Francisco, 99, 101
Roberts, John, 20
Robinson, David, 20
Robinson, Jennifer, 19
Rockefeller, Nelson, 189
Rome and the Romans, 2–3, 39, 139
Romeo and Juliet, 46, 64
Roosevelt, 188
Rose, Nikolas, 44
Rotterdam, 109, 117–18
Rudd, Kevin, 68
Ruins of Empire, 212
Rush, Emma, 79
Rybczynski, Witold, 155

Salo or *120 Days of Sodom*, 38
Sánchez, Raymundo, 99, 102

Sandoval, 90, 99, 101
Sandwell, B., 62, 66
scandal, 56, 60, 66–7
Scandinavian, 113
scatology, 180
schizophrenia, 42, 44
schooling, 10, 13–14, 31, 39, 45–56, 58–61, 63–7, 74, 93, 140–1, 156, 163, 185, 199–200
Schuessler, Michael, 100, 102
Schumacher, Joel, 151
science, 18, 44, 65, 107–8, 122, 124, 142, 158, 168. 184, 186, 208, 215
self, the, 3, 5, 7, 16, 18, 25–6, 28, 30, 32, 34–5, 41–2, 44, 59, 111, 120, 129, 140, 142, 150, 157–8, 160, 164–5, 178–9, 183, 206, 208–9, 212, 214, 217–20
semiotics, 36, 78, 133–4
Serrano, Andreas, 193
Sesame Street, 187
Seven Beauties, 38
sex, 1, 5–10, 13–14, 17, 25, 27, 36–41, 43, 45–61, 47–53, 63–7, 72, 75–83, 87–95, 97–9, 106, 145–6, 168, 174–5, 177, 179–81, 183, 186, 190, 196–7, 199, 210
Sex in the City, 196
sexism, 47, 153–4
sexlessness, 36
sexualisation, 1, 5, 14, 48, 54, 56–7, 60, 64–5, 69, 72, 75, 78–9
sexuality, 1, 5, 8, 11, 13, 17, 31, 36, 39–40, 45–6, 48–50, 53, 55–60, 64–6, 71, 77–8, 171, 182
Shelley, Mary Wollstonecraft, 211–14, 221–2
Shiban, John, 166
Singer, Peter, 222
Sinnerbrink, Robert, 133–4
Sitcoms, 144–5, 151
Skidmore, P., 66
Skyler, 159, 162
smoking, 15, 55, 112–13, 119, 119–25, 127–34, 129–30, 131
society, 1–2, 4, 8–10, 14–16, 18–19, 28, 31, 35, 38, 40, 43–4, 48, 53, 56, 61, 63, 66–7, 70, 77, 80–2, 84–7,

89, 91–9, 104, 106, 108, 110–12, 114, 119–22, 129–34, 137, 140–1, 144, 147, 150, 153–5, 162, 170–1, 176, 180, 182, 184–5
Sodomy, 88
Soylent Green, 220
Spanish, 88–9
spanking, 59, 64
Spinoza, 125–6
spirituality, 106, 115, 189
Stevenson, Richard J, 186
stigmatisation, 94, 109, 114–15
Stonewall Riot, 6
Stransky, 201–2
structuralism, 9
subculture, 15, 104–5, 107–9, 113, 116
subjectivation, 32
subjectivities, 13, 33, 54, 58, 66, 126, 170
suicide, 28, 36, 115
Surin, Kenneth, 134
Surinam, 114
Surinamese, 108–9, 114
Surrey, 54
surveillance, 52–3, 120, 131
Sweden, 88, 103, 145
Swirski, Peter, 186
Sydney, 68–9
Sylvania Waters, 145

tabloid news, 46, 59, 67, 89
taboo, 8, 13, 23, 57, 82, 113–14, 146, 174, 193, 196
teaching, 7, 13, 45–51, 54–7, 59–60, 63–7, 75, 115, 156, 159, 189
technocracy, 108
technology, 7, 10, 18, 20, 45, 220
teenagers, 45–6, 55–6, 67–8, 73–6, 77, 160, 195, 197
television, 5, 13, 16–17, 60, 68, 92, 137, 143–5, 152, 156, 165–6, 187, 192, 197–9, 203
temperance, 3
territory, 74, 78–9, 163
Texas, USA, 150–1, 200, 202
The 120 Days of Sodom, 170
The Lost Boys, 151
theodicy, 205, 207, 209–11, 216, 219

theology, 3, 13, 23, 32–3, 41, 212–13
This Film is Not Yet Rated, 195, 201–2
Thomas, Deborah, 165, 167
Thomson, George, 133
titillation, 56, 59, 172
tobacco, 122–3, 132
tolerance, 10–11, 15, 19–20, 39, 89, 91–2, 99, 111–12, 117–18, 128, 145
torture, 3, 29, 38, 130, 171, 172, 177, 182, 214
transgender, 6, 47, 66
transgression, 1, 9, 13, 16–17, 23, 40, 54, 55, 57, 66, 162, 168, 170, 175–8, 181
Tunisia, 151
Turkey, 107, 109
Turowski, Jan, 155

U.S. Congress, 75, 82, 187, 193
Ulysses, 5
unacceptability, 1–18, 21, 23–6, 28–9, 30–8, 40–2, 44–6, 48–9, 52–4, 56–62, 64, 66, 69–70, 72, 74, 76, 78, 80–2, 84, 86, 88, 90, 92, 94–6, 98–100, 102–4, 106, 108, 110, 112, 114, 116, 118–20, 122, 124, 126, 128–32, 134–5, 137–8, 140, 142, 144, 146–8, 150–4, 156–7, 158, 160, 162, 164–6, 168, 170, 172, 174–6, 178, 180, 182–4, 186, 188, 190, 192, 194, 196–8, 200, 202–4, 206–8, 210, 212–14, 215, 216, 218–22
unconscious, 7–9, 77, 126, 138, 210, 221–2
underage, 51, 56, 64, 67
unemployment, 23, 107, 142, 146, 194
United Kingdom, 1, 4–5, 13, 42–3, 45, 48, 65, 72, 133, 202
United States, 17, 27, 33, 36–7, 187–8, 192, 194, 199
university, 19–20, 44, 64–6, 69, 78–9, 101, 117–20, 123–4, 128, 132–4, 155, 165–7, 185–6, 200–2, 221–2
University of Sydney, 120
utilitarianism, 126, 128

vagina, 25, 172
vampirism, 151, 218–20
Vancouver, 63
Viacom, 198
Viagra, 152
vice, 81, 115, 157, 172, 181, 183
victimisation, 15, 28, 31, 32, 38, 55, 58, 60, 67, 110, 120, 122, 125, 151, 172, 177, 220
Victorian, the, 3–4, 37, 52, 65, 69, 71–2, 78–9, 185
Vienna, 29
Vietnam, 105, 196
vilification, 4, 32–3, 57, 137
villainy, 18, 157, 218–19
Vinkenoog, Simon, 105–6, 118
violence, 10, 15, 17–20, 24, 32–3, 35, 53, 59–60, 77, 88, 94, 109, 121, 145–6, 148–9, 162, 199, 205–6, 208–10, 212–17, 219
virginity, 56, 58, 179
Visconti, Luchino, 38
Voight, Jon, 196
Von Trier, Lars, 26
voyeurism, 2

Walley-Beckett, Moira, 165–66
Walters, James, 165, 167
Warmoesstraat, De, 109

Warshow, Robert, 158, 165, 167
WASP (White Anglo-Saxon Protestant), 147, 149
WBAI (NYC Radio Station), 192
wealth, 143–4, 217–18
Welles, Orson, 188
Wertmuller, Lina, 38
Western genre, 165–7
Western World, the 2, 4–6, 8, 14–16, 18, 20, 26, 29, 34, 53, 68, 81, 90, 95, 98, 103–4, 106–8, 113, 125, 137–9, 141–2, 146–7, 151–2, 154, 156–8, 161, 176
WikiLeaks, 4
Winfrey, Oprah, 206
Wise, Sue 67
Wolf, Susan, 222
Women, 5–6, 25, 42, 46, 57, 59, 60, 64–6, 73, 74, 76, 77, 79, 87, 93, 97–8, 138–41, 144–5, 150, 153, 172, 182, 183, 185–6, 191, 196–8
World Health Organisation, 122

Youth, 5, 14, 55, 70, 73, 79, 103, 106–7, 110–11, 115–17, 173, 182
YouTube, 42, 187

Zizek, Slavoj, 20